Japanese Loanword Phonology

Hituzi Linguistics in English

No. 1 Lexical Borrowing and its Impact on English   Makimi Kimura-Kano
No. 2 From a Subordinate Clause to an Independent Clause
                                                          Yuko Higashiizumi
No. 3 ModalP and Subjunctive Present   Tadao Nomura
No. 4 A Historical Study of Referent Honorifics in Japanese
                                                            Takashi Nagata
No. 5 Communicating Skills of Intention   Tsutomu Sakamoto
No. 6 A Pragmatic Approach to the Generation and Gender
       Gap in Japanese Politeness Strategies   Toshihiko Suzuki
No. 7 Japanese Women's Listening Behavior in Face-to-face Conversation
                                                         Sachie Miyazaki
No. 8 An Enterprise in the Cognitive Science of Language
                                                         Tetsuya Sano et al.
No. 9 Syntactic Structure and Silence   Hisao Tokisaki
No. 10 The Development of the Nominal Plural Forms in Early Middle English
                                                            Ryuichi Hotta
No. 11 Chunking and Instruction   Takayuki Nakamori
No. 12 Detecting and Sharing Perspectives Using Causals in Japanese
                                                              Ryoko Uno
No. 13 Discourse Representation of Temporal Relations in the So-Called
       Head-Internal Relatives   Kuniyoshi Ishikawa
No. 14 Features and Roles of Filled Pauses in Speech Communication
                                                        Michiko Watanabe
No. 15 Japanese Loanword Phonology   Masahiko Mutsukawa

Hituzi Linguistics in English No. 15

Japanese Loanword Phonology
The Nature of Inputs and the Loanword Sublexicon

Nanzan University Monograph Series

Masahiko Mutsukawa

Hituzi Syobo Publishing

Copyright © Masahiko Mutsukawa 2009
First published 2009

Author: Masahiko Mutsukawa

All rights reserved. Except for the quotation of short passages for the purposes of criticism and review, no part of this publication may be reproduced, stored in a retrieval system, or transmitted in any form or by any means, electronic, mechanical, photocopying, recording or otherwise, without the written prior permission of the publisher.
In case of photocopying and electronic copying and retrieval from network personally, permission will be given on receipts of payment and making inquiries. For details please contact us through e-mail. Our e-mail address is given below.

Book Design © Hirokazu Mukai (glyph)

Hituzi Syobo Publishing
Yamato bldg. 2F, 2-1-2 Sengoku Bunkyo-ku Tokyo, Japan
112-0011

phone +81-3-5319-4916 fax +81-3-5319-4917
e-mail: toiawase@hituzi.co.jp
http://www.hituzi.co.jp/
postal transfer 00120-8-142852

ISBN978-4-89476-442-2
Printed in Japan

To my parents,
Hiromi and Naomi Mutsukawa

Acknowledgements

This book is a slightly revised version of my Ph.D. dissertation submitted to Michigan State University in 2006. The publication of this book was funded by Nanzan University.

This book represents my graduate student life in Michigan. I would like to thank all the people who helped me in the course of my graduate studies. First and foremost, I am grateful to Yen-Hwei Lin, chair of my dissertation committee, for reading more partial drafts of this work than anyone else and accepting appointments at a short notice. This study benefited immensely from her inspiration, feedback, and encouragement. She was the best advisor I could imagine throughout my graduate years at Michigan State University. I would also like to thank the other members of my committee: Mutsuko Endo Hudson, Grover Hudson, and Anne Violin-Wigent. Mutsuko Endo Hudson provided invaluable comments from the perspective of a Japanese linguist. She also gave me opportunities of teaching Japanese and finding the joy of Japanese language teaching. I am grateful to Grover Hudson, and Anne Violin-Wigent for their insightful suggestions and invaluable comments. Besides my committee members, a number of people in the Department of Linguistics at Michigan State University deserve special thanks. I want to thank every member of the faculty and staff and my fellow students. In particular, I am grateful to the Japanese teaching assistants for their comments and friendship.

I would like to thank Mark Kaufman, my best friend in the U.S. I am lucky to have him as my friend. He made my life in Michigan enjoyable. I am also glad that I have a friend with whom I do not talk about linguistics. He helped me a lot in life outside the university throughout my days in Michigan. I am grateful for his friendship.

I want to thank my wife, Yoko, and my sons, Miiru, Fuga, and Towa, for their patience and love during the last few years in Michigan. They were always my most enthusiastic supporters. I cannot imagine having completed this study without them.

Last, but not least, I would like to express my deepest gratitude to my parents: Hiromi and Naomi Mutsukawa. They have given me unfailing love and constant support. I am proud of being their son. This book is dedicated to them.

Nagoya, Japan
February 2009

Contents

Acknowledgements ... i

Chapter 1 Introduction ... 1
1.1. Introduction ... 1
1.2. Organization of the Book ... 3

Chapter 2 Background ... 5
2.1. Introduction ... 5
2.2. Optimality Theory ... 5
2.3. Models of Loanword Adaptation ... 7
    2.3.1. Phonetic-based Model ... 7
    2.3.2. Phonology-based Model ... 8
2.4. Japanese Phonology ... 9
    2.4.1. Japanese Phonetic Inventory ... 9
    2.4.2. Adjustments Observed in English Loanwords in Japanese ... 10
    2.4.3. Japanese Lexicon ... 12

Chapter 3 Accentuation of English Loanwords ... 15
3.1. Introduction ... 15
3.2. Accentuation of Non-loanwords in Japanese ... 16
    3.2.1. Accentuation of Non-loanwords in Tokyo Japanese ... 16
    3.2.2. Accentuation of Non-loanwords in Kansai Japanese ... 18
3.3. Previous Studies ... 21
    3.3.1. McCawley (1968) ... 21
    3.3.2. Nakai (1988) ... 22
    3.3.3. Ono (1991) ... 22
    3.3.4. Asano (1999) ... 24

3.4. Kansai Japanese	26
3.4.1. Data	26
3.4.2. Analysis	31
3.5. Tokyo Japanese	43
3.5.1. Data	43
3.5.2. Analysis	46
3.6. Conclusion	52

Chapter 4 The Realization of English /r/ — 57
4.1. Introduction	57
4.2. Data	58
4.2.1. Onset /r/	58
4.2.2. Coda /r/	59
4.3. Analysis	63
4.3.1. The Inputs to Phonological Processes	63
4.3.2. Analysis	66
4.4. Conclusion	75

Chapter 5 The Realization of the English Plural Morpheme — 77
5.1. Introduction	77
5.2. Data	78
5.3. Analysis	80
5.3.1. Previous Studies	80
5.3.2. Analysis	90
5.4. Conclusion	103

Chapter 6 English Compound Abbreviation — 107
6.1. Introduction	107
6.2. Sympathy Theory vs. Weakly Parallel Model	108
6.2.1. Sympathy Theory	109
6.2.2. Weakly Parallel Model	110
6.3. Data	116

6.4. Previous Studies 117
    6.4.1. Itô (1990) 117
    6.4.2. Nishihara et al. (2001) 117
    6.4.3. Itô and Mester (1997b) 121
6.5. Analysis 124
6.6. Conclusion 142

Chapter 7   Conclusion   147
7.1. The Nature of Inputs 147
7.2. Japanese Phonology 149
7.3. Future Research 150

Appendix 151
Bibliography 177
Index 185

Chapter 1
Introduction

1.1. Introduction

This book discusses issues surrounding loanword phonology, more specifically issues surrounding the phonology of English loanwords in Japanese. In the past decade, loanword phonology has become a major field of phonology, due to the conceptual shift from rules to a constraints and repair model of sound change (Kenstowicz and Suchato 2004). Especially in Japanese phonology, the study of loanwords has been of great importance, since most of the new words in the Japanese lexicon are loanwords, more specifically American English loanwords (Kay 1995). A number of issues have arisen in this field, but many of them are still under debate. Among them, discussing four phonological phenomena observed in English loanwords in Japanese within the framework of Optimality Theory (OT: Prince and Smolensky 1993/2004), this book especially focuses on issues regarding the nature of inputs to loanword adaptation and the Loanword sublexicon, one of the four sublexica in the Japanese lexicon. The four phonological phenomena are: accentuation of English loanwords (Chapter 3), the realization of English /r/ (Chapter 4), the realization of the English plural morpheme (Chapter 5), and English compound abbreviation (Chapter 6).

This book will discuss the following issues. With regard to the nature of inputs, it is not clear whether the input is based on the phonetic representation of the source language (Silverman 1992, Peperkamp and Dupoux 2003) or the phonological one (Paradis and LaCharité 1997, LaCharité and Paradis 2005). In this book, adopting Silverman's (1992) idea that there is an intermediate level (the Perceptual Level) between the input, i.e. the output of the source language, and the Operative Level, where phonological changes take place (see Chapter 2), I will claim that the input to the Operative Level is the perceived segment, i.e. the output of the Perceptual Level, and that it is closely related to the phonetic representation of the source language. As will be argued in detail in Chapter 4, this claim is based on the realization of English [r] in Japanese. Chapter 4 will reveal that the purely phonetic or phonological representation as the input does not explain the realization of English [r] in Japanese.

Second, regarding the input of loanwords, it is not clear what information is included in the input. In this book, I will argue that Japanese borrowers have access to the information on the locus of English stress and English morphology. It has not been fully discussed in the literature what information is included in the input. Based on the accentuation of English loanwords (Chapter 3) and the realization of the English plural morpheme (Chapter 5), I claim that the information on the locus of stress and morphology in the source language is included in the input.

Third, with respect to loanword adaptation, it is not clear who borrows loanwords. Paradis and LaCharité (1997) and LaCharité and Paradis (2005) claim that loanwords are borrowed by bilinguals. In this book, I will elaborate their claim and argue that English loanwords in Japanese are introduced by limited bilinguals, i.e. Japanese-English bilinguals with the knowledge of English morphology but not necessarily with the knowledge of English phonology. As will be discussed in Chapter 5, this claim is based on the fact that the stem and the plural morpheme are treated differently. Furthermore, the fact that all the Japanese people study English at secondary school supports the idea that English loanwords in Japanese are introduced by the Japanese speakers with some knowledge of English.

Fourth, this book will discuss the assimilation process to the core part of the Japanese lexicon and the structure of the Loanword sublexicon in Japanese. It has been agreed in the literature (McCawley 1968, Itô and Mester 1995, 1999, among others) that the Japanese lexicon consists of sublexica. But the structure of the Loanword sublexicon, one of the four sublexica, has not been fully discussed. Analyzing four phonological phenomena of English loanwords, this book discusses the structure of the Loanword sublexicon and how loanwords can be assimilated with regard to some particular aspects.

Finally, this book will also discuss issues regarding OT such as how phonological opacity can be accounted for within the framework of OT. English compound abbreviation reveals a case of phonological opacity. This book will show that the Weakly Parallel Model (Itô and Mester 2001b, 2003a), a subtheory of OT, accounts for a case of phonological opacity observed in English compound abbreviation straightforwardly.

1.2. Organization of the Book

This book is organized as follows. Chapter 2 introduces the background relevant to this book: Optimality Theory, models of loanword phonology, and introduction to Japanese phonology including Japanese phonetic inventory, context-free phonological adjustments observed in English loanwords in Japanese, and the Japanese lexicon.

Chapter 3 explores accentuation of English loanwords in two major dialects of Japanese, i.e. Kansai Japanese and Tokyo Japanese, within the framework of OT. In this chapter, I will show the following: (i) English loanwords in Japanese preserve English stress, which suggests that the information on the locus of English stress is included in the input, (ii) the pitch pattern, i.e. the contour, of loanwords in Kansai Japanese is highly predictable, although it has been claimed that the pitch pattern of non-loanwords is unpredictable (Pierrehumbert and Beckman 1988: 214), and (iii) Kansai Japanese and Tokyo Japanese are the same with respect to the accent assignment, although they are different with regard to the pitch pattern.

Chapter 4 discusses the realization of English /r/ in Japanese. English /r/ is a unique segment in English loanwords in Japanese in the sense that it is the only consonant that can correspond to zero as well as a consonant [ɾ] and vowels, [a] or [o], in the output. In this chapter, I will claim the following: (i) the perceived segment, which is closely related to the phonetic representation of the source language, is the input to loanword phonology, (ii) an input segment can be perceived differently based on the location it appears, and (iii) the diachronic change with regard to the realization of English /r/ in Japanese can be understood as the result of the constraint reranking between two constraints *[aː]]$_{PW}$, i.e. no word-final [aː], and M<small>AX</small>, i.e. no deletion.

Chapter 5 deals with the realization of the English plural morpheme in Japanese. Three phonological phenomena related to the English plural morpheme are observed in Japanese: devoicing, diachronic change, and deletion. In this chapter, my major claims will be the following: (i) the devoicing of the plural morpheme is a phenomenon in the affixes in the Loanword sublexicon, (ii) Japanese borrowers have access to the morphological information of English, which means that morphological information is included in the input, and (iii) the accessibility to the morpho-phonological information of English is different between the older and younger generations.

Chapter 6 concerns English compound abbreviation in Japanese. This chapter deals with a case of phonological opacity, which has not been discussed in the literature, and explains it within the framework of the Weakly Parallel Model of Itô and Mester (2001b, 2003a). In this chapter, I will show that there are two types of coda conditions in Japanese. Based on the structure of trimoraic abbreviated compounds, this chapter also claims that an abbreviated compound is not a prosodic word consisting of two abbreviated prosodic words but a prosodic word by itself. This chapter will also reveal that the Light-Heavy structure is systematically disfavored in Japanese.

Finally, this book is closed in Chapter 7 by summarizing the discussion and claims developed in this study. Major claims of this book will be as follows: (i) loanwords are adapted by limited bilinguals, (ii) the perceived segments, which are closely related to the phonetic representation but not to the phonological representation of the source language, are the inputs to loanword phonology, and (iii) the input includes the information on the locus of stress and morphology of the source language.

Chapter 2
Background

2.1. Introduction

This chapter introduces the background relevant to this book. This chapter consists of three parts. In the first part, I will present a brief overview of Optimality Theory, which is adopted in this book to analyze the four phonological phenomena observed in English loanwords in Japanese. Then, in the second part, I will illustrate two models of loanword adaptation: one is phonetic-based (Silverman 1992, Peperkamp and Dupoux 2003) and the other is phonology-based (Paradis and LaCharité 1997, LaCharité and Paradis 2005). Finally, the last part is an introduction to Japanese phonology, where Japanese phonetic inventory, context-free phonological adjustments observed in English Loanwords in Japanese, as well as the Japanese lexicon, will be introduced.

2.2. Optimality Theory

This section briefly overviews the basic concepts of Optimality Theory (OT: Prince and Smolensky 1993/2004). OT is an output-oriented, constraint-based theory. In this theory, there are no rules and no serial derivations, and the set of constraints plays a central role. The set of constraints is provided by Universal Grammar. In OT, constraints are all considered to be universal whereas the ranking of constraints is language-specific. This concept is called 'Richness of the Base' (Prince and Smolensky 1993: 191). The formulation in (1) is Smolensky's (1996: 5). 'Richness of the Base' means that there is no restriction on inputs and cross-linguistic variation attributed to the difference of constraint ranking.

(1) Richness of the Base
 The source of all systematic cross-linguistic variation is constraint reranking. In particular, the set of inputs to the grammars of all languages is the same.

The grammatical inventories of a language are the outputs, which emerge from the grammar when it is fed the universal set of all possible inputs.

There is another significant property of the OT grammar, which is relevant to language acquisition. That is called 'Lexicon Optimization'. 'Lexicon Optimization' means that the input form is assumed to be identical to the output whenever there is no overt evidence of existence of a specific lexical form, because it is the easiest strategy to build a lexicon.

(2) Lexicon Optimization (Prince and Smolensky 1993: 192)
Suppose that several different inputs $I_1, I_2..., I_n$ when parsed by a grammar G lead to corresponding outputs $O_1, O_2..., O_n$, all of which are realized as the same phonetic form Φ – these inputs are phonetically equivalent with respect to G. Now one of these outputs must be the most harmonic, by virtue of incurring the least significant marks: suppose this optimal one is labeled O_k. Then the learner should choose, as the underlying form for Φ, the input I_k.

All the constraints in OT, in principle, are violable, but the violation must be minimal. A candidate is considered to be optimal when it violates constraints minimally and best satisfies the constraint hierarchy. Output candidates are evaluated and the best output form is determined in a tableau, as in (3).

(3)

Input		Constraint 1	Constraint 2
a. ☞	Output Candidate A		**
b.	Output Candidate B	*!	*

In a tableau, output candidates are shown vertically in the leftmost column in random order, while constraints are given horizontally in the top row in a descending ranking from left to right, i.e. Constraint 1 is ranked higher than Constraint 2 in the tableau (3). Candidate A satisfies Constraint 1 but violates Constraint 2 twice, whereas Candidate B violates both Constraint 1 and Constraint 2 once. Candidate A is the optimal output in the tableau (3), because Candidate B's violation of Constraint 1 is fatal, which is indicated by the exclamation mark '!'.

With respect to Constraint 2, Candidate A violates it more than Candidate B does. But Candidate A's violation of Constraint 2 is irrelevant to the choice of the output form, since Constraint 2 is ranked lower than Constraint 1.

2.3. Models of Loanword Adaptation

This section introduces two models of loanword adaptation: phonetic-based (Silverman 1992, Peperkamp and Dupoux 2003) and phonology-based models (Paradis and LaCharité 1997, LaCharité and Paradis 2005). The nature of inputs to loanword adaptation is still under debate in the literature: the input is based on the phonetic representation of the source language in phonetic-based model whereas Paradis and LaCharité (1997) and LaCharité and Paradis (2005) claim that it is phonology-based.

2.3.1. Phonetic-based Model

Silverman (1992) proposes a phonetic-based model of loanword adaptation. In loanword phonology, the nature of inputs is unclear: for instance, it is not clear whether the inputs to phonological processes are phonologically faithful to the source language or they are somewhat affected by the host language. Silverman (1992) assumes that the speakers of the host language have no access to the phonological representation of the source language and provides the following diagram.

(4) Silverman's Model (1992: 293)

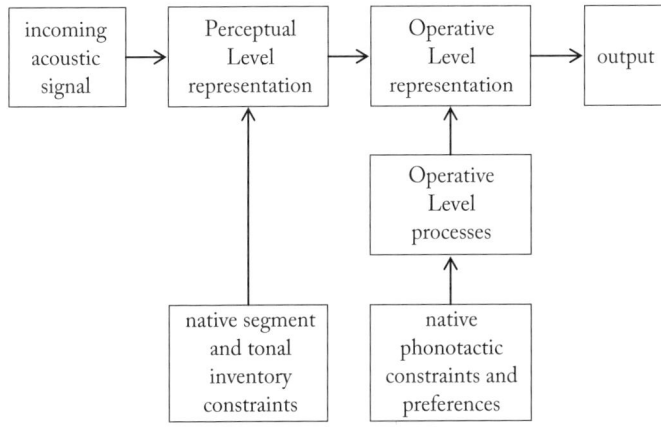

In Silverman's model shown in (4), the input is merely a linguistically unanalyzed acoustic signal and the speakers of the host language cannot have access to the phonological representation of the source language. At the Perceptual Level, the native segment and tonal inventory constraints apply, and restrict the representation of perceived segments. Then, it is at the Operative Level that "perceived segments may undergo true phonological operations, triggered by native phonotactic constraints" (Silverman 1992: 293). That is, the speakers of the host language perceive the inputs in accordance with the phonological system of the host language and fit "the superficial input into the native phonological system as closely as possible" (Silverman 1992: 289). This model accounts for why the identical input can be "perceived, represented, and ultimately produced in a distinct manner in each language it enters" (Silverman 1992: 289).

There is another hypothesis that plays a role in Silverman's model, which is the Perceptual Uniformity Hypothesis. This hypothesis means that, at the Perceptual Level, an incoming acoustic signal cannot have more than one acoustic correspondent.

(5) Perceptual Uniformity Hypothesis
At the Perceptual Level, the native segment inventory constrains segmental representation in a uniform fashion, regardless of string position.
However, an input whose acoustic phonetic properties cannot be discerned due to its presence in an impoverished context (a context to be determined on a language-specific basis) is not supplied representation at the Perceptual Level of the loanword phonology.

Peperkamp and Dupoux (2003) also propose a phonetic-based model of loanword adaptation, which draws on theories of speech perception, and a research program to test their model. Their model of loanword adaptation is quite similar to Silverman's.

2.3.2. Phonology-based Model

Paradis and LaCharité (1997) and LaCharité and Paradis (2005) take the opposite position of Silverman (1992) and propose a phonology-based model of loanword adaptation. Paradis and LaCharité's model of loanword phonology is shown in (6).

(6) Paradis and LaCharité's Model (1997: 394)

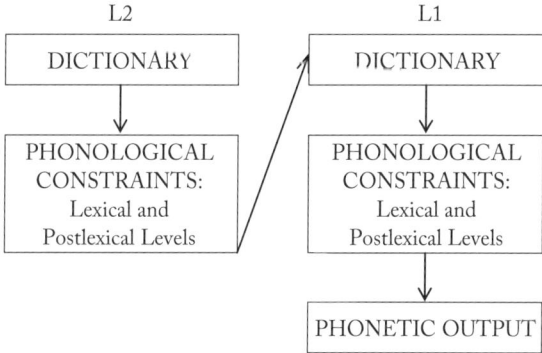

Paradis and LaCharité assume that loanwords are introduced by bilinguals who have competencies in both the source and host languages. In this model, the phonological output of the source language, which is based on the phonemic representation, is the input to the host language and the input is incorporated directly into the lexicon of the host language.

2.4. Japanese Phonology

This section gives a brief introduction to Japanese phonology: Japanese phonetic inventory, context-free phonological adjustments observed in English Loanwords in Japanese, and the Japanese lexicon.

2.4.1. Japanese Phonetic Inventory

The following is the chart of Japanese consonants, which is the revised version of Tsujimura's (1996: 16) (See also Bloch (1950: 107)). Among the consonants in (7), Japanese phonemes are /b/, /p/, /d/, /t/, /g/, /k/, /z/, /s/, /h/, /r/, /y/, /w/, /m/, and /n/, and the others are allophones.[1] The chart in (8) shows Japanese vowels (Tsujimura 1996: 18, Nakajo 1989).

(7) Japanese Consonants

		bilabial	alveolar	alveo-palatal	palatal	velar	uvular	glottal
Stops:	[+V]	b	d			g		ʔ
	[-V]	p	t			k		
Fricatives:	[+V]		z	ž²				
	[-V]	ɸ	s	š	ç			h
Affricates:	[+V]		dᶻ	ǰ				
	[-V]		tˢ	č				
Approximants:								
Liquid	[+V]		ɾ					
Glide	[-V]				y	w		
Nasals:	[+V]	m	n	ñ³	ɲ³	ŋ	N	

(8) Japanese Vowels

	front	central	back
high	i		ɯ⁴
mid	e		o
low		a	

2.4.2. Adjustments Observed in English Loanwords in Japanese

Some English phonemes do not exist in the Japanese phonemic inventory and Japanese possible syllable structures, i.e. (C)(G)V(V)(C) where G is a glide [y] and coda consonant is either a nasal or the first half of a geminate, are different from English possible syllable structures. These facts lead to a number of adjustments having taken place in the borrowing English words into Japanese. The adjustments are divided into two categories: phonetic adjustments and vowel epenthesis. The major phonetic adjustments are shown in (9)–(11) (National Language Institute 1990, Ohso 1991, Tsuchida 1995).[5]

(9) Consonants

English   Japanese
a. [f] → [ɸ] (fur → [ɸaː])
b. [v] → [b] (view → [bʸɯː])
c. [θ] → [s] (Ithaca → [isaka])
d. [ð] → [z] (mother → [mazaː])

e. [l] → [ɾ]   (fly → [ɸɯɾai])

(10) Lax Vowels[6]
    English   Japanese
    a. [ɪ] → [i]   (pin → [piɴ])
    b. [ɛ] → [e]   (pen → [peɴ])
    c. [æ] → [a]   (rally → [ɾaɾi:])
    d. [ʌ] → [a]   (cut → [katto])
    e. [a] → [a]   (top → [toppɯ])
    f. [ɔ] → [o:]   (call → [ko:ɾɯ])
    g. [ʊ] → [ɯ]   (book → [bɯkkɯ])

(11) Tense Vowels
    English   Japanese
    a. [i] → [i:]   (key → [ki:])
    b. [o] → [o:]   (zone → [zo:ɴ])
    c. [u] → [ɯ:]   (cue → [kʲɯ:])

As mentioned above, Japanese possible syllable structures are (C)(G)V(V)(C), and possible syllable structures in English and Japanese are different. This leads to the second type of the adjustment: vowel epenthesis. That is, since the sequence of consonants and coda consonants are highly restricted in Japanese, vowels are epenthesized to avoid the illegitimate structures. The epenthetic vowels are determined as in (12) (Ohso 1991, Kobayashi et al. 1991, Jorden et al. 1976, among others).

(12) Epenthetic Vowels
    a. [o] is inserted after [t] and [d]
        (travel → [toɾabeɾɯ])
        (road → [ɾo:do])
    b. [i] is inserted after [č], [ǰ], and [š]
        (bench → [benči])
        (brush → [bɯɾaši])
    c. [ɯ] is inserted elsewhere
        (three → [sɯɾi:])
        (noise → [noidᶻɯ])

In the rest of this book, the orthography-based representation of loanwords, which is based on the Japanese orthography, will be adopted unless the phonetic representation is relevant to the discussion.

2.4.3. Japanese Lexicon

It has been agreed in the literature that the Japanese lexicon consists of sublexica (McCawley 1968, Itô and Mester 1995, Itô and Mester 1999, Fukuzawa, Kitahara, and Ota 1998, among others). Itô and Mester (1995) claim that the Japanese lexicon consists of four sublexica, i.e. Yamato, Sino-Japanese, Mimetic, and Loanword, and those sublexica are organized in a core-periphery structure. Sublexica are characterized by three constraints that apply. The relevant constraints are *P (no single [p]), *NT (no post-nasal voiceless obstruent), and *DD (no voiced obstruent geminate). As illustrated in (13), the Yamato sublexicon is the most restricted while the Loanword sublexicon is the least.

(13) (Itô and Mester 1995: 820)

	*P	*NT	*DD
a. Yamato	✓	✓	✓
b. Sino-Japanese	✓		✓
c. Mimetic		✓	✓
d. Loanword			

In the core-periphery model, it has been assumed that the Yamato, Sino-Japanese, and Mimetic sublexica exist as strata and form the core part of the lexicon, whereas the Loanword sublexicon does not constitute a uniform stratum and loanwords exist in less central areas of the lexicon where more constraints can be violated.

Sublexica in the Japanese lexicon are not always defined by etymology. The Portuguese loanword *karuta* '(playing) card' is etymologically a loanword but it is considered as a Yamato item because it has phonological characteristics of Yamato items (e.g. Rendaku (Sequential Voicing): *hana* 'flower' + *karuta* → *hana-garuta* (*hana-karuta) 'flower card game'). Also, items in the Japanese lexicon, which are etymologically loanwords, can phonologically behave like the items in the core part of the lexicon with respect to some particular aspects. For example, the English word 'bag' behave like a core item with regard to the constraint *DD, which, as illustrated in (13), does not apply to the items in the Loanword sublexicon ('bag' → *bakku* (or *baggu*); cf. 'rod' → *roddo* (*rotto)).[7] Based on this, Itô and Mester (1999) divide the Loanword sublexicon into two constituents, "Assimilated" Loanword sublexicon and "Unassimilated" Loanword sublexicon. The items in the "Assimilated" Loanword sublexicon behave like core items with regard to some particular aspects, while the items in the "Unassimilated" Loanword sublexicon do not. The distinction between "Assimilated" and "Unassimilated" better explains the structure of the Loanword sublexicon. But, as Itô and Mester (1999: 70) point out, "many finer distinctions are hidden beneath this coarse classification: the less nativized an item is, the more it disobeys lexical constraints, i.e. the more it falls outside of various constraint domains and is located towards the periphery of the lexical space." This book further discusses the structure of the Japanese lexicon, especially the structure of the Loanword sublexicon and how a loanword can be assimilated.

Endnotes

1. [m] is a phoneme, but it also can appear as an allophone of /n/.
2. Tsujimura (1996: 19) points out that "some native speakers seem to have [ž] in rapid speech." Bloch (1950) discusses this sound in more detail. According to Bloch (1950: 101), "Most phrases containing [ž] are paralleled by otherwise identical synonymous phrases containing [dž] instead; [ž] is less common than [dž], and in the speech of many persons does not occur at all. Examples: [mižíkái] *short*, [nížuu] *twenty*, [sān·žuu] *thirty*." Bloch distinguishes mediovelar stop and nasal, i.e. [g] and [ŋ], from prevelar stop and nasal, i.e. [g̣] and [ŋ̣]. Bloch (1950: 109) mentions that "[i]n three pairs of phones—[g, ŋ],[g̣, ŋ̣],[dž, ž]—the members are in partially free variation with each other, but must nevertheless be kept apart." "Since the alternation between [g, g̣, dž] and [ŋ, ŋ̣, ž] respectively are limited to certain phrases only, and since their common environments do not form a phonetically or phonemically definable set, the three pairs of phones must be treated separately in the phonemic analysis."
3. With regards to [ñ] and [ɲ], Tsujimura (1996: 20) explains as follows: "The coarticulation involving the nasal consonants can also be observed before alveo-palatal and palatal consonants. In these situations, the nasal is realized as alveo-palatal nasal [ñ] and palatal nasal [ɲ], respectively. Examples include *ken zya* (*nai*) [keñ ǰa (nai)] 'it is not a ticket' and *ken ya* (*kane*) [keɲ ya (kane)] 'things like ticket and (money)'."
4. The symbol [ɯ] indicates the unrounded high back vowel. Whereas the lack of lip rounding is more prominent in the Tokyo dialect, the high back vowel tends to be rounded in the Western dialects (Tsujimura 1996: 18; Shibatani 1990: 161). The symbol for rounded high back vowel is [u].

5   The adjustment of English [r] will be discussed in detail in Chapter 4.
6   As far as I know, the realization of [ə] has not got attention in the literature and no one has studied it systematically. Interestingly, however, [ə] in English words can correspond to the five vowels in Japanese, as illustrated below. In the examples below, the vowels corresponding to English [ə] are shown in bold. The realization of English [ə] seems relevant to English orthography.
    a. [ə] → [i] (terminal   → [ta:minaɾɯ])
    b. [ə] → [e] (entrepreneur → [antoɾepuɾena])
    c. [ə] → [a] (away   → [awe:])
    d. [ə] → [o] (vision   → [biǰoɴ])
    e. [ə] → [ɯ] (even   → [i:bɯɴ])
7   The application of *DD to 'bag' is optional and subject to individual differences, although *bakku* seems more common than *baggu*.

Chapter 3
Accentuation of English Loanwords[*]

3.1. Introduction

This chapter explores accentuation of English loanwords in two major dialects of Japanese, i.e. Kansai Japanese and Tokyo Japanese, within the framework of Optimality Theory (OT: Prince and Smolensky 1993/2004).[1] Accentuation is one of the major issues in Japanese loanword phonology and many studies have been conducted (McCawley 1968, Kubozono 1994, Labrune 2002, others). Most of the studies, however, are on the loanword accentuation in Tokyo Japanese and the loanword accentuation in other dialects such as Kansai Japanese has been studied little.

This chapter examines the accentuation of English loanwords in Kansai Japanese and Tokyo Japanese with three goals in mind. The first goal of this chapter is to discuss the pitch pattern, i.e. the contour, of English loanwords in Kansai Japanese. In Tokyo Japanese, given the locus of the accent, the pitch pattern of the whole word is predictable. In Kansai Japanese, on the other hand, the pitch pattern preceding the accented mora has not been explained in the literature (Pierrehumbert and Beckman 1988: 214). This chapter analyzes the pitch pattern of English loanwords in Kansai Japanese within the OT framework and shows that the pitch pattern preceding the accented mora is mostly predictable.

The second goal is to examine the locus of the accent of English loanwords in Kansai Japanese. Regarding the location of the accent of loanwords in Kansai Japanese, few studies (Nakai 1988) have been conducted. The data collected for this study shows that about 50% of 1090 English loanwords in Kansai Japanese have the antepenultimate accent, which is considered the default accent of loanwords in Tokyo Japanese in the literature (Ono 1991, Tanaka 1992, Katayama 1995, Kubozono 1995b, Kubozono and Ohta 1998, others). This chapter reveals that most of English loanwords retain the English accent, i.e. the accent on the syllable stressed in English, which indicates that the information on the locus of

English stress is included in the input.

Finally, this chapter reanalyzes English loanwords in Tokyo Japanese and compares Kansai Japanese and Tokyo Japanese. This chapter shows that Kansai Japanese and Tokyo Japanese are the same with respect to the accent assignment, although they are different with regard to the pitch pattern.

This chapter is organized as follows. After illustrating an overview of the accentuation of non-loanwords in Tokyo Japanese and Kansai Japanese in section 2, section 3 reviews four previous studies of the loanword accentuation. Then, in section 4 and section 5, English loanwords in Kansai Japanese and Tokyo Japanese are analyzed. Finally, this chapter concludes in section 6 by summarizing the analysis and pointing to further issues.

3.2. Accentuation of Non-loanwords in Japanese

Japanese is considered as a pitch-accent language, which means that the pitch pattern of the whole word is predictable given the locus of the accent of the word. Japanese is divided into four big groups based on accentuation systems. Among them, this chapter focuses only on Kansai Japanese and Tokyo Japanese. The accent in Japanese is marked by an abrupt falling pitch where, following the convention, the accent is marked by an apostrophe placed immediately after the accented mora and high- and low-pitched morae are indicated by 'H' and 'L' respectively.

(1) a. tebu'kuro   LHLL   'glove'   (Tokyo Japanese)
    b. tebuku'ro   LLHL   'glove'   (Kansai Japanese)

The rest of this section introduces the accentuation of non-loanwords in Tokyo Japanese and Kansai Japanese.

3.2.1. Accentuation of Non-loanwords in Tokyo Japanese

The location of the accent of non-loanwords in Tokyo Japanese is lexically determined and unpredictable, as illustrated in (2).

(2) a. ha'si   HL   'chopsticks'   (accent on the first syllable)
    b. hasi'   LH   'bridge'   (accent on the last syllable)
    c. hasi   LH   'edge'   (unaccented)

3 Accentuation of English Loanwords

Each word is either accented (e.g. (2a) and (2b)) or unaccented (e.g. (2c)). The word with the accent on the final mora, i.e. (2b), and the unaccented word, i.e. (2c), in isolation have the same pitch pattern. When they are followed by a particle such as the nominative marker *ga*, however, they show distinctive pitch patterns, as illustrated in (3).

(3) a. hasi´   'bridge' (accent on the last syllable)
       hasi´ga   LHL
    b. hasi   'edge'   (unaccented)
       hasiga   LHH

The possible pitch patterns of words of one to four light syllables are shown in (4)–(7), where both the pattern of the word in isolation and the pattern followed by the nominative marker *ga* are given. The examples below are from Sugito (1982: 3), except for (7b) and (7d), which were collected by the author.

(4) Monomoraic Words
    a. na   H   'name'   (unaccented)
       naga   LH
    b. na´   H   'eating greens' (accented)
       na´ga   HL

(5) Bimoraic Words
    a. hasi   LH   'edge'   (unaccented)
       hasiga   LHH
    b. ha´si   HL   'chopsticks' (accent on the first syllable)
       ha´siga HLL
    c. hasi´   LH   'bridge'   (accent on the last syllable)
       hasi´ga LHL

(6) Trimoraic Words
    a. kodomo   LHH   'child'   (unaccented)
       kodomoga   LHHH
    b. mi´dori   HLL   'green'   (accent on the first syllable)
       mi´doriga HLLL
    c. koko´ro   LHL   'spirit' (accent on the second syllable)

          koko´roga   LHLL
    d.   kagami´   LHH   'mirror'   (accent on the last syllable)
          kagami´ga LHHL

(7) Quadrimoraic Words
    a. tomodati   LHHH   'friend'   (unaccented)
       tomodatiga   LHHHH
    b. ma´tibari   HLLL   'pin'   (accent on the first syllable)
       ma´tibariga HLLLL
    c. tebu´kuro   LHLL   'glove'   (accent on the second syllable)
       tebu´kuroga LHLLL
    d. zeita´ku   LHHL   'extravagance'   (accent on the penultimate syllable)
       zeita´kuga   LHHLL
    e. kaminari´   LHHH   'thunder'   (accent on the last syllable)
       kaminari´ga LHHHL

The following five generalizations can be made from (4)–(7). First, the accented mora is high-pitched. Second, the morae following the accented mora are low-pitched throughout. Third, the morae preceding the accented mora are high-pitched, but the word-initial pitch and the pitch of the second mora must be distinct. That is, the first mora is low-pitched and the second mora is high-pitched unless the first mora is accented, otherwise the first mora is high-pitched and the second mora is low-pitched. Fourth, a prosodic word cannot have more than one accented mora. Finally, a prosodic word must have at least one high-pitched mora.

When a heavy syllable is accented, only the first mora of the syllable can be accented, as illustrated in (8).

(8) a. to´oki[2]   HLL   'pottery'   (*too´ki   LHL)
    b. ge´ndai   HLLL   'today'   (*gen´dai LHLL)
    c. ka´kkoo   HLLL   'cuckoo'   (*kak´koo LHLL)

3.2.2. Accentuation of Non-loanwords in Kansai Japanese
The location of the accent of non-loanwords in Kansai Japanese is lexically determined and unpredictable, as in Tokyo Japanese (cf. (2)).

(9) a. ha´si   HL   'bridge'   (accent on the first syllable)
    b. hasi   HH   'edge'   (unaccented)
    c. hasi   LH   'chopsticks' (unaccented)

As illustrated in (9), each word is either accented (e.g. (9a)) or unaccented (e.g. (9b) and (9c)). Unlike Tokyo Japanese (cf. (2)), Kansai Japanese has two types of unaccented words: high-pitched unaccented words (e.g. (9b)) and unaccented words with the word-final high-pitched mora (e.g. (9c)). When an unaccented word of the second type (e.g. (9c)) is followed by a particle such as the nominative marker *ga*, the high pitch moves to the word-final position, i.e. onto the nominative marker, as shown in (10c).

(10) a. ha´si   HL   'bridge'   (accent on the first syllable)
        ha´siga   HLL
     b. hasi   HH   'edge'   (unaccented)
        hasiga   HHH
     c. hasi   LH   'chopsticks'   (unaccented)
        hasiga   LLH

The examples in (11)–(14) show the possible pitch patterns of words of one to four light syllables. The accentuation system of Kansai Japanese is more complex than that of Tokyo Japanese (cf. (4)–(7)). In the examples below, both the pattern in isolation and the pattern followed by the nominative marker *ga* are given. The examples below are from Sugito (1982: 3) except for (14b), (14c), (14e) and (14f), which were collected by the author.

(11) Monomoraic Words[3]
     a. ko   H   'child'   (unaccented)
        koga   HH
     b. ee   LH   'picture'   (unaccented, lengthened)
        ega   LH
     c. ke´e   HL   'hair'   (accented, lengthened)
        ke´ga   HL

(12) Bimoraic Words
     a. hasi   HH   'edge'   (unaccented)

       hasiga   HHH
- b. hasi   LH   'chopsticks' (unaccented)
    hasiga   LLH
- c. ha´si   HL   'bridge'   (accent on the first syllable)
    ha´siga   HLL
- d. ame´e   LHL   'rain'   (accented, lengthened)
    ame´ga   LHL

(13) Trimoraic Words
- a. kodomo   HHH   'child'   (unaccented)
    kodomoga HHHH
- b. tokai   LLH   'city'   (unaccented)
    tokaiga   LLLH
- c. ko´koro   HLL   'spirit'   (accent on the first syllable)
    ko´koroga HLLL
- d. kaga´mi   HHL   'mirror'   (accent on the second syllable)
    kaga´miga HHLL
- e. kata´na   LHL   'sword'   (accent on the second syllable)
    kata´naga LHLL

(14) Quadrimoraic Words
- a. tomodati   HHHH 'friend'   (unaccented)
    tomodatiga HHHHH
- b. jagaimo   LLLH   'potato'   (unaccented)
    jagaimoga LLLLH
- c. ma´tibari   HLLL   'pin'   (accent on the first syllable)
    ma´tibariga HLLLL
- d. mago´koro   HHLL   'sincerity' (accent on the second syllable)
    mago´koroga HHLLL
- e. kitu´tuki   LHLL   'woodpecker' (accent on the second syllable)
    kitu´tukiga LHLLL
- f. tetuda´i   HHHL   'help'   (accent on the penultimate syllable)
    tetuda´iga HHHLL
- g. tebuku´ro   LLHL   'glove'   (accent on the penultimate syllable)
    tebuku´roga LLHLL

The following six generalizations can be drawn from (11)–(14). First, the accented mora is high-pitched. Second, a prosodic word cannot have more than one accent, and a prosodic word must have at least one high-pitched mora. Third, the morae following the accented mora are low-pitched throughout. Fourth, the morae preceding the accented mora can be either high- or low-pitched throughout (e.g. (14f) and (14g)). Fifth, when a prosodic word has a low-pitched mora word-initially, only the accented mora of the accented word (e.g. (14g)) or the last mora of unaccented word (e.g. (14b)) can be high-pitched. Finally, the accent on the final mora is not allowed.[4]

When a heavy syllable is accented, unlike Tokyo Japanese (cf. (8)), both the first mora (e.g. (15a)) and the second mora of the syllable, i.e. the second half of a long vowel (e.g. (15b)) and the coda (e.g. (15c)), can be accented.

(15) a. ge′ndai   HLLL   'modern times'
     b. kyoo′dai LHLL   'brother'
     c. kon′ban   LHLL   'tonight'

3.3. Previous Studies

Accentuation is one of the main issues in Japanese loanword phonology and many studies have been conducted. But, most of them are about the loanword accentuation in Tokyo Japanese, and the loanword accentuation in Kansai Japanese has been studied little. This section gives an overview of four previous studies on the loanword accentuation in Japanese: McCawley (1968), Nakai (1988), Ono (1991), and Asano (1999).

3.3.1. McCawley (1968)

McCawley (1968) is a milestone in the study of loanword accentuation in Tokyo Japanese. He observes the characteristics of the loanword accentuation in Tokyo Japanese given in (16).

(16) McCawley (1968: 134 fn. 6)
     Loanwords fall into three classes based on the accentuation: i) unaccented words, ii) words accented on the syllable containing the antepenultimate mora, iii) words accented on the syllable which was stressed in the source language.

Following the observation above, many researchers claim that the antepenultimate accent is the default loanword accent in Tokyo Japanese (Ono 1991, Tanaka 1992, Katayama 1995, among others).

In addition, McCawley (1968: 134 fn. 6) refers to Tashiro's (1953) interesting observation regarding the antepenultimate accent that "this ante-penultimate accent is also the normal pronunciation for lists of meaningless syllables; for example, the *kana* syllabary is recited: *ʔaʔiʔu˙ʔeʔo, kakiku˙ keko, tatitu˙ teto, …*"

3.3.2. Nakai (1988)

Nakai (1988) is a descriptive study that deals with accentuation of English loanwords in Kyoto Japanese, a variety of Kansai Japanese. He reports that the majority of loanwords in Kyoto Japanese and Tokyo Japanese are the same with respect to the accent assignment. Nakai claims that the accent in the source language does not play the major role in determining the locus of the accent in Kyoto Japanese and that the antepenultimate accent with the word-initial high pitch is the default loanword accent and pitch in Kyoto Japanese.

3.3.3. Ono (1991)

Ono (1991) discusses the accentuation of loanwords in Tokyo Japanese, comparing with that in other languages: English, Russian, Turkish, Polish, and Macedonian. From the studies of the loanword accentuation in the five languages, he finds three common features in (17), and shows that these common features apply to the loanword accentuation in Tokyo Japanese as well.

(17) Common Features of Loanword Accentuation
 a. The accentuation of loanwords is different from that of native words.
 b. The accentuation of loanwords is as simple as that of non-loanwords (e.g. Polish and Macedonian), or simpler than that of non-loanwords (e.g. English, Russian, Turkish).
 c. The accent on loanwords can appear only on the syllable following the preantepenultimate syllable: on the last, penultimate, or antepenultimate syllable.

Ono claims that the default loanword accent in Tokyo Japanese is the antepenultimate accent. He accounts for the exceptions to his claim as follows. First, some loanwords have the accent on the mora preceding the antepenultimate mora, e.g. preantepenultimate accent, as shown in (18).

(18) a. bo´onasu   HLLL   'bonus'
     b. a´kusesu   HLLL   'access'
     c. te´kisasu   HLLL   'Texas'
     d. yu´nion   HLLL   'union'
     e. si´gunaru   HLLL   'signal'
     f. ra´gubii   HLLL   'rugby'

Exceptions of this type can be divided into two classes: class 1 ((18a) and (18b)) and class 2 ((18c)–(18f)). In class 1, either the second half of a heavy syllable (e.g. (18a)) or a devoiced vowel (e.g. (18b)) is the antepenultimate mora. The loanwords of class 1 do not have the accent on the antepenultimate mora because the accent on the second half of a heavy syllable or a devoiced vowel is not allowed. Therefore, the accent in class 1 words moves one mora left from the antepenult. Kanno (1971) observes that the loanwords ending with -*su*, -*n*, -*ru*, or a long vowel have the accent not on the antepenultimate mora but on the preantepenultimate mora (e.g. (18c)–(18f)). Those are the exceptions of class 2. Ono claims that they do not have the antepenultimate accent because -*su*, -*n*, -*ru*, and the second half of a long vowel are extrametrical elements in Japanese.

Second, the loanwords in (19) have the accent not on the antepenultimate mora but on the penultimate mora. The locus of the accent of the loanwords of this type corresponds to that of the source words. That is, these words retain the original accent in the source language.

(19) a. supa´i   LHL   'spy'
     b. tora´i   LHL   'try'
     c. gure´e   LHL   'gray'

Finally, the loanwords in (20) are unaccented. Following Kanno (1971), Ono claims that unaccented loanwords are the loanwords borrowed long time ago and they are the result of nativization.

(20) a. botan   LHH   'button'
     b. sutamina   LHHH   'stamina'
     c. guraundo   LHHHH   'ground'

Based on the examples above, Ono hypothesizes that the nativization process of loanword accentuation has three stages. First, when a word is borrowed, the word is accented on the syllable stressed in the source language. Then, in the second stage, the accent changes to the default pattern, i.e. the antepenultimate accent. Finally, the word loses the accent and becomes an unaccented word.

3.3.4. Asano (1999)

Asano (1999) claims that the basic loanword accent in Tokyo Japanese is the accent on the syllable stressed in the source language. According to Asano, the locus of the accent is determined by the two groups of rules: rules of footing and rules of accent shift.

Feet in Japanese are bimoraic (Poser 1984, 1990, Tateishi 1989, Itô 1990, Itô and Mester 1992, Katayama 1995, Kubozono 1995a, Asano 1999, among others). Feet are assigned by the three steps in (21).

(21) Step 1: Assign a foot to the last two morae, regardless of their syllabic position.

a. ... μ μ # → ... (μ μ) #
     | | | |
     σ σ   σ σ

b. ... μ μ # → ... (μ μ) #
       \ /   \ /
        σ   σ

c. ... μ μ μ# → ... μ (μ μ) #
       \ / | \ / |
        σ σ   σ σ

Step 2: Parse heavy syllables into feet.

d. ... σ σ σ...σ σ σ...σ# → ...σ σ σ...σ σ σ...σ#
       | /\ | /\ | | /\ | /\ | /\ | | /\
       μ μ μ μ μ μ μ μ(μ μ)   μ(μ μ)μ (μ μ)μ μ (μ μ)

Step 3: Parse light syllables into feet iteratively from left to right. Degenerate feet are not allowed.

e. ...σ σ σ σ σ σ σ σ...# → ...σ σ σ σ σ σ σ σ...#
    ∧ | | | ∧ | | ∧   ∧ | | | ∧ | | ∧
    (μ μ) μ μ μ (μ μ) μ μ (μ μ)   (μ μ)(μ μ) μ (μ μ)(μ μ) (μ μ)

There are four rules that move the locus of the accent, as given in (22). In the examples below, the accents are indicated by the apostrophes.

(22) a. Move the accent to the antepenultimate mora when it is in the last foot.

i) ... σ   σ#   ...σ   σ#
     | ∧ | ∧
     μ   (μ´ μ)   →   μ´ (μ μ)

ii) ... σ   σ σ#   ... σ   σ σ#
      ∧ | | ∧ | |
     μ μ (μ´ μ)   →   μ´ μ (μ μ)

b. Move the accent to the antepenultimate mora when it is on the foot preceding the penultimate foot.

i) ...σ   σ   σ σ#   ...σ   σ   σ σ#
     | ∧ | | | ∧ | |
     μ´ (μ μ)(μ μ)   →   μ   (μ´ μ)(μ μ)

ii) ... σ   σ σ   σ#   ... σ   σ σ   σ#
      ∧ | | ∧   ∧ | | ∧
     μ´ μ (μ μ)(μ μ)   →   μ μ (μ μ´)(μ μ)

c. Move the accent to the mora immediately preceding it when it is on the devoiced vowel. In the example below, /i/ in italic bold is the devoiced vowel.

i) ofi´syaru → o´fisyaru 'official'

d. Move the accent to the head of the syllable when it is in coda position.

i) tinpanji´i 'chimpanzee'   ii) e´rebeetaa 'elevator'

tinpanˊjii	Rule (22a)	erebeeˊtaa	Rule (22b)
tinpaˊnjii	Rule (22d)	erebeˊetaa	Rule (22d)

In sum, Asano claims that, due to the rules in (21) and (22), the accent falls on the antepenultimate, the preantepenultimate, or the fifth mora from the last.

3.4. Kansai Japanese

This section analyzes the location of accent and the pitch pattern of English loanwords in Kansai Japanese within the framework of OT.

3.4.1. Data

For this study, 1090 unabbreviated English loanwords of three to eight morae (two to eight syllables) were collected.[5] The main source of the data is Horiuchi (1996). Adjectives and verbs are not included in the data because the majority of the loanwords in Japanese are nouns and verbs are made from nouns by adding a verb *suru* 'to do' (e.g. tesuto 'test' + suru 'to do' → tesutosuru 'to test'). The locus of the accent and the pitch pattern of the loanwords in Kansai Japanese are mainly based on the author's knowledge, who is a native speaker of Kansai Japanese. Bimoraic loanwords are excluded from the data since no loanword has the accent on the final mora, and the locus of the accent and the pitch pattern of accented bimoraic loanwords is always HˊL (H = high pitch, L = low pitch). Also there is no monomoraic loanword in the data simply because monomoraic loanwords do not exist in the Japanese lexicon.

The present study focuses only on unabbreviated English loanwords and ignores abbreviated ones. I will leave the accentuation of abbreviated loanwords for future study. Also, since the accentuation of compounds have different characteristics from that of non-compounds, compounds are excluded from the data.[6]

The present study categorizes the unabbreviated English loanwords in Kansai Japanese into three types, and each type is divided into two subgroups based on the word-initial pitch, as shown in (23).

(23) (H = word-initial high pitch, L = word-initial low pitch)
    a. (i)   English Type H
       (ii) English Type L
    b. (iii) Non-English Type H

(iv) Non-English Type L
c. (v) Unaccented Type H
   (vi) Unaccented Type L

3.4.1.1. English Type

The accented loanwords that have the accent on the syllable stressed in English belong to English Type. The loanwords of this type are divided into two subgroups based on the word-initial pitch: high (see (24)) or low (see (25)).

English Type H consists of 460 words of three to nine morae (two to six syllables), whereas English Type L consists of 272 words of three to eight morae (two to six syllables). In total, 732 words out of 1090, i.e. 67.2%, belong to English Type. This type of accentuation is most common in English loanwords in Kansai Japanese.

(24) English Type H

	Kansai J.	Tokyo J.	Gloss	
a.	ba´taa	(ba´taa)	'butter'	(3-mora, 2-syllable)
	HLL	(HLL)		
b.	me´rodii	(me´rodii)	'melody'	(4-mora, 3-syllable)
	HLLL	(HLLL)		
c.	pi´kunikku	(pi´kunikku)	'picnic'	(5-mora, 3-syllable)
	HLLLL	(HLLLL)		
d.	konse´nsasu	(konse´nsasu)	'consensus'	(6-mora, 4-syllable)
	HHHLLL	(LHHLLL)		
e.	paasona´ritii	(paasona´ritii)	'personality'	(7-mora, 5-syllable)
	HHHHLLL	(LHHHLLL)		
f.	furasutore´eshon	(furasutore´eshon)	'frustration'	(8-mora, 6-syllable)
	HHHHHLLL	(LHHHHLLL)		
g.	entaate´imento	(entaate´imento)	'entertainment'	(9-mora, 6-syllable)
	HHHHHLLLL	(LHHHHLLLL)		

(25) English Type L

	Kansai J.	Tokyo J.	Gloss	
a.	kuru´u	(kuru´u)	'crew'	(3-mora, 2-syllable)
	LHL	(LHL)		
b.	suna´kku	(suna´kku)	'snack'	(4-mora, 3-syllable)

	LHLL	(LHLL)		
c.	ame´nitii	(ame´nitii)	'amenity'	(5-mora, 4-syllable)
	LHLLL	(LHLLL)		
d.	wisuko´nsin	(wisuko´nsin)	'Wisconsin'	(6-mora, 4-syllable)
	LLHLLL	(LHHLLL)		
e.	imajine´eshon	(imajine´eshon)	'imagination'	(7-mora, 5-syllable)
	LLLHLLL	(LHHHLLL)		
f.	insutora´kutaa	(insutora´kutaa)	'instructor'	(8-mora, 6-syllable)
	LLLLHLLL	(LHHHHLLL)		

3.4.1.2. Non-English Type

The accented loanwords that do not have the accent on the syllable stressed in English are categorized into Non-English Type. The loanwords of this type are divided into two subgroups based on the word-initial pitch: high (see (26)) or low (see (27)).

Non-English Type H consists of 150 words of three to eight morae (two to eight syllables), while Non-English Type L consists of 65 words of three to seven morae (two to six syllables). In total, 215 words out of 1090 English loanwords, i.e. 19.7%, belong to this category. Interestingly, 180 words out of 215 loanwords of this type, i.e. 83.7%, have the accent on the syllable containing the antepenultimate mora, i.e. on the antepenultimate mora when the syllable is light (e.g. (26g)) or on the preantepenultimate when the syllable is heavy (e.g. (27e)). This strongly suggests that the accent moves onto the syllable containing the antepenultimate mora when a loanword does not have the English accent, i.e. the accent on the syllable stressed in English. I will further discuss this below.

(26) Non-English Type H

	Kansai J.	Tokyo J.	Gloss	
a.	ka´nuu	(ka´nuu)	'canoe'	(3-mora, 2-syllable)
	HLL	(HLL)		
b.	ro´mansu	(ro´mansu)	'romance'	(4-mora, 3-syllable)
	HLLL	(HLLL)		
c.	baruko´nii	(baruko´nii)	'balcony'	(5-mora, 4-syllable)
	HHHLL	(LHHLL)		
d.	jaanari´zumu	(jaanari´zumu)	'journalism'	(6-mora, 5-syllable)
	HHHHLL	(LHHHLL)		

e. koresutero´oru   (koresutero´oru)   'cholesterol'   (7-mora, 6-syllable)
   HHHHHLL   (LHHHHLL)
f. indianapo´risu   (indianapo´risu)   'Indianapolis' (8-mora, 7-syllable)
   HHHHHHLL   (LHHHHHLL)
g. erekutoroni´kusu (erekutoroni´kusu) 'electronics'   (8-mora, 8-syllable)
   HHHHHHHLL   (LHHHHHLL)

(27) Non-English Type L
     Kansai J.   Tokyo J.   Gloss
  a. gau´n   (ga´un)   'gown'   (3-mora, 2-syllable)
     LHL   (HLL)
  b. ime´eji   (ime´eji)   'image'   (4-mora, 3-syllable)
     LHLL   (LHLL)
  c. edi´nbara   (edi´nbara)   'Edinburgh'   (5-mora, 4-syllable)
     LHLLL   (LHLLL)
  d. supeshari´suto   (supeshari´suto)   'specialist' (6-mora, 6-syllable)
     LLLHLL   (LHHHLL)
  e. konpure´kkusu   (konpure´kkusu)   'complex'   (7-mora, 5-syllable)
     LLLHLLL   (LHHHLLL)

3.4.1.3. Unaccented Type

Finally, all the unaccented loanwords in Kansai Japanese belong to Unaccented Type. Unaccented Type is also divided into two subgroups based on the word-initial pitch: high (see (28)) or low (see (29)).

Unaccented Type H consists of 134 words of three to six morae (two to six syllables), while Unaccented Type L consists of 9 words of three to six morae (two to four syllables). Among the six groups of accentuation in Kansai Japanese introduced so far, Unaccented Type L is the least common.

(28) Unaccented Type H
     Kansai J.   Tokyo J.   Gloss
  a. baajon   (ba´ajon)   'version'   (4-mora, 2-syllable)
     HHHH   (HLLL)
  b. botoru   (botoru)   'bottle'   (3-mora, 3-syllable)
     HHH   (LHH)
  c. supuringu   (supuringu)   'spring'   (5-mora, 4-syllable)

   HHHHH (LHHHH)
 d. bakuteria (bakuteria) 'bacteria' (5-mora, 5-syllable)
   HHHHH (LHHHH)
 e. kariforunia (kariforunia) 'California' (6-mora, 6-syllable)
   HHHHHH (LHHHHH)

(29) Unaccented Type L
  Kansai J. Tokyo J. Gloss
 a. karee (karee) 'curry' (3-mora, 2-syllable)
  LLH (LHH)
 b. marason (marason) 'marathon' (4-mora, 3-syllable)
  LLLH (LHHH)
 c. sutookaa (suto´okaa) 'stalker' (5-mora, 3-syllable)
  LLLLH (LHLLL)
 d. rekoodingu (reko´odingu) 'recording' (6-mora, 4-syllable)
  LLLLLH (LHLLLL)

3.4.1.4. Summary

As illustrated in the previous subsections, English loanwords in Kansai Japanese fall into three types and six groups, as summarized in (30). The table (30) shows two things. First, the majority of English loanwords, i.e. 67.2%, have the English accent. Second, the low-pitched mora in the word-initial position is less common.

(30) English Loanwords in Kansai Japanese

a. English Type H	460 (42.2%)	732 (67.2%)
b. English Type L	272 (25.0%)	
c. Non-English Type H	150 (13.7%)	215 (19.7%)
d. Non-English Type L	65 (6.0%)	
e. Unaccented Type H	134 (12.3%)	143 (13.1%)
f. Unaccented Type L	9 (0.8%)	
Word-initial H	744 (68.3%)	1090 (100%)
Word-initial L	346 (31.7%)	

 Distribution of accented morae is summarized as in (31). In (31), the top row shows the location of the accented mora, i.e. '0' = unaccented, '1' = the accent on the first mora, while the leftmost column indicates the word-initial pitch ('H' = high and 'L' = low). As shown in bold in (31), among 346 English loanwords with the word-initial low pitch, 252 words, i.e. 72.8%, have the accent on the second mora and all the English loanwords with the accent on the second mora have the word-initial low pitch. It has been said in the literature that the word-initial pitch of non-loanwords in Kansai Japanese is unpredictable (Pierrehumbert and Beckman 1988: 214). But the data suggests that the word-initial low pitch of English loanwords in Kansai Japanese is highly predictable and the accent on the second mora seems relevant to the word-initial low pitch. I will discuss this more in detail within the OT framework in the following section.

(31) Distribution of Accented Morae

	0	1	2	3	4	5	6	7	8	9		
H	134	455	**0**	91	48	14	2	0	0	0	744	1090
L	9	0	**252**	62	20	3	0	0	0	0	346	
	143	455	252	153	68	17	2	0	0	0	1090	

3.4.2. Analysis

In the following subsections, I will account for the locus of the accent and the pitch pattern of English loanwords in Kansai Japanese within the OT framework.

3.4.2.1. The Locus of Accent
3.4.2.1.1. Accented Loanwords

947 words out of 1090 English loanwords in the data, i.e. 86.9%, are accented loanwords. As introduced in the previous subsection, accented loanwords fall into two groups: English Type, which has the English accent, i.e., the accent on the syllable stressed in English, and Non-English Type, which does not have the English accent.

First, let us consider Non-English Type. 215 words out of 947 accented loanwords, i.e. 22.7%, fall into Non-English Type. 180 words out of 215 loanwords of Non-English Type, i.e. 83.7%, have the accent on the syllable containing the antepenultimate mora. This strongly suggests that the original accent moves onto the syllable containing the antepenultimate mora when a loanword does not preserve the English accent.

The next question to be considered is: What triggers the accent shift? The accent shift occurs to keep the accent within the last two feet. Among the loanwords belonging to Non-English Type, only 10 words out of 215, i.e. 4.7%, do not have the accent within the last two feet, although there are 120 words out of 215, i.e. 55.8%, that do not have the mora corresponding to the English original stress within the last two feet. Based on this, I claim that the restriction on the locus of the accent triggers the accent shift. The fact that the majority of the loanwords belonging to English Type (604 words out of 732, i.e. 82.5%) satisfy this restriction supports the claim.

My analysis is based on the foot structure in Japanese. It has been agreed in the literature that foot size in Japanese is bimoraic (Poser 1984 and 1990, Tateishi 1989, Itô 1990, Itô and Mester 1992, Katayama 1995, Kubozono 1995a, Asano 1999, among others). As cited in (32), however, other questions related to the foot structure in Japanese have not been settled.

(32) Kubozono (1999: 57–58)
The formation of "foot", for example, raises many interesting questions: e.g. whether it proceeds from left to right or from right to left, whether (or when) it permits a monomoraic (i.e. degenerate) foot, whether an unfooted syllable may be allowed, and whether it is entirely independent of syllable structure as assumed by Poser (1990). None of these questions has been settled in the literature.

In this chapter, therefore, I assume the following: (i) the foot distribution is right to left, (ii) the degenerate foot is not allowed, and (iii) following Poser (1990), the foot structure is independent of the syllable structure. That is, I assume that feet are assigned by the constraints FT-BIN (Prince 1980), PARSE-SYL (Hayes 1980), and ALL-FT-RIGHT (McCarthy and Prince 1993a), which are defined as in (33)–(35) and are ranked as in (36). The ranking in (36) determines the foot structure in Japanese, as illustrated in (37). In this chapter, I will not include those constraints in tableaux for simplification.

(33) FT-BIN: Feet are bimoraic or disyllabic.

(34) PARSE-SYL: Syllables are parsed by feet.

(35) ALL-FT-RIGHT: Every foot is at the right edge of the prosodic word.

(36) Constraint Ranking for Foot Assignment

    FT-BIN
    |
    PARSE-SYL
    |
    ALL-FT-RIGHT

(37) FT-BIN >> PARSE-SYL >> ALL-FT-RIGHT

$\sigma_\mu\sigma_\mu\sigma_\mu\sigma_\mu\sigma_\mu$	FT-BIN	PARSE-SYL	ALL-FT-R
a. $(\sigma_\mu)(\sigma_\mu\sigma_\mu)(\sigma_\mu\sigma_\mu)$	*!		**, ****
b. $\sigma_\mu\sigma_\mu\sigma_\mu(\sigma_\mu\sigma_\mu)$		**!*	
c. ☞ $\sigma_\mu(\sigma_\mu\sigma_\mu)(\sigma_\mu\sigma_\mu)$		*	**

Within the OT framework, the accent shift can be explained by six constraints: NONFINALITY (Prince and Smolensky 1993: 52), RIGHTMOST (Prince and Smolensky 1993: 39), FAITHLOC(ACCENT) (Smith 1998), ALIGN-R(PENULT F, ACCENT), ACCENT(PROMINENT μ), and LEFTMOST (Prince and Smolensky 1993: 39). These constraints are defined as in (38)–(43).

(38) NONFINALITY: No accent falls on the word-final foot.

(39) RIGHTMOST: The accented foot is rightmost of the word.

(40) FAITHLOC(ACCENT): Output accent is faithful to its location in the input.

(41) ALIGN-R(PENULT F, ACCENT): The last mora of the penultimate foot is accented.

(42) ACCENT(PROMINENT μ): Accent is on the most prominent nucleus of the syllable, i.e. on the first part of a long vowel.

(43) LEFTMOST: The accented foot is leftmost of the word.

NonFinality prohibits the accent on the word-final foot, while Rightmost requires the accented foot be rightmost of the word. As mentioned above, the accent that is not within the last two feet is avoided. The interaction of these two constraints accounts for this restriction on the locus of the accent, as illustrated in (44). In (44), the candidates that have the accent within the last two feet (e.g. (44a) and (44b)) are optimal, although they violate one of the two constraints once. The candidates (44c) and (44d), which have the accent in the antepenultimate foot or preantepenultimate foot, on the other hand, are ruled out, because they violate Rightmost more than twice.

(44)

	μμμμμμμμ	NonFinality	Rightmost
a. ☞	(μμ)(μμ)(μμ)(μ´μ)	*	
b. ☞	(μμ)(μμ)(μ´μ)(μμ)		*
c.	(μμ)(μ´μ)(μμ)(μμ)		**!
d.	(μ´μ)(μμ)(μμ)(μμ)		**!*

FaithLoc (Accent) (Smith 1998) says that the locus of the accent in the output is faithful to the locus of the accent in the input. The English accent is most common in English loanwords in Kansai Japanese. They preserve the English accent when it is within the last two feet. This suggests that the constraints for the restriction on the locus of the accent, i.e. NonFinality and Rightmost, are ranked higher than FaithLoc(Accent). Align-R(Penult F, Accent) is a member of the constraint family Align (McCarthy and Prince 1993a). This constraint requires that the last mora of the penultimate foot, i.e. the antepenultimate mora, be accented. The English accent shifts to the antepenultimate accent when English loanwords do not preserve the English accent. This suggests that FaithLoc(Accent) is ranked higher than Align-R(Penult F, Accent). Accent(prominent μ) militates against the accent on the second half of the long vowel or on the coda. Accent(prominent μ) is the highest-ranked constraint because no loanword violates this constraint. Finally, Leftmost requires that the accented foot be leftmost of the word. When the antepenultimate mora is assigned to the second half of a long vowel or a coda consonant, the accent on it moves leftward but not rightward. This accent shift is explained by Leftmost, as illustrated in (45) where only the relevant constraints are shown. In (45), the candidate (45a), which has the accent on the antepenultimate mora, cannot be the optimal because of the violation of the highest-ranked constraint Accent(prominent μ). The candidates (45b) and (45c) satisfy Accent(prominent μ), but the candidate (45b) loses to the candidate (45c), since the candidate (45b) violates Leftmost more than the candidate (45c) does.

(45) Accent(prominent μ) >> Align-R(Penult F, Accent) >> Leftmost

	complex	Accent	Align-R	L-most
a.	ko(n.pu.)(rek´.)(ku.su.)	*!		*
b.	ko(n.pu.)(rek.)(ku´.su.)		*	**!
c. ☞	ko(n.pu.)(re´k.)(ku.su.)		*	*

In sum, the six constraints introduced above are ranked as in (46). The ranking in (46) produces the loanwords of Non-English Type, as exemplified in (47) and (48). The optimal candidates in (47) and (48) do not preserve the English accent because their English accents are not within the last two feet.

(46) Constraint Ranking

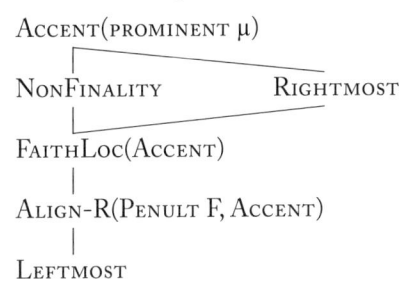

Accent(prominent μ)

NonFinality   Rightmost

FaithLoc(Accent)

Align-R(Penult F, Accent)

Leftmost

(47) Non-English Type H

	journalism	Accent	NonFin	R-most	FaithLoc	Align-R	L-most
a.	(jaa´.)(na.ri.)(zu.mu.)	*!		**	*	*	
b.	(ja´a.)(na.ri.)(zu.mu.)		**!			*	
c.	(jaa.)(na.ri.)(zu´.mu.)			*		*!	**
d.	(jaa.)(na´.ri.)(zu.mu.)			*	*	*!	*
e. ☞	(jaa.)(na.ri´.)(zu.mu.)			*	*		*

(48) Non-English Type L

	specialist	Accent	NonFin	R-most	FaithLoc	Align-R	L-most
a.	(su.pe´.)(sha.ri.)(su.to.)			**!		*	
b.	(su.pe.)(sha.ri.)(su´.to.)		*		*	*!	**
c.	(su.pe.)(sha´.ri.)(su.to.)			*	*	*!	*
d. ☞	(su.pe.)(sha.ri´.)(su.to.)			*	*		*

Next, consider English Type. 732 words out of 947 accented loanwords, i.e. 77.3%, belong to English Type. The constraint ranking in (46), which accounts for Non-English Type, explains English Type as well, as illustrated in (49) and (50). In (49) and (50), the optimal candidates preserve the English accent because they have the English accent within the last two feet.

(49) English Type H

	personality	Accent	NonFin	R-most	FaithLoc	Align-R	L-most
a.	pa(a.so´.)(na.ri.)(tii.)			**!	*	*	*
b.	pa(aso)(nari)(tii´)	*!	*		*	*	***
c.	pa(aso)(nari´)(tii)			*	*!		**
d. ☞	pa(aso)(na´ri)(tii)			*		*	**

(50) English Type L

	snack	Accent	NonFin	R-most	FaithLoc	Align-R	L-most
a.	(su.na)(kˊ.ku.)	*!	*		*	*	*
b.	(suˊ.na)(k.ku.)			*	*!	*	
c. ☞	(su.naˊ)(k.ku.)			*			

3.4.2.1.2. Unaccented Loanwords

143 words out of 1090 English loanwords in the data, i.e. 13.1%, are unaccented loanwords. Unaccented loanwords are subcategorized: Unaccented Type H and Unaccented Type L.

Kubozono and Ohta (1998: 39–42) analyze the accentuation of place name loanwords, and show that the majority of unaccented place name loanwords in Tokyo Japanese are quadrimoraic and their last two syllables are light. However, an examination of English loanwords in Kansai Japanese reveals that these generalizations do not explain the unaccented loanwords in Kansai Japanese. First, among 1090 English loanwords in Kansai Japanese, quadrimoraic words form the largest group, i.e. 445 words (40.8%). Among the quadrimoraic words, however, only 88 words, i.e. 19.8%, are unaccented. That is, the majority of quadrimoraic loanwords are not unaccented. Second, among 342 loanwords in Kansai Japanese whose last two syllables are light, only 58 words, i.e. 17.0%, are unaccented. That is, the majority of the loanwords whose last two syllables are light are not unaccented. These facts suggest that the generalizations by Kubozono and Ohta do not explain why the 145 words in Kansai Japanese do not have accents.

How can unaccented loanwords be explained? The majority of non-loanwords in Tokyo Japanese are unaccented (Hayashi 1982) and unaccentedness is the default situation in Tokyo Japanese (Akinaga 1958, Katayama 1995). These observations seem to apply to Kansai Japanese as well, and the number of unaccented non-loanwords in Kansai Japanese seems to be increasing. Based on this, following Ono (1991), I assume that English loanwords become unaccented as a result of assimilation to the core part of the Japanese lexicon with respect to accentuation. Deaccentuation can be explained by the constraint *HL (Itô and Mester 2003b: 58) in (51). *HL is ranked highest in the constraint ranking for the assimilated loanwords as shown in (52), while it is ranked lowest in the ranking for the accented loanwords as illustrated in (53). The ranking in (52) accounts for unaccented loanwords, as exemplified in (54) and (55). In (54) and (55), the optimal candidates are unaccented because of the highest-ranked constraint *HL.

(51) *HL: No accent.

(52) Constraint Ranking for Unaccented Loanwords

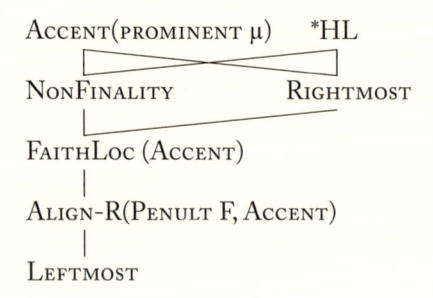

    Accent(prominent μ)   *HL
    NonFinality   Rightmost
    FaithLoc (Accent)
    |
    Align-R(Penult F, Accent)
    |
    Leftmost

(53) Constraint Ranking for Accented Loanwords

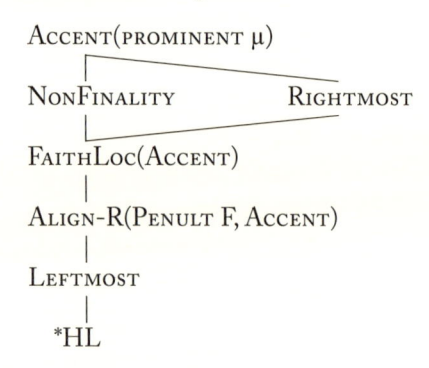

    Accent(prominent μ)
    NonFinality   Rightmost
    FaithLoc(Accent)
    |
    Align-R(Penult F, Accent)
    |
    Leftmost
    |
    *HL

(54) Unaccented Type H

	California	*HL	Accent	NonFin	R-most	FaithLoc	Align-R	L-most
a.	(ka.ri.)(fo´.ru.)(ni.a.)	*!			*		*	*
b.	(ka.ri.)(fo.ru´.)(ni.a.)	*!			*	*		*
c. ☞	(ka.ri.)(fo.ru.)(ni.a.)					*		

(55) Unaccented Type L

marathon	*HL	Accent	NonFin	R-most	FaithLoc	Align-R	L-most
a. (ma´.ra.)(son.)	*!			*		*	
b. (ma.ra´.)(son.)	*!			*	*		
c. ☞ (ma.ra.)(son.)					*		

3.4.2.2. Pitch Pattern

I have introduced the pitch pattern of non-loanwords in Kansai Japanese in 3.2.2. Non-loanwords and English loanwords in Kansai Japanese are basically the same with respect to the pitch pattern, and they share the same characteristics in (56), which is the summary of 3.2.2. The significant difference between them is the word-initial pitch. With regard to non-loanwords, Pierrehumbert and Beckman (1988: 214) claim that the word-initial pitch is unpredictable. In English loanwords, on the other hand, it is highly predictable, as shown in (31) (repeated in (57)). The table in (57) suggests that the accent on the second mora triggers the word-initial low pitch.

(56) a. The accent is marked by a falling pitch.
 b. The accented mora is high-pitched.
 c. A prosodic word cannot have more than one accented mora.
 d. A prosodic word must have at least one high-pitched mora.
 e. The morae following the accented mora are low-pitched throughout.
 f. The morae preceding the accented mora can be either high- or low-pitched throughout.
 g. When a loanword has a low-pitched mora word-initially, only the accented mora of the accented word or the last mora of the unaccented word can be high-pitched.
 h. When the unaccented word with the word-initial low pitch is followed by a particle such as the nominative marker *ga*, the location of the high pitch moves to the word-final, i.e. onto the nominative marker.

(57) Distribution of Accented Morae (= (31))

	0	1	2	3	4	5	6	7	8	9	
H	134	455	0	91	48	14	2	0	0	0	744
L	9	0	252	62	20	3	0	0	0	0	346
	143	455	252	153	68	17	2	0	0	0	1090

The pitch pattern of English loanwords in Kansai Japanese is determined by the following six markedness constraints.

(58) HEAD=H: Head mora should be high-pitched.

(59) *NonHd/H: No High pitch on non-head mora.

(60) *[HH: No word-initial HH.

(61) *[LL: No word-initial LL.

(62) *[LH: No word-initial LH.

(63) LH´: The mora immediately precedes the accented mora is low-pitched.

HEAD=H (Yip 2002: 85) in (58) requires that the accented mora be high-pitched and *NonHd/H (Yip 2002: 98) in (59) militates against high pitch on non-accented mora. HEAD=H is ranked highest since no loanword violates this constraint, while *NonHd/H is ranked lowest. The constraints *[HH in (60) and *[LL in (61) prohibit the word-initial HH and the word-initial LL, respectively. These constraints are members of the constraint family OBLIGATORY CONTOUR PRINCIPLE in the sense of McCarthy (1986), i.e. no adjacent identical elements except across morpheme boundaries. *[LH in (62) militates against the word-initial LH. This is a positional markedness version of *LH. Versions of the constraint *LH play significant roles in Japanese. For example, the constraint *LH^2, the self-conjoined version of *LH, is a highest-ranked in Japanese, since a prosodic word cannot have more than one rising pitch. The sequence of low-high in the word-initial position is not allowed in Kansai Japanese unless the high is on the accented mora. As mentioned above, the word-initial low pitch is less common than the word-initial high pitch. This indicates that *[LL and *[LH are ranked higher than *[HH. The ranking between *[LL and *[LH is *[LL >> *[LH, because most of the loanwords with the word-initial low pitch have the accent on the second mora and the accented mora is high-pitched. The constraint LH´ in (63) requires that the mora immediately preceding the accented mora be low-pitched. In Kansai Japanese, the rising of the pitch is possible only in the position immediately preceding the accented mora. This constraint makes the accented mora the only high-pitched mora of the word, i.e. ...LH´L... vs. ...HH´L.... That is, this constraint makes the accent of a prosodic word more prominent. The constraint LH´ is ranked higher than *[LH. The constraints in (60)–(63) determine the pitch pattern of the morae preceding the accented mora.

In sum, the six constraints are ranked as in (64). This ranking determines the pitch pattern of English loanwords in Kansai Japanese, as exemplified in (65)–(68). The optimal candidates in (65), (66), and (67) have the word-initial high pitch because of the high-ranked constraints HEAD=H and *[LL, whereas the optimal candidate in (68) have the word-initial low pitch due to the constraint LH´.

(64) Constraint Ranking
HEAD=H >> *[LL >> LH´ >> *[LH >> *[HH >> *NonHd/H

(65) Unaccented Loanword

	bottle	HEAD=H	*[LL	LH´	*[LH	*[HH	*NonHd/H
a.	botoru LLL		*!				
b. ☞	botoru HHH					*	***

(66) Accented Loanword (the accent on the first mora)

	canoe	Head=H	*[LL	LH´	*[LH	*[HH	*NonIᴅ/H
a.	ka´nuu HHH					*!	**
b. ☞	ka´nuu HLL						
c.	ka´nuu LLL	*!	*				

(67) Accented Loanword (the accent on the second mora)

	amenity	Head=H	*[LL	LH´	*[LH	*[HH	*NonHᴅ/H
a.	ame´nitii HHLLL			*!		*	*
b. ☞	ame´nitii LHLLL				*		

(68) Accented Loanword (the accent on the third mora)

	consensus	Head=H	*[LL	LH´	*[LH	*[HH	*NonHd/H
a.	konse´nsasu LHHLLL			*	*!		*
b.	konse´nsasu LLHLLL		*!				
c. ☞	konse´nsasu HHHLLL			*		*	**

3.4.2.3. Summary

In this section, I have discussed the locus of the accent and the pitch pattern of English loanwords in Kansai Japanese and showed that the rankings in (69)–(71) account for them. The rankings in (69) and (71) and the rankings in (70) and (71) determine the accentuation and the pitch pattern of English accented loanwords in Kansai Japanese and the accentuation and the pitch pattern of English unaccented loanwords in Kansai Japanese, respectively.

(69) Constraint Ranking for Accented Loanwords

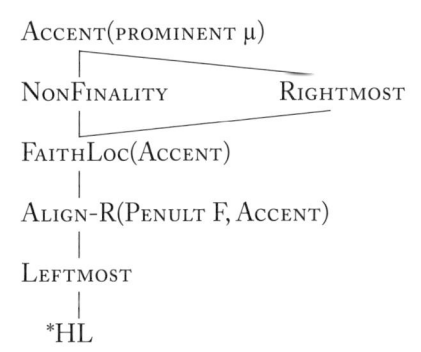

Accent(prominent μ)
⌐――――――――――┐
NonFinality   Rightmost
└――――┘
FaithLoc(Accent)
|
Align-R(Penult F, Accent)
|
Leftmost
|
*HL

(70) Constraint Ranking for Unaccented Loanwords

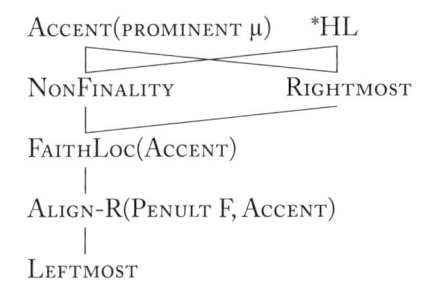

Accent(prominent μ)   *HL
⌐――――――――――×――――┘
NonFinality   Rightmost
└――――┘
FaithLoc(Accent)
|
Align-R(Penult F, Accent)
|
Leftmost

(71) Constraint Ranking for the Pitch Pattern
Head=H >> *[LL >> LH´ >> *[LH >> *[HH >> *NonHd/H

3.5. Tokyo Japanese

This section discusses the locus of the accent and the pitch pattern of English loanwords in Tokyo Japanese within the OT framework.

3.5.1. Data

1090 unabbreviated English loanwords of three to eight morae (two to eight syllables) were collected mainly from a loanword dictionary (Horiuchi 1996). Adjectives and verbs are not included in the data because most of the loanwords in Japanese are nouns and verbs are made from nouns by adding a verb *suru* 'to do' (e.g. tesuto 'test' + suru 'to do' → tesutosuru 'to test'). The locus of the accent and the pitch pattern of the loanwords in Tokyo Japanese are based on two accent dictionaries of Tokyo Japanese (Nihon Hoso Kyokai 1998 and Kindaichi and Akinaga 2001). In the Japanese accent dictionaries, there are words that have more than one possible location of the accent, as exemplified in (72). In such cases, the present study deals only with the most common accent (e.g. (72a)), which is indicated in the dictionaries. The difference in the loci of the accent will be the subject of future research.

(72) 'accordion'   (Kindaichi and Akinaga 2001: 10)
    a. ako´odion
    b. akoodi´on

As in Kansai Japanese, English loanwords in Tokyo Japanese can be divided into three types: English Type, Non-English Type, and Unaccented Type. First, the accented loanwords that have the English accent, i.e. the accent on the syllable stressed in English, are categorized into English Type. This type consists of 749 words of three to nine morae (two to six syllables).

(73) English Type

	Tokyo J.	Kansai J.	Gloss	
a.	kuru´u LHL	(kuru´u) (LHL)	'crew'	(3-mora, 2-syllable)
b.	suna´kku LHLL	(suna´kku) (LHLL)	'snack'	(4-mora, 3-syllable)
c.	pi´kunikku HLLLL	(pi´kunikku) (HLLLL)	'picnic'	(5-mora, 3-syllable)
d.	wisuko´nsin LHHLLL	(wisuko´nsin) (LLHLLL)	'Wisconsin'	(6-mora, 4-syllable)
e.	imajine´esyon LHHHLLL	(imajine´esyon) (LLLHLLL)	'imagination'	(7-mora, 5-syllable)
f.	furasutore´esyon LHHHHLLL	(furasutore´esyon) (HHHHHLLL)	'frustration'	(8-mora, 6-syllable)
g.	entaate´imento LHHHHLLLL	(entaate´imento) (HHHHHLLLL)	'entertainment'	(9-mora, 6-syllable)

Second, the accented loanwords that do not have the English accent are categorized into Non-English Type. This group consists of 216 words of three to eight morae (two to eight syllables). As in Kansai Japanese, most (79.6%, i.e. 172 words out of 216 loanwords) of the loanwords belonging to this type have the accent on the syllable containing the antepenultimate mora, i.e. on the antepenultimate mora when the syllable is light or on the preantepenultimate when the syllable is heavy. This strongly suggests that the accent moves onto the syllable containing the antepenultimate mora when a loanword does not preserve the English accent.

(74) Non-English Type
    Tokyo J.   Kansai J.   Gloss
 a. ka′nuu   (ka′nuu)   'canoe'   (3-mora, 2-syllable)
    HLL   (HLL)
 b. ime′eji   (ime′eji)   'image'   (4-mora, 3-syllable)
    LHLL   (LHLL)
 c. edi′nbara   (edi′nbara)   'Edinburgh' (5-mora, 4-syllable)
    LHLLL   (LHLLL)
 d. jaanari′zumu (jaanari′zumu) 'journalism' (6-mora, 5-syllable)
    LHHHLL   (HHHHLL)
 e. koresutero′oru (koresutero′oru) 'cholesterol' (7-mora, 6-syllable)
    LHHHHLL   (HHHHHLL)
 f. indianapo′risu (indianapo′risu) 'Indianapolis' (8-mora, 7-syllable)
    LHHHHHLL   (HHHHHHLL)
 g. erekutoroni′kusu (erekutoroni′kusu) 'electronics' (8-mora, 8-syllable)
    LHHHHHLL   (HHHHHHLL)

Finally, all the unaccented loanwords in Tokyo Japanese fall into Unaccented Type. Unaccented Type consists of 125 words of three to six morae (two to six syllables).

(75) Unaccented Type
    Tokyo J.   Kansai J.   Gloss
 a. karee   (karee)   'curry'   (4-mora, 2-syllable)
    LHH   (LLH)
 b. marason   (marason) 'marathon' (3-mora, 3-syllable)
    LHHH   (LLLH)

  c. supuringu (supuringu) 'spring' (5-mora, 4-syllable)
    LHHHH (HHHHH)
  d. bakuteria (bakuteria) 'bacteria' (5-mora, 5-syllable)
    LHHHH (HHHHH)
  e. kariforunia (kariforunia) 'California' (6-mora, 6-syllable)
    LHHHHH (HHHHHH)

In summary, English loanwords in Tokyo Japanese are divided into three types as shown in (76). In Tokyo Japanese, unlike Kansai Japanese, the word-initial pitch is totally predictable and each of these types needs not be divided into subcategories based on the word-initial pitch.

(76) English Loanwords in Tokyo Japanese

a. English Type	749 (68.7%)
b. Non-English Type	216 (19.8%)
c. Unaccented Type	125 (11.5%)
	1090 (100.0%)

3.5.2. Analysis

In this section, I will account for the locus of the accent and the pitch pattern of English loanwords in Tokyo Japanese within the OT framework.

3.5.2.1. The Locus of Accent

965 words out of 1090 English loanwords in the data, i.e. 88.5%, are accented. Accented loanwords fall into two groups: English Type and Non-English Type. With respect to the locus of the accent, Tokyo Japanese and Kansai Japanese share the three features: (i) English accent as the most common accent among accented loanwords, (ii) the antepenultimate accent as the most common accent among the loanwords of Non-English Type, and (iii) dispreference for the accent that is not within the last two feet. As a result, 891 words out of 965 accented loanwords in Tokyo Japanese, i.e. 92.3%, are identical with their corresponding words in Kansai Japanese with regard to the locus of the accent.[7] This means that the accentuation of accented loanwords in Tokyo Japanese can be explained by the constraint ranking for the accentuation of accented loanwords in Kansai

Japanese in (69) (repeated here in (77)). The constraint ranking in (77) produces the correct outputs of English Type and Non-English Type, as exemplified in (78) and (79).[8] In (78), the optimal candidate has the English accent since it is in the penultimate foot, whereas the optimal candidate in (79) does not have it because it is in the antepenultimate foot.

(77) Constraint Ranking for Accented Loanwords

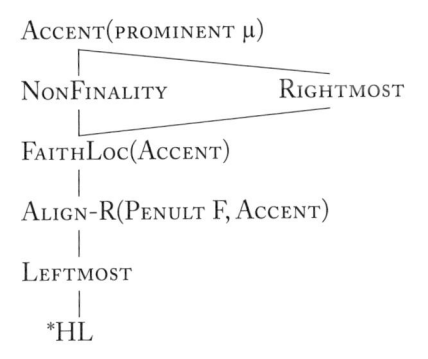

Accent(prominent μ)

NonFinality   Rightmost

FaithLoc(Accent)

Align-R(Penult F, Accent)

Leftmost

*HL

(78) English Type

imagination	Accent	NonFin	R-most	FaithLoc	Align-R	L-most
a. i(maji)(nee´)(syon)	*!		*	*		**
b. i(ma´ji)(nee)(syon)		**!	*	*	*	
c. i(maji)(nee)(syo´n)		*		*!	*	***
d. ☞ i(maji)(ne´e)(syon)		*			*	**

(79) Non-English Type

journalism	Accent	NonFin	R-most	FaithLoc	Align-R	L-most
a. (jaa´)(nari)(zumu)	*!		**	*	*	
b. (ja´a)(nari)(zumu)		**!		*		
c. (jaa)(nari)(zu´mu)		*		*	*!	**
d. (jaa)(na´ri)(zumu)		*	*	*	*!	*
e. ☞ (jaa)(nari´)(zumu)			*	*		*

There is one more issue I need to address: the treatment of devoiced vowels.

In Tokyo Japanese, high vowels are devoiced when preceded and followed by voiceless obstruents or when they are in the word-final position and preceded by a voiceless obstruent.[9] Asano (1999:74) claims that the accent shift occurs to avoid the accent on a devoiced vowel (e.g. o´fisharu 'official' (*ofi´sharu)). But, the accent shift Asano claims is not observed in the data.[10] In fact, many studies show that the accent shift to avoid the accent on the devoiced vowel has become rare (Vance 1987: 50, Kindaichi and Akinaga 2001: Appendix (8), among others). For examples, the words in (80), which are from Kindaichi and Akinaga (2001), have the accent on the devoiced vowel. Based on this, I claim that devoiced vowels in Tokyo Japanese do not trigger the accent shift and, as discussed in this chapter, accent shift occurs only when the accent is not within the last two feet.

(80) Counterexamples to Asano (1999)
 (Devoiced vowels are italicized.)
 a. t*i*´kin   HLL   'chicken'
 b. k*i*´ttin   HLLL   'kitchen'
 c. p*i*´kunikku HLLLL   'picnic'

Finally, let us consider unaccented loanwords. 125 words out of 1090 English loanwords in the corpus, i.e. 11.5%, belong to Unaccented Type. Regarding the unaccented loanwords in Tokyo Japanese, Kubozono and Ohta (1998: 39–42) make two generalizations: (i) the majority of unaccented loanwords in Tokyo Japanese are quadrimoraic and (ii) their last two syllables are light. As in the case of Kansai Japanese, however, these generalizations do not explain why the 125 words in Tokyo Japanese do not have accents. First, as Kubozono and Ohta observe, the majority (77 words out of 125, i.e. 61.6%) of unaccented loanwords in Tokyo Japanese are quadrimoraic. Among 445 quadrimoraic loanwords in the data, however, only 77 words, i.e. 17.3%, are unaccented. That is, the majority of quadrimoraic loanwords are accented. Second, 342 loanwords in the data have the sequence of two light syllables word-finally. Among them, however, only 57 words, i.e. 16.7%, are unaccented. In other words, the majority of the loanwords whose last two syllables are light are accented. These facts suggest that the generalizations by Kubozono and Ohta do not explain unaccented loanwords in Tokyo Japanese.

The majority of non-loanwords in Tokyo Japanese are unaccented (Hayashi 1982) and unaccentedness is the default situation in Tokyo Japanese (Akinaga

1958, Katayama 1995). Based on these, following Ono (1991), I assume that English loanwords become unaccented as a result of assimilation to the core part of the Japanese lexicon with respect to accentuation. The assimilated loanwords do not have the accent due to the highest-ranked constraint *HL. That is, the constraint ranking in (70) (repeated in (81)), which is developed for unaccented loanwords in Kansai Japanese, accounts for unaccented loanwords in Tokyo Japanese as well, as exemplified in (82). In (82), the optimal candidate is unaccented due to the highest ranked constraint *HL.

(81) Constraint Ranking for Unaccented Loanwords

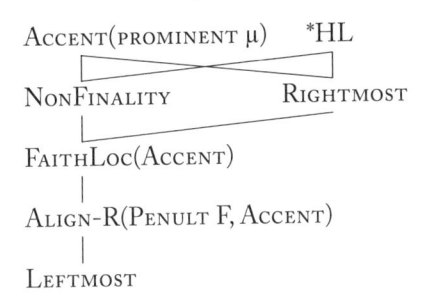

     Accent(prominent μ)   *HL

     NonFinality   Rightmost

     FaithLoc(Accent)

     Align-R(Penult F, Accent)

     Leftmost

(82) Unaccented Type

bacteria	*HL	Accent	NonFin	R-most	FaithLoc	Align-R	L-most
a. ba´(kute)(ria)	*!			**	*	*	
b. ba(kute´)(ria)	*!			*			*
c. ba(kute)(ri´a)	*!		*		*	*	**
d. ☞ ba(kute)(ria)				*	*	*	*

3.5.2.2. Pitch Pattern

With regard to the pitch pattern, there is no difference between Non-loanwords and English loanwords in Tokyo Japanese. They share the same characteristics in (83), which is the summary of 3.2.1.

(83) a. The accent is marked by a falling pitch.
    b. The accented mora is high-pitched.
    c. A prosodic word cannot have more than one accented mora.
    d. The morae following the accented mora are low-pitched throughout.

e. The word-initial pitch and the pitch on the second mora must be distinct.

The pitch pattern of English loanwords in Tokyo Japanese is determined by the six constraints introduced in the analysis of English loanwords in Kansai Japanese: Head=H, *NonHd/H, LH´, *[LL, *[LH, and *[HH. The characteristic (83e) suggests that the constraints *[LL and *[HH are highest-ranked. The constraint Head=H is also highest-ranked because no loanwords in Tokyo Japanese violate it. In sum, the six constraints are ranked as in (84). The constraint ranking in (84) determines the pitch pattern of English loanwords in Tokyo Japanese, as exemplified in (85)–(88). In (85), (86), and (87), the optimal candidates have the word-initial low pitch because of the high-ranked constraints *[LL and *[HH, whereas the optimal candidate in (88) have the word-initial high pitch due to the constraint *[HH. There is no irregularity with regard to the pitch pattern of English loanwords in Tokyo Japanese. The constraint ranking in (84) explains all the loanwords in the data.

(84) Constraint Ranking

```
    Head=H      *[LL      *[HH
    
    *[LH        LH´       *NonHd/H
```

(85) Unaccented Loanword

	curry	Head=H	*[LL	*[HH	*[LH	LH´	*NonHd/H
b.	karee LLL		*!				
b.	karee HHH			*!			***
c. ☞	karee LHH				*		**

3 Accentuation of English Loanwords   51

(86) Accented Loanword (the accent on the first mora)

canoe	Head=H	*[LL	*[HH	*[LH	LH´	*NonHd/H
c. ka´nuu HHH			*!			**
b. ☞ ka´nuu HLL						

(87) Accented Loanword (the accent on the second mora)

image	Head=H	*[LL	*[HH	*[LH	LH´	*NonHd/H
d. ime´eji HHLL			*!		*	*
b. ☞ ime´eji LHLL				*		

(88) Accented Loanword (the accent on the third mora)

Wisconsin	Head=H	*[LL	*[HH	*[LH	LH´	*NonHd/H
e. wisuko´nsin LLHLLL		*!				
b. wisuko´nsin HHHLLL			*!		*	**
c. ☞ wisuko´nsin LHHLLL				*	*	*

3.5.2.3. Summary

In this section, I have discussed that the rankings in (89)–(91) account for the locus of the accent and the pitch pattern of English loanwords in Tokyo Japanese. The rankings (89) and (91) and the rankings (90) and (91) account for the accentuation and the pitch pattern of English accented loanwords in Tokyo Japanese and the accentuation and the pitch pattern of English unaccented loanwords in Tokyo Japanese, respectively.

(89) Constraint Ranking for Accented Loanwords

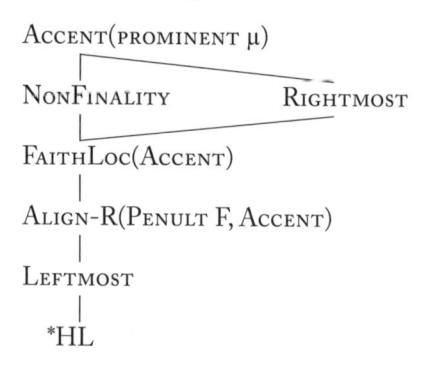

　　Accent(prominent μ)
　　┌─────────────┐
　　NonFinality　　　Rightmost
　　└─────────────┘
　　FaithLoc(Accent)
　　　│
　　Align-R(Penult F, Accent)
　　　│
　　Leftmost
　　　│
　　*HL

(90) Constraint Ranking for Unaccented Loanwords

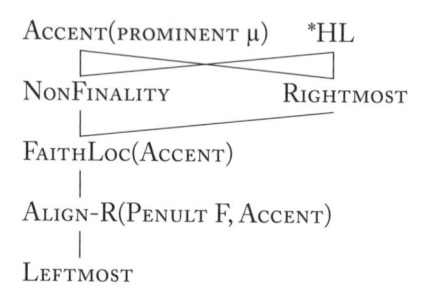

　　Accent(prominent μ)　　*HL
　　┌──────────────────┐
　　　　　　×
　　NonFinality　　　Rightmost
　　└─────────────┘
　　FaithLoc(Accent)
　　　│
　　Align-R(Penult F, Accent)
　　　│
　　Leftmost

(91) Constraint Ranking for the Pitch Pattern

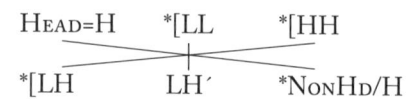

　　Head=H　　*[LL　　*[HH
　　　　　　　×
　　*[LH　　　LH´　　*NonHd/H

3.6. Conclusion

This chapter discussed the locus of the accent and the pitch pattern of English loanwords in Kansai Japanese and Tokyo Japanese within the framework of OT. The present study is summarized as follows.

First, Kansai Japanese and Tokyo Japanese are the same with regard to accent assignment: (i) the English accent, i.e. the accent on the syllable stressed in English, is the most common, and (ii) the accent moves onto the syllable containing the antepenultimate mora when the English accent is not within the last two feet.

Second, the information on the locus of accent is included in the input, although Nakai (1988) claims that the accent in the source language does not play the major role in determining the locus of the accent in Kyoto Japanese, a variety of Kansai Japanese. As mentioned above, the English accent is the most common and the non-English accent is due to the restriction on the locus of the accent, i.e. the accent must be within the last two feet. This suggests that the information on the locus of English stress is included in the input and Japanese borrowers have access to the information.

Third, in OT, the difference between dialects can be explained in terms of the ranking difference. Tokyo Japanese and Kansai Japanese are different with respect to the pitch pattern. In Kansai Japanese, the pitch pattern of English loanwords can be explained by the constraint ranking in (92), where constraints *[LL and LH´ play significant roles. In Kansai Japanese, because of these constraints, the word-initial high pitch is more common than the low pitch. In Tokyo Japanese, on the other hand, the pitch pattern of English loanwords can be explained by the constraint ranking in (93), where the constraints *[HH and *[LL play crucial roles. In Tokyo Japanese, the pitch on the first mora and the pitch on the second mora are distinct due to these constraints.

(92) Constraint Ranking for the Pitch Pattern in Kansai Japanese
 Head=H >> *[LL >> LH´ >> *[LH >> *[HH >> *NonHd/H

(93) Constraint Ranking for the Pitch Pattern in Tokyo Japanese

 Head=H   *[LL   *[HH

 *[LH   LH´   *NonHd/H

Finally, the word-initial pitch of English loanwords in Kansai Japanese is predictable. Because of the two possible word-initial pitches, high and low, the pitch pattern in Kansai Japanese is more complicated and it has been said that the pitch pattern of the whole word in Kansai Japanese is unpredictable. The present study revealed that the word-initial high pitch is more common and the word-initial low pitch is triggered by the accent on the second mora, which is due to the constraint LH´.

In future research, the following issues should be further studied. First, the ranking for accented loanwords developed in this chapter accounts for most of English loanwords in both Kansai Japanese and Tokyo Japanese, but there are exceptions to it. Especially, the ranking does not explain the accentuation of short words belonging to Non-English Type consisting of four or fewer morae. In this study, I claimed that the restriction on the locus of the accent triggers the accent shift. The ranking accounts for the accent shift in the loanwords consisting of five or more morae but does not explain the accent shift in the loanwords consisting of four or fewer morae, since all the loanwords consisting of four or fewer morae have the English accent within the last two feet. That is, the ranking predicts the wrong output, as illustrated in (94), and does not account for why they do not preserve the English accent. Among accented loanwords consisting of four or fewer morae (504 words in Kansai Japanese and 530 in Tokyo Japanese), the analysis developed in this chapter does not explain 58 loanwords, i.e. 11.5%, in Kansai Japanese and 60 loanwords, i.e. 11.3%, in Tokyo Japanese. I will leave these exceptions for future research.

(94) sapphire → safa´ia (Wrong Prediction)

sapphire	ACCENT	NONFIN	R-MOST	FAITHLOC	ALIGN-R	L-MOST
a. ☹ (sa´fa)(ia)			*		*	
b. (safa´)(ia)			*	*!		
c. (safa)(i´a)		*		*!	*	*
d. (safa)(ia´)		*		*!	*	*

Second, the ranking in (92) explains the pitch pattern of most English loanwords in Kansai Japanese. But the word-initial low pitch has not been completely explained yet. The present study claims that the word-initial low pitch is triggered by the accent on the second mora. But, there are words that have the word-initial low pitch without having the accent on the second mora. Among 94 counterexamples, 54 words, i.e. 57.4%, have the accent on the heavy syllable. The weight of the syllable might also be relevant to the word-initial low pitch. This question needs to be further pursued.

Third, this chapter focused only on the most common accent of the word. In Tokyo Japanese, there are words that have more than one possible accent, as illustrated in (95), and the difference between the possible accents was not discussed. This should be studied in the future.

(95) 'accordion' (Kindaichi and Akinaga 2001: 10)
   a. ako´odion
   b. akoodi´on

Finally, this chapter dealt with unabbreviated English loanwords and ignored abbreviated ones. Labrune (2002) finds that apocope and aphaeresis generally occur just before the accented mora of a base. This suggests that the accentuation of abbreviated words is different from that of unabbreviated ones. The difference between abbreviated and unabbreviated words with regard to the accentuation should be further researched.

Endnotes

* Earlier versions of parts of this chapter appear in Penn Working Papers in Linguistics 11.1 and CLS 40-I.
1 Kansai is an area in Japan where cities such as Kobe, Osaka, Nara, and Kyoto are included.
2 In this and the following chapters, instead of phonetic representation (e.g. [o:]), long vowels in examples are represented by the sequence of two vowels (e.g. 'oo') for convenience.
3 In Kansai Japanese, unlike Tokyo Japanese, lexically-monomoraic-words can be lengthened (e.g. (11b) and (11c)).
4 Yoshida and Zamma (2001: 216) give an example of the word-final accent, *kaki*´ 'oyster'. As Yoshida and Zamma point out, however, this is historically pronounced as *kaki*´*i* where the final mora is lengthened, and the pronunciation without lengthening is the result of a recent dialectal change. In this chapter, I will ignore this type of examples.
5 The complete list is given in the Appendix.
6 It has been claimed in the literature that the location of the accent and the length of the second element of a compound determine the locus of the accent of the compound. For the detailed discussion of the accentuation of compounds in Japanese, see Kubozono's series of studies (Kubozono 1994, Kubozono 1995b, Kubozono and Ohta 1998, among others).
7 See the Appendix for words whose accentuation in Tokyo Japanese is different from that in Kansai Japanese.
8 The constraint *HL is not shown in the tableaux, because it plays little role in determining the optimal output.
9 Some examples are shown below. In the examples, devoiced vowels are shown in italic.
   f*u*ku   (unaccented)   clothes
   ka´k*i*   (accented)   oyster
10 The word *ofisharu* 'official' is not included in the data because it is an adjective.

Chapter 4
The Realization of English /r/[*]

4.1. Introduction

This chapter explores the realization of English /r/ in Japanese within the framework of Optimality Theory (OT: Prince and Smolensky 1993/2004). English /r/ is a unique segment in English loanwords in Japanese in the sense that it is the only consonant that can correspond to zero, a consonant [r] or a vowel, i.e. [a] or [o], depending on its location.

This chapter examines the realization of English /r/ in Japanese with three goals in mind. First, this chapter discusses the nature of inputs. With regard to the nature of inputs, it is not clear whether the input is based on the phonetic representation of the source language or the phonological one. In this study, adopting Silverman's (1992) idea that there is an intermediate level (the Perceptual Level) between the input, i.e. the output of the source language, and the Operative Level (see Chapter 2 and 4.3.1 below), I will claim that the input to the Operative Level is the perceived segment, i.e. the output of the Perceptual Level.

The second goal of this chapter is to argue that an input segment can be perceived differently at the Perceptual Level based on its location, i.e. the English onset /r/, word-medial coda /r/, and word-final coda /r/ are perceived as [r], [a] or [o], and [a], respectively. The onset /r/ and the coda /r/ are treated differently in Japanese. This fact suggests that the inputs to phonological processes are based on the perception, which is closely related to the phonetic representation of the source language but not phonological one.

Finally, this chapter explores the process of assimilation of loanwords to the core part of the Japanese lexicon. Itô and Mester (1995) claim that recent loanwords violate more constraints and are less assimilated. But this is not the case for the recent English loanwords with the word-final coda /r/. In recent loanwords, the English word-final coda /r/ in the input is deleted in Japanese. The deletion occurs to avoid the word-final long vowel [a:], which is disfavored in the core strata of the Japanese lexicon. The fact that the English word-final coda /r/ is deleted in recent loanwords indicates that they are more assimilated to the core part of the Japanese lexicon with respect to the treatment of the word-final [aː].

This chapter is organized as follows. Section 2 presents the data on the realization of English /r/ in Japanese. Section 3 consists of two parts. The first part discusses the inputs to phonological processes. Then, in the second part, I account for the realization of English /r/ in Japanese within the OT framework. Finally, this chapter concludes in section 4.

4.2. Data

The loanwords analyzed in this chapter were mainly collected from five Japanese dictionaries: Shimmura (1955, 1969, 1983, and 1991) and Akahori (1999). The examples below are represented phonemically and the location of accent is not shown unless it is relevant.

English /r/ is a unique segment in Japanese loanword phonology in the sense that it is the only consonant that has more than one possible corresponding segment, depending on the location it occurs. English /r/ has five possible corresponding patterns in Japanese, as illustrated in (1). Among them, only the corresponding pattern (1a) applies to the English onset /r/ and the others apply to the coda /r/.

(1) Five Possible Corresponding Patterns
    a. /r/ → [ɾ] [1]
    b. /r/ → [o](the second half of a long vowel [oː])
    c. /r/ → [a](including the second half of a long vowel [aː])
    d. /r/ → Ø (deletion)
    e. /r/ → [a] or Ø (free variation)

4.2.1. Onset /r/

As introduced above, the English onset /r/ has only one possible correspondent in Japanese, namely [ɾ]. Examples are given in (2). The corresponding pattern in (2) is simple. English /r/ corresponds to the closest sound in the Japanese phonemic inventory, namely [ɾ]. This is the only corresponding pattern for the English onset /r/. The English onset /r/ always corresponds to the onset [ɾ] in Japanese.

(2) /r/ → [r]
    a. bureeki   'break'
    b. ribon   'ribbon'
    c. torakku   'truck'
    d. kontorakuto 'contract'
    e. risaikuru   'recycle'

4.2.2. Coda /r/

As illustrated in (1), the English coda /r/ never corresponds to a consonant but corresponds to vowels, or it is deleted. The English coda /r/ has three possible corresponding segments including the null segment, and four possible corresponding patterns in Japanese.

First, as shown in (1b), i.e. /r/ → [o] (the second half of a long vowel [o:]), the English coda /r/ corresponds to the second half of a long vowel [o:]. In the examples of this corresponding pattern given in (3), the nucleus preceding coda /r/ in the input corresponds to the nucleus [o] in Japanese and the coda /r/ appears as the second half of [o:]. This corresponding pattern applies only to the word-medial coda /r/ and the word-final coda /r/ does not correspond to the second half of [o:], even when the nucleus preceding the coda /r/ in English corresponds to [o] (see (6) below).[2] This indicates that the word-medial coda /r/ and the word-final coda /r/ are treated differently in Japanese.

(3) Word-medial /r/ → [o] (a part of [o:])
    a. pooku   'pork'
    b. hoosu   'horse'
    c. noosu   'north'
    d. inpooto 'import'
    e. soosu   'source'

Second, the corresponding pattern (1c), i.e. /r/ → [a] (including the second half of a long vowel [a:]), is the most common among the four corresponding patterns for the English coda /r/. This pattern is further divided into two groups: the English coda /r/ appears as a short vowel [a] when the nucleus preceding the English coda /r/ corresponds to a vowel other than [a], while it appears as the second half of a long vowel [a:] when the nucleus preceding the English coda /r/ corresponds to [a] in Japanese. Examples are given in (4)–(7).

(4) Word-final /r/ → [a] (a part of [a:])
    a. saa 'sir'
    b. sutaa 'star'
    c. tawaa 'tower'
    d. sentaa 'center'
    e. furawaa 'flower'

(5) Word-medial /r/ → [a] (a part of [a:])
    a. sutaato 'start'
    b. pataan 'pattern'
    c. kaatuun 'cartoon'
    d. haamonii 'harmony'
    e. chaati 'church'

(6) Word-final /r/ → [a] (short vowel)
    a. doa 'door' (*doo)
    b. furoa 'floor' (*furoo)
    c. pia 'pier' (*pii)
    d. pyua 'pure' (*pyuu)
    e. kea 'care' (*kee)

(7) Word-medial /r/ → [a] (short vowel)
    a. tiariidaa 'cheerleader'
    b. giasifuto 'gearshift'
    c. eabasu 'airbus'

As illustrated in (3), the word-medial coda /r/ corresponds to the second half of [o:] when the nucleus preceding the /r/ in the input corresponds to [o] in Japanese. But, the examples (6a) and (6b) indicate that the word-final coda /r/ does not correspond to the second half of [o:] even when the nucleus corresponds to [o] in Japanese. The English coda /r/ corresponds to a short vowel [a] when the nucleus preceding the English coda /r/ corresponds to a vowel other than [a], i.e. [i], [u], or [e] in the word-medial syllable and [i], [u], [e] or [o] in the word-final syllable.

Third, in the corresponding pattern (1d), i.e. /r/ → Ø (deletion), the English coda /r/ does not have an apparent correspondent in the output. This pattern is observed in the loanwords that were recently brought into the Japanese lexicon.[3] Examples of this type are shown in (8).

(8) Word-final /r/ → Ø (deletion)
    a. konekuta   'connector'   (*konekutaa)
    b. weha   'wafer'[4]   (*wehaa)
    c. siikensa   'sequencer'   (*siikensaa)
    d. kurasuta   'cluster'   (*kurasutaa)
    e. sukyana   'scanner'   (*sukyanaa)

In the examples in (8), the nucleus preceding the word-final /r/ in the input corresponds to [a] and the word-final /r/ does not have an apparent correspondent in the output. The examples in (8) do not mean that the English coda /r/ in recent loanwords never has a counterpart in the output. As illustrated in (9), the word-medial coda /r/ in the input corresponds to the second half of [a:] in recent loanwords, as in the corresponding pattern (1c) (see (5)), and the word-medial coda /r/ is never deleted in the output. Furthermore, the word-final long vowels other than [a:] are not prohibited in recent loanwords, as shown in (10). The examples in (8)–(10) suggest that the only difference between the recent and less recent loanwords is the treatment of the English word-final /r/ and only the word-final English /r/ in recent loanwords does not have an apparent correspondent in the output.

(9) Word-medial /r/ → [a] (a part of [a:])
    a. intaanetto   'internet'   (*intanetto)
    b. intaariibu   'interleave'   (*intariibu)
    c. wizaado   'wizard'   (*wizado)
    d. komaasu   'commerce'   (*komasu)
    e. insaata   'inserter'   (*insata)

(10) No Shortening of Long Vowels
    a. fakutorii   'factory'   (*fakutori)
    b. kyuu   'queue'   (*kyu)
    c. kyarii   'carry'   (*kyari)
    d. jagii   'jaggy'   (*jagi)

Finally, the corresponding pattern (1e), i.e. /r/ → [a] or Ø, is free variation. This is also a recent phenomenon (Inaba 2001). In the other corresponding patterns introduced thus far, English /r/ has only one corresponding segment in an output including the null correspondent. In this pattern, on the other hand, English /r/ has two possible correspondents in Japanese. As illustrated in (11), the nucleus preceding the coda /r/ in the input always corresponds to [a] whereas the coda /r/ has two possible correspondents in an output, i.e. the second half of [a:] or the null correspondent.

(11) Word-final /r/ → [a] or Ø (free variation)
    a. erebe´eta(a)   'elevator'
    b. kompyu´uta(a)   'computer'
    c. puri´nta(a)   'printer'
    d. koodine´eta(a)   'coordinator'
    e. kompure´ssa(a)   'compressor'

The examples in (11) have two common characteristics: (i) the accent in Japanese is on the syllable containing the antepenultimate mora, which is a favored landing site for the loanword accent as discussed in Chapter 3, and (ii) the syllable containing the antepenultimate mora is heavy. The free variation introduced above is observed only word-finally. As illustrated in (12), the word-medial coda /r/ does not have more than one possible correspondent in an output and it always corresponds to the second part of [a:], even when the word has the two common characteristics above.

(12) Word-medial /r/ → [a] (no deletion)
    a. ha´ara(a)   'hurler'   (*hara(a))
    b. ma´aka(a)   'marker'   (*maka(a))
    c. pa´ara(a)   'parlor'   (*para(a))
    d. supa´ato   'spurt'   (*supato)
    e. taamine´eta(a)   'terminator'   (*tamineeta(a))

As illustrated in (13), furthermore, other word-final consonants or vowels in the input never have more than one correspondent in the output, even when the word has the two common characteristics observed in (11).

(13) No Word-final Free Variation
   a. u´ddii   'woody' (*uddi(i))
   b. ku´kkii   'cookie' (*kukki(i))
   c. ta´akii   'turkey' (*taaki(i))
   d. ge´kkoo   'gecko' (*gekko(o))

The examples in (11)–(13) suggest that only the word-final /r/ can have more than one correspondent in Japanese.

4.3. Analysis

This section discusses the realization of English /r/ in Japanese within the OT framework. Before analyzing the data, let us consider the inputs to phonological processes.

4.3.1. The Inputs to Phonological Processes

As introduced in Chapter 2, Paradis and LaCharité (1997) and LaCharité and Paradis (2005) propose a phonology-based model of loanword adaptation where the inputs to phonological processes are based on the phonemic representation of the source language. In this model, all the allophones of a phoneme in the source language are treated identically in the host language.

The realization of English /r/ in Japanese is problematic for their model. In their model, both the onset /r/ and the coda /r/ should be treated identically in Japanese. As introduced in the previous section (see (14)), however, the onset /r/ and the coda /r/ are treated differently in Japanese: the onset /r/ corresponds to [ɾ], the closest sound in the Japanese phonemic inventory, whereas the coda /r/ never corresponds to /r/ but corresponds to vowels or it is deleted.

(14) Five Possible Corresponding Patterns (= (1))
   a. Onset /r/ → [ɾ]
   b. Coda /r/   → [o] (the second half of a long vowel [oː])
   c. Coda /r/   → [a] (including the second half of a long vowel [aː])
   d. Coda /r/   → Ø (deletion)
   e. Coda /r/   → [a] or Ø (free variation)

With regard to the realization of the coda /r/, one question arises: Why does the English coda /r/ correspond to vowels in Japanese? As introduced in the previous section, the English coda /r/ can correspond to [a] or [o]. For example, the English coda /r/ corresponds to [a] in the loanwords such as *paaku* 'park' and *doa* 'door' and corresponds to [o] in the loanwords such as *pooku* 'pork' and *foomu* 'form'. As illustrated in (15), however, all the other English consonants correspond to consonants in Japanese. That is, English /r/ is the only consonant that corresponds to vowels as well as a consonant in Japanese. If all the allophones of a phoneme in the source language are treated identically in the input to the phonological process in the host language, as Paradis and LaCharité (1997) and LaCharité and Paradis (2005) claim, it is not clear why only the English coda [r] corresponds to vowels in Japanese and what distinguishes the onset [r] and the coda [r].

(15) Consonantal Adjustments Observed in English Loanwords
English   Japanese
a. [f] → [ɸ] (leaf   → [riːɸɯ])
b. [v] → [b] (love   → [rabɯ])
c. [θ] → [s] (cloth   → [kurosu])
d. [ð] → [z] (mother → [mazaː])
e. [l] → [r] (reel   → [riːru])

As discussed above, the phonology-based model proposed by Paradis and LaCharité (1997) and LaCharité and Paradis (2005) does not explain the realization of English /r/ in Japanese. In this study, therefore, adopting Silverman's (1992) model (see (16)), I will assume that the inputs to the phonological processes are the perceived segments and that the different realization of the onset /r/ and the coda /r/ in Japanese is due to the perception. As introduced in Chapter 2, Silverman proposes a phonetic-based model of loanword adaptation and hypothesizes that the speakers of the host language have no access to the phonological representation of the source language. In this model, the input is merely a linguistically unanalyzed acoustic signal and it is distinguished from the Perceptual Level, where the native segment and tonal inventory constraints apply and they restrict the representation of perceived segments.

(16) Silverman's Model (1992: 293)

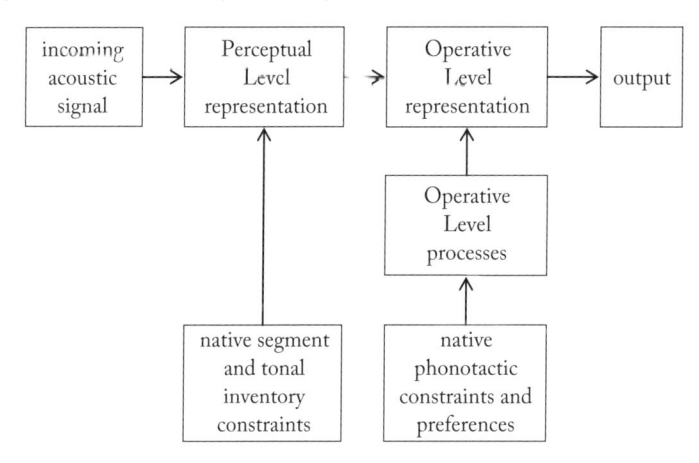

```
┌──────────┐    ┌──────────────┐    ┌──────────────┐    ┌──────┐
│ incoming │    │  Perceptual  │    │  Operative   │    │      │
│ acoustic │ →  │    Level     │ →  │    Level     │ →  │output│
│  signal  │    │representation│    │representation│    │      │
└──────────┘    └──────────────┘    └──────────────┘    └──────┘
                       ↑                    ↑
                       │            ┌──────────────┐
                       │            │  Operative   │
                       │            │    Level     │
                       │            │  processes   │
                       │            └──────────────┘
                       │                    ↑
                ┌──────────────┐    ┌──────────────┐
                │native segment│    │    native    │
                │   and tonal  │    │  phonotactic │
                │   inventory  │    │constraints and│
                │  constraints │    │  preferences │
                └──────────────┘    └──────────────┘
```

Next, let us consider how English /r/ is perceived in Japanese. With respect to the input status of English /r/, I assume that English loanwords in Japanese are borrowed from rhotic dialects of American English, since most of the English loanwords in Japanese are borrowed from American English (Kay 1995) and American English is rhotic in general (Downes 1998: Ch 3).[5] In this study, I hypothesize that an input segment can be perceived differently at the Perceptual Level based on its location and that the onset /r/ and the word-final coda /r/ are perceived as [ɹ] and [a] in Japanese, respectively. Regarding the perception of the English onset [ɹ] in Japanese, it is plausible to assume that the onset /r/ is perceived as [ɹ] at the Perceptual Level, since it is pronounced as [ɹ] in American English and it always corresponds to [r] in Japanese. With respect to the perception of the word-medial coda /r/, I hypothesize that the word-medial coda /r/ can be perceived as [o] or [a]. As shown in the previous section, the word-medial coda /r/ corresponds to [o] when the nucleus preceding coda /r/ in the input corresponds to the nucleus [o] in Japanese (e.g. 'pork' → pooku). The output [o] in those examples is due to the perception. The word-medial coda /r/ in examples such as 'pork' is perceived as [o], probably because the word-medial post-vocalic (and pre-consonantal) position is less salient. In sum, the inputs, perceptions, and outputs of English /r/ are summarized as in (17).

(17) Inputs, Perceptions, and Outputs of English /r/

	Onset /r/	Word-final Coda /r/	Word-medial Coda /r/
Inputs	[r]	[r]	[r]
Perceptions	[r]	[a]	[a] or [o]
Outputs	[r]	[a] (including the second part of [a:]) or zero	[a] (including the second part of [a:]) or [o] (the second part of [o:])

4.3.2. Analysis

In the previous subsection, I have argued that the different realization of the onset /r/ and the coda /r/ in Japanese is due to the perception and that English /r/ can be perceived differently in Japanese depending on the syllabic position it appears. In this subsection, I will discuss the realization of English /r/ in Japanese within the OT framework.

4.3.2.1. Word-final Coda /r/

As introduced in the previous section, the word-final coda /r/ in English has four possible corresponding patterns, which are repeated in (18)–(21). The vowel [a] is the most common corresponding segment to the English coda /r/ and, among (18)–(21), the corresponding pattern in (18) is most common. The corresponding pattern in (19) is observed only when the nucleus preceding the coda /r/ in English corresponds to a vowel other than [a]. The deletion of /r/ is possible only in recent loanwords and the free variation is also a recent phenomenon observed not only in recent loanwords but also in less recent loanwords.

(18) Word-final /r/ → [a] (a part of [a:]) (= (4))
    a. saa   'sir'
    b. sutaa   'star'
    c. tawaa   'tower'
    d. sentaa   'center'
    e. furawaa   'flower'

(19) Word-final /r/ → [a] (short vowel) (= (6))
    a. doa   'door'   (*doo)
    b. furoa   'floor'   (*furoo)
    c. pia   'pier'   (*pii)

  d. pyua   'pure'   (*pyuu)
  e. kea   'care'   (*kee)

(20) Word-final /r/ → Ø (deletion) (= (8))
  a. konekuta   'connector'   (*konekutaa)
  b. weha   'wafer'   (*wehaa)
  c. siikensa   'sequencer'   (*siikensaa)
  d. kurasuta   'cluster'   (*kurasutaa)
  e. sukyana   'scanner'   (*sukyanaa)

(21) Word-final /r/ → [a] or Ø (free variation) (= (11))
  a. erebe´eta(a)   'elevator'
  b. kompyu´uta(a)   'computer'
  c. puri´nta(a)   'printer'
  d. koodine´eta(a)   'coodinato'
  e. kompure´ssa(a)   'compressor'

Within the OT framework, the realization of the English word-final coda /r/ in Japanese can be explained by the six constraints Max, Dep, Ident(consonantal), *Complex-Onset, Coda-Cond, and *[a:]]$_{PW}$, which are defined as in (22)–(27).

(22) Max: No deletion.

(23) Dep: No epenthesis.

(24) Ident(consonantal): An output segment has the identical feature values for [consonantal] as its input correspondent.

(25) *Complex-Onset: No complex onset.

(26) Coda-Cond: Codas cannot have independent place of articulation.

(27) *[a:]]$_{PW}$: No word-final long vowel [a:].

Max (McCarthy and Prince 1995) in (22) is the anti-deletion constraint that ensures every element in the input is preserved in the output, whereas Dep (McCarthy and Prince 1995) in (23) is the anti-insertion constraint that requires every element in the output to have a correspondent in the input. Ident(consonantal) in (24) is a member of the constraint family Ident (Prince and Smolensky 1993/2004). This constraint stipulates that an element of the input and its correspondent in the output must be identical with regard to the feature [consonantal]. *Complex-Onset (Itô 1986) in (25) does not allow complex onsets, while Coda-Cond (Itô 1989) in (26) prohibits a coda with independent place of articulation. *[a:]]$_{PW}$ (Mutsukawa 2004) in (27) prohibits the word-final [a:]. Only the word-final, but not the word-medial, [a:] is prohibited because the final position is the least marked position for phonological changes crosslinguistically (e.g. word-final devoicing in German and Russian) and the vowel [a] has the greatest sonority, or the longest, among the five vowels in Japanese (see Ladefoged 1993: Ch 10). That is, the distinction between a short vowel [a] and a long vowel [a:] makes little difference in the word-final position. As will be shown later in this section, this constraint plays a significant role in the core part of the Japanese lexicon.

In Japanese, no words have a complex onset or a coda consonant with independent place of articulation. This suggests that the constraints *Complex-Onset and Coda-Cond are highest-ranked. To avoid complex onset consonants or coda consonants, there are two possible ways: vowel epenthesis or consonant deletion. In Japanese, the former is adopted to avoid complex onset consonants and coda consonants. This indicates that Max is ranked higher than Dep (see (28)). The constraint Ident(consonantal) is also highest-ranked, since the word-final /r/ in English, which is perceived as [a] in Japanese, never corresponds to [r].

(28) Max >> Dep
'foom ('form') → foomu'

foom[6]	Max	Dep
a. ☞ foomu		*
b. foo	*!	

As introduced above, the English word-final coda /r/ has four possible corresponding patterns: short vowel [a], the second half of [a:], null correspondent, and free variation (the second half of [a:] or null correspondent). The realization of the English word-final coda /r/ suggests that the constraint ranking between MAX and *[a:]]$_{PW}$ has been changing, as shown below.

First, consider the corresponding patterns in (18) (e.g. 'tower' →tawaa) and in (19) (e.g. 'door' → doa (*doaa, *doo)). In these cases, English /r/ in the input, which is perceived as [a] at the Perceptual Level, corresponds to [a] in Japanese. In other words, the output [a], the counterpart of English /r/, is faithful to the perception. Within the OT framework, this pattern is explained by the constraint ranking MAX >> *[a:]]$_{PW}$ in (29), as illustrated in (30). In (30), the candidate (30c), which has the word-final long vowel [a:], is the optimal candidate because the candidate (30b), which does not have the long vowel word-finally, violates the higher-ranked constraint MAX. The candidate (30a) also cannot be the optimal due to its violation of CODA-COND. Among the corresponding patterns for the word-final English /r/, this pattern is most common.

(29) Ranking for '/r/ → [a]'

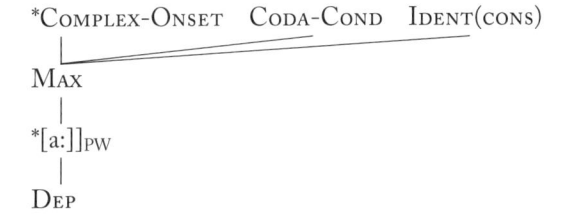

*COMPLEX-ONSET   CODA-COND   IDENT(CONS)

MAX

*[a:]]$_{PW}$

DEP

(30) Tableau for 'tawaa ('tower') → tawaa'

tawaa	*COMPLEX -ONSET	CODA- COND	IDENT (CONS)	MAX	*[a:]]$_{PW}$	DEP
a. tawar		*!	*			
b. tawa				*!		
c. ☞ tawaa					*	

Second, the corresponding pattern in (20) (e.g. 'cluster' → kurasuta (*kurasutaa)) is observed only in recent loanwords. This pattern occurs due to the constraint *[a:]]$_{PW}$. This constraint plays a crucial role in the core strata of the Japanese lexicon as well. The table (31) shows the result of a dictionary research I conducted.[7] As illustrated in (31), 1426 Japanese words have the long vowel [a:] word-finally. Among them, 1382 words, i.e. 96.9%, are loanwords and only

44 words, i.e. 3.1%, are non-loanwords. That is, the word-final [aː] is highly disfavored in the core part of the Japanese lexicon, i.e. Yamato, Sino-Japanese, and Mimetic sublexica. The fact that recent loanwords do not have the word-final [aː] indicates that they are more assimilated to the core part of the Japanese lexicon with respect to the constraint *[aː]]$_{PW}$, although Itô and Mester (1995) claim that recent loanwords violate more constraints and are less assimilated.

(31) The Number of the Words with Word-final [aː]

Total #	# of Loanwords	# of Non-loanwords
1426	1382 (96.9%)	44 (3.1%)

(The majority of non-loanwords are interjections, onomatopoeia, non-standard words, etc.)

The fact that the deletion of the English word-final /r/ occurs only in recent loanwords suggests that the ranking between MAX and *[aː]]$_{PW}$ has been changing as in (32) and that the ranking in (33), where *[aː]]$_{PW}$ is ranked higher than MAX, is the constraint ranking for recent loanwords. The constraint ranking for recent loanwords selects the optimal candidate without the word-final [aː], as illustrated in (34). In the tableau in (34), the candidate (34d), which does not have the word-final long vowel [aː], is the optimal candidate because the candidate (34c), which has the long vowel word-finally, is ruled out due to the violation of *[aː]]$_{PW}$.

(32) MAX >> *[aː]]$_{PW}$ → *[aː]]$_{PW}$ >> MAX

(33) Ranking for '/r/ → Ø'

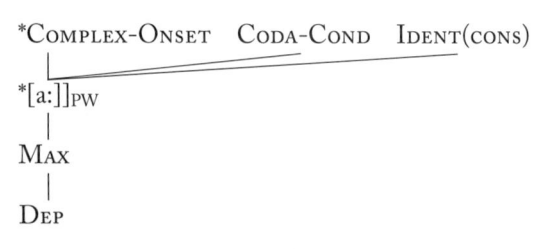

*COMPLEX-ONSET   CODA-COND   IDENT(CONS)
|
*[aː]]$_{PW}$
|
MAX
|
DEP

(34) Tableau for 'krastaa ('cluster') →kurasuta (*kurasutaa)'

krastaa	*Complex Onset	Coda-Cond	Ident (cons)	*[aː]]_PW	Max	Dep
a. krastaa	*!			*		
b. kurasutar		*!	*			**
c. kurasutaa				*!		**
d. ☞ kurasuta					*	**

Finally, the corresponding pattern in (21) (e.g. 'computer' → kompyuuta(a)) shows free variation. As Inaba (2001) points out, this free variation is also a recent phenomenon. This phenomenon is observed both in recent and less recent loanwords. Free variation is due to the freely-ranked constraints *[aː]]$_{PW}$ and Max. The constraint ranking in (35), where *[aː]]$_{PW}$ and Max are freely ranked, predicts the optimal outputs, as illustrated in (36). In (36), both candidates (36b) and (36c) are optimal, since each of them violates one of the freely-ranked constraints once.

(35) Ranking for Free Variation
   a. Ranking for '/r/ → [a]'

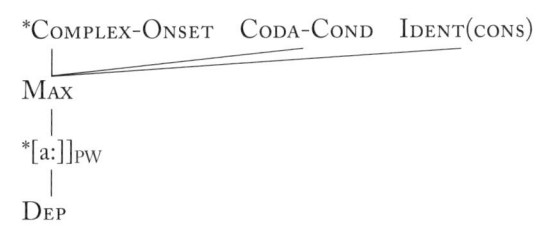

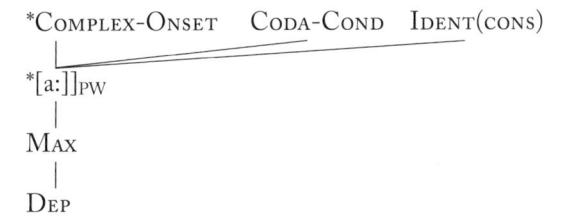

   *Complex-Onset   Coda-Cond   Ident(cons)
   |
   Max
   |
   *[aː]]$_{PW}$
   |
   Dep

   b. Ranking for '/r/ → Ø'

   *Complex-Onset   Coda-Cond   Ident(cons)
   |
   *[aː]]$_{PW}$
   |
   Max
   |
   Dep

(36) Tableau for 'kompyuutaa ('computer') → kompyuuta(a)'
(*[a:]]$_{PW}$ and M$_{AX}$ are freely ranked.)

kompyuutaa	*C OMPLEX -O NSET	C ODA - C OND	I DENT (CONS)	M AX	*[a:]]$_{PW}$	D EP
a. kompyuutar		*!	*			
b. ☞ kompyuuta				*		
c. ☞ kompyuutaa					*	

4.3.2.2. Word-medial Coda /r/

In the previous subsection, I have discussed the realization of the English word-final coda /r/. In this subsection, I will discuss the realization of the English word-medial coda /r/. The word-medial coda /r/ in English has three possible corresponding patterns, as in (37)–(39).

(37) Word-medial /r/ → [o] (a part of [o:]) (= (3))
    a. pooku   'pork'
    b. hoosu   'horse'
    c. noosu   'north'
    d. inpooto   'import'
    e. soosu   'source'

(38) Word-medial /r/ → [a] (a part of [a:]) (= (5))
    a. sutaato   'start'
    b. pataan   'pattern'
    c. kaatuun   'cartoon'
    d. haamonii   'harmony'
    e. chaati   'church'

(39) Word-medial /r/ → [a] (a short vowel) (= (7))
    a. tiariidaa   'cheerleader'
    b. giasifuto   'gearshift'
    c. eabasu   'airbus'

The only difference between the word-final coda /r/ and the word-medial coda /r/ is that the latter can correspond to [o] as in (37) while the former cannot.

The word-medial coda /r/ corresponds to [o] when the nucleus preceding coda /r/ in the input corresponds to the nucleus [o] in Japanese. The corresponding pattern in (37) is due to the perception. The only difference between [a] and [o] lies in the feature [round], i.e. [a] has [-round] and [o] has [+round]. The word-medial coda /r/ in examples such as 'pork' does not correspond to [a] in the output because of the highest-ranked constraint Ident(round) in (40). Within the framework of OT, the examples in (37)–(39) can be explained, as illustrated in (41)–(43). In the tableaux in (41)–(43), the ranking between *[a:]]$_{PW}$ and Max does not affect the selection of the optimal output, since *[a:]]$_{PW}$ does not apply to the word-medial segments.

(40) IDENT(ROUND): An output segment has the identical feature values for [round] as its input correspondent.

(41) Tableau for 'pook ('pork') → pooku'
(*[a:]]$_{PW}$ and Max are freely ranked.)

pook	*COMPLEX -ONSET	CODA- COND	IDENT (CONS)	IDENT (ROUND)	MAX	*[a:]]$_{PW}$	DEP
a. porku		*!	*				*
b. poaku				*!			*
c. ☞ pooku							*

(42) Tableau for 'staat ('start') → sutaato'
(*[a:]]$_{PW}$ and Max are freely ranked.)

staat	*COMPLEX -ONSET	CODA- COND	IDENT (CONS)	IDENT (ROUND)	MAX	*[a:]]$_{PW}$	DEP
a. sutarto		*!	*				**
b. ☞ sutaato							**
c. sutaoto				*!			**

(43) Tableau for 'tiariidaa ('cheerleader') → tiariidaa'
(*[a:]]$_{PW}$ and M<small>AX</small> are freely ranked.)

tiariidaa	*C<small>OMPLEX</small>-O<small>NSET</small>	C<small>ODA</small>-C<small>OND</small>	I<small>DENT</small> (<small>CONS</small>)	I<small>DENT</small> (<small>ROUND</small>)	M<small>AX</small>	*[a:]]$_{PW}$	D<small>EP</small>
a. tirriidaa		*!	*				
b. ☞ tiariidaa							
c. tioriidaa				*!			

4.3.2.3. Onset /r/

Finally, this subsection deals with the realization of the English onset /r/. As illustrated in (44), the English onset /r/ always corresponds to [r] in Japanese. This corresponding pattern is also due to the perception. The constraint ranking developed in the previous subsection accounts for the examples in (44) as well, as shown in (45). In (45), English /r/ does not correspond to a vowel in the output because of the constraint I<small>DENT</small>(<small>CONSONANTAL</small>). In the case of the realization of the onset /r/, the ranking between M<small>AX</small> and *[a:]]$_{PW}$ does not affect the selection of the optimal output, since the onset /r/ is perceived as [r] and never corresponds to [a] in Japanese.

(44) /r/ → [r] (= (2))
    a. bureeki   'break'
    b. ribon   'ribbon'
    c. torakku   'truck'
    d. kontorakuto   'contract'
    e. risaikuru   'recycle'

(45) Tableau for 'breek ('break') → bureeki'
(*[a:]]$_{PW}$ and M<small>AX</small> are freely ranked.)

breek	*C<small>OMPLEX</small>-O<small>NSET</small>	C<small>ODA</small>-C<small>OND</small>	I<small>DENT</small> (<small>CONS</small>)	I<small>DENT</small> (<small>ROUND</small>)	M<small>AX</small>	*[a:]]$_{PW}$	D<small>EP</small>
a. ☞ bureeki							**
b. buaeeki			*!				**
c. buoeeki			*!				**

4.4. Conclusion

This chapter has discussed the realization of English /r/ in Japanese within the OT framework. The chapter is summarized as follows.

First, this chapter revealed that the recent and less recent loanwords are different with respect to the realization of the word-final English [r]. In recent loanwords, the word-final English [r] is deleted, while in less recent loanwords it corresponds to [a]. This diachronic change can be explained in terms of the constraint reranking between *[a:]]$_{PW}$ and MAX. The deletion of English /r/ in Japanese is triggered by *[a:]]$_{PW}$.

Second, the recent English loanwords with the word-final coda /r/ are more assimilated to the core part of the Japanese lexicon with respect to the constraint *[a:]]$_{PW}$. Itô and Mester (1995) claim that recent loanwords violate more constraints and are less assimilated. But this is not the case for the recent English loanwords with the word-final coda /r/. A dictionary research revealed that the constraint *[a:]]$_{PW}$, which triggers the deletion of the English word-final coda /r/, plays a crucial role in the core part of the Japanese lexicon. The fact that the English word-final coda /r/ is deleted in recent loanwords indicates that they are more assimilated to the core part of the Japanese lexicon with respect to the constraint *[a:]]$_{PW}$, which is contrary to Itô and Mester's claim.

Third, the inputs to phonological processes in loanword adaptation are the perceived segments, which are closely related to the phonetic representation of the source language. The nature of the inputs is still under debate in the literature. Based on the realization of English /r/ in Japanese, this study argued that the inputs to phonological processes in loanword adaptation are not the phonetic or phonemic representation of the source language but are based on the perception. This study supports Silverman's (1992) idea that the phonetic representation of the source language and the input to loanword phonology are different and need to be distinguished.

Finally, this chapter argued that the different realization of the onset /r/ and the coda /r/ in Japanese is due to the perception and that an input segment can be perceived differently at the Perceptual Level based on its location. In this study, I hypothesized that English /r/ can be perceived differently in Japanese depending on the syllabic position it appears and that the English onset /r/, word-medial coda /r/, and word-final coda /r/ are perceived as [r], [a] or [o], and

[a], respectively.

Endnotes

* An earlier version of parts of this chapter appears in University of Washington Working Papers in Linguistics 23.
1 In this chapter, instead of the symbol [ɾ] for the tap, [r] is used for convenience.
2 The loanword *woo* 'war' is the only exception I found.
3 The definition of 'recent loanwords' in this chapter is the loanwords that are found only in Akahori (1999), which is the latest dictionary among the five dictionaries used as the source for this study. The fact that computer-related words tend to undergo deletion leads to the possibility that the orthography set by Japanese Industrial Standards Committee is relevant to the deletion of the word-final coda /r/. In this book, however, I will explain this phenomenon phonologically, since the corresponding pattern /r/ → Ø (including free variation) is observed in non-computer-related words as well (see (11)).
4 This word was borrowed from English more than once. In this case, the output *weha* means 'a component of a computer' and does not have the other meaning 'a thin biscuit'. In the latter case, this word is pronounced as *wehaa* with the long vowel [a:]
5 In varieties of American and British English, the onset /r/ is different from the coda /r/.
6 In the tableaux in this chapter, the input is based on the perception.
7 The source is Shimmura (1991).

Chapter 5
The Realization of the English Plural Morpheme*

5.1. Introduction

This chapter explores the realization of the English plural morpheme in Japanese within the framework of Optimality Theory (OT: Prince and Smolensky 1993/2004). Three phonological phenomena related to the English plural morpheme are observed in Japanese: devoicing (e.g. tigers → taigaas̥u), diachronic change (e.g. raions̥u → raionzu 'lions'), and deletion (e.g. the Lord of the Rings → roodo obu za ringu). Among these, there are a few previous studies discussing the devoicing (Tateishi 2001, 2003, Fukazawa and Kitahara 2005) and the diachronic change (Tateishi 2003), but the deletion has been studied little in the literature. Also, the previous studies dealing with the devoicing of the plural morpheme have one common problem. They claim that the devoicing is a phenomenon in affixes (Fukazawa and Kitahara 2005) or in the Yamato sublexicon (Tateishi 2001, 2003), which is one of the four sublexica in the Japanese lexicon. These studies, however, do not explain why only the English plural morpheme undergoes devoicing in Japanese.

The goals of this chapter are fourfold. First, this chapter argues that the devoicing of the plural morpheme is a phenomenon in the affixes in the Loanword sublexicon. The previous studies claim that the devoicing is a phenomenon in the Yamato sublexicon or in affixes. But, based on the facts that the English plural morpheme is the only affix that undergoes devoicing in Japanese and the consonant devoicing is not observed in the Yamato sublexicon, this chapter claims that both etymological and morphological categories are relevant to the devoicing of the English plural morpheme.[1]

The second goal is to show that Japanese borrowers have access to the morphological information of English in borrowing. The devoicing of the English plural morpheme is a phenomenon in the affix, which is a morphological category. This fact suggests that Japanese borrowers have access to the morphological information and distinguish the stem and the affix.

Third, this chapter discusses the diachronic change with regard to the realization of the English plural morpheme in Japanese. The older and younger generations are different with respect to the treatment of the plural morpheme in Japanese. In the older generation, the English plural morpheme is always devoiced when it is in the word whose singular form also exists as a loanword in the Japanese lexicon. But it is faithful to the input when it is in a word whose singular form does not exist in the Japanese lexicon. In the younger generation, on the other hand, the plural morpheme can be devoiced only in the word whose input contains more than one voiced obstruent. This chapter argues that the accessibility to the morpho-phonological information of English has been changing: the older generation does not have access (or has limited access) to the morpho-phonological information of English whereas the younger generation has access to the morpho-phonological information of English.

Finally, this chapter explores the difference between the word-level and the phrase-level with respect to the realization of the plural morpheme. The English plural morpheme does not have a counterpart in Japanese when it is in the phrase-final position in English, while it always has a correspondent at the word-level. This suggests that the plural morpheme at the word-level needs to be distinguished from the plural morpheme at the phrase-level. The present study claims that the deletion of the plural morpheme at the phrase-level is triggered by the constraint DEP-IO(PH AFF).

This chapter is organized as follows. Section 2 presents the data on the devoicing of the English plural morpheme. In section 3, after illustrating an overview of three previous studies, I will analyze the three phenomena related to the English plural morpheme: devoicing, diachronic change, and deletion. Finally, this chapter concludes in section 4.

5.2. Data

The phonological realizations of the plural morpheme in English are determined by the last segment of the stem, as summarized in (1).[2] The phonological realizations of the plural morpheme in English loanwords in Japanese, however, do not necessarily follow English realizations, as illustrated in (2)–(4).[3]

(1) a. -s → [ɪz]: when it follows a sibilant; e.g. crashes [kræšɪz], quizzes [kwɪzɪz], bridges [brɪjɪz].
   b. -s → [s]: when it follows any other voiceless consonant; e.g. beliefs [bəlifs], books [bʊks], plates [plets], .
   c. -s → [z]: otherwise; e.g. dreams [drimz], hills [hɪlz], trees [triz].

(2) [s] → su
   a. sokkusu   'socks'
   b. supootsu   'sports'
   c. hookusu   '(Atlanta) Hawks' (an NBA team)

(3) [z] → zu
   a. shuuzu   'shoes'
   b. jiinzu   'jeans'
   c. indianzu   '(Cleveland) Indians' (an MLB team)

(4) [z] → su
   a. buruusu   'blues'
   b. taigaasu   '(Detroit) Tigers' (an MLB team)
   c. kabusu   '(Chicago) Cubs' (an MLB team)

The examples in (2)–(4) show that English [s] always corresponds to *su* whereas English [z] corresponds to either *zu* or *su*. The corresponding pattern [z] → *su* in (4) is not a simple consonant devoicing, since *zu* in the word-final position, which is faithful to the input [z] in terms of voicing, is possible as exemplified in (3). Moreover, voiced obstruents in other positions, i.e. the word-initial and word-medial positions, as well as the word-final non-derivational *zu*, which is not the counterpart of the English plural morpheme, do not undergo devoicing, as illustrated in (5)–(7).

(5) Word-initial Voiced Obstruents
   a. gareeji   *kareeji   'garage'
   b. zukkiini   *sukkiini   'zucchini'
   c. juusu   *shuusu   'juice'

(6) Word-medial Voiced Obstruents
   a. nozuru   *nosuru   'nozzle'
   b. rajio   *rashio   'radio'
   c. puroguramu *purokuramu   'program'

(7) Word-final *zu* (non-derivational)
   a. chiizu   *chiisu   'cheese'
   b. saizu   *saisu   'size'
   c. poozu   *poosu   'pose'

Devoicing is a highly disfavored phonological phenomenon in Japanese.[4] The examples above indicate that devoicing is allowed only in affixes, more precisely in suffixes.

5.3. Analysis

5.3.1. Previous Studies

This subsection presents an overview of three previous studies on the devoicing of the English plural morpheme in Japanese: Tateishi (2001, 2003) and Fukazawa and Kitahara (2005).

5.3.1.1. Tateishi (2001, 2003)

Tateishi (2001) is the first study discussing the devoicing of the English plural morpheme in Japanese. In Tateishi (2001, 2003), he points out that the relevant constraints for this phenomenon are *NC and Lyman's Law, which are defined as in (8) and (9).

(8) *NC: Post-nasal obstruents must be voiced.

(9) Lyman's Law: No two voiced obstruents in a morpheme.

It has been agreed in the literature (Itô and Mester 1995, 1999, and others) that these two constraints play significant roles in the Yamato sublexicon ((10)–(11)) but not in the Loanword sublexicon ((12)–(13)).

(10) *NC: Effective in the Yamato Sublexicon
    a. kaku – kaita   'write – wrote'
    b. toru – totta   'take – took'
    c. kamu – kanda, *kanta 'bite – bit'
    d. tobu – tonda, *tonta 'fly – flew'

(11) Lyman's Law: Effective in the Yamato Sublexicon
    a. futa   'lid'
    b. buta   'pig'
    c. fuda   'card'
    d. *buda

(12) *NC: Ineffective in the Loanword Sublexicon
    a. rantan   *randan   'lantern'
    b. atoranta *atoranda 'Atlanta'
    c. tento   *tendo   'tent'

(13) Lyman's Law: Ineffective in the Loanword Sublexicon
    a. bideo   *biteo, *pideo   'video'
    b. doragon *dorakon, *toragon 'dragon'
    c. jazu   *jasu, *shazu   'jazz'

However, these two constraints seem to apply to the loanwords with the English plural morpheme. In (14), the loanwords with the English plural morpheme immediately following the nasal never undergo devoicing, whereas the examples in (15) undergo devoicing because each of them has a voiced obstruent in the stem.

(14) *NC Effects on Loanwords with the English Plural Morpheme
    a. jiinzu   *jiinsu   'jeans'
    b. indianzu *indiansu '(Cleveland) Indians' (an MLB team)
    c. penginzu *penginsu '(Pittsburgh) Penguins' (an NHL team)

(15) Lyman's Law Effects on Loanwords with the English Plural Morpheme (= (4))
    a. buruusu *buruuzu 'blues'
    b. taigaasu *taigaazu '(Detroit) Tigers' (an MLB team)

c. kabusu   *kabuzu   '(Chicago) Cubs' (an MLB team)

Based on the examples above, Tateishi concludes that the constraints *NC and Lyman's Law are relevant to the devoicing of the plural morpheme, although it has been agreed in the literature that they are inactive in the Loanword sublexicon, and that the fact that these constraints apply to the English plural morpheme suggests that the plural morpheme falls not in the Loanword sublexicon but in the Yamato sublexicon despite its origin.

Tateishi's analysis seems to account for the realizations of the English plural morpheme. But, his analysis has a problem. That is, it does not account for other suffixes in the Yamato sublexicon such as the negative suffix *zu* in (16). As illustrated in (17), Lyman's Law does not apply to the Yamato words with the negative suffix, although both the English plural morpheme *zu* and the negative suffix *zu* are suffixes and appear word-finally.

(16) *zu* (negative)
  a. shirazu   'know-not'
  b. kaerazu   'return-not'
  c. yomazu   'read-not'

(17) No Lyman's Law Effects on *zu* (negative)
  a. tabezu   *tabesu   'eat-not'
  b. shinjizu   *shinjisu   'believe-not'
  c. kangaezu   *kangaesu   'think-not'

If Tateishi's analysis is correct, Lyman's Law should apply to the negative suffix as well, since both the English plural morpheme and the negative suffix are Yamato suffixes and are phonetically identical. But the examples in (17) show that Lyman's Law does not apply to the negative suffix, although it applies to the English plural morpheme, as illustrated in (15). The fact that the English plural morpheme and the negative suffix are different with respect to the application of Lyman's Law suggests that they are not in the same sublexicon. Since the negative suffix *zu* is undoubtedly a Yamato suffix, the plural morpheme *zu* should be in different sublexicon, presumably in the Loanword sublexicon. Also, notice that devoicing is a highly disfavored phonological phenomenon in Japanese. It is plausible to assume that a highly disfavored phonological phenomenon occurs not in the core part of the lexicon, i.e. Yamato, but in the periphery of the lexicon, i.e. Loanword. This also suggests that the plural morpheme is not a Yamato suffix but a Loanword suffix.

5.3.1.2. Fukazawa and Kitahara (2005)
Fukazawa and Kitahara (2005) account for the devoicing of the plural morpheme *zu* within the OT framework. They claim that this devoicing reveals three paradoxical cases for the ranking for Rendaku (Sequential Voicing) developed in Itô and Mester (2001a), which is given in (18).[5] The constraints in (18) are defined as in (19)–(23) (cited from Fukazawa and Kitahara (2005) except (23), which is slightly modified by the author).

(18) Ranking for Rendaku (slightly modified from Fukazawa and Kitahara (2005))[6]

Ident(voice)-Loanword
|
No-D$^2_{STEM}$
|
Ident(voice)-Sino-Japanese (SJ)
|
ExpressAffix
|
Ident(voice)-Common-Sino-Japanese (CSJ)
|
*NC
|
Ident(voice)-Yamato
|
No-D

(19) No-D$^2_{STEM}$: No double obstruent voicing in a stem.[7] (=Lyman's Law)

(20) ExpressAffix: Affixes must be realized in the output.

(21) *NC: No voiceless obstruent after a nasal.

(22) No-D: No voiced obstruents.

(23) IDENT(VOICE)-X: In the sublexicon X, an output segment has the identical feature value for [voice] as its input correspondent.

Among the constraints above, relevant here are *NC, No-D$^2_{STEM}$, IDENT(VOICE)-YAMATO, and IDENT(VOICE)-LOANWORD. Itô and Mester (2001a) claim that these four constraints are ranked as in (24) and (25), which are extracted from (18).

(24) Ranking for the Yamato Sublexicon
No-D$^2_{STEM}$ >> *NC >> IDENT(VOICE)-YAMATO

(25) Ranking for the Loanword Sublexicon
IDENT(VOICE)-LOANWORD >> No-D$^2_{STEM}$ >> *NC

Fukazawa and Kitahara claim that, although it is etymologically a suffix in the Loanword sublexicon, the plural morpheme *zu* contradicts the ranking for the Loanword sublexicon in (25) in the following three respects. First, No-D$^2_{STEM}$ must be ranked higher than IDENT(VOICE)-LOANWORD to account for the examples in (26), although the ranking between them in Itô and Mester (2001a) is IDENT(VOICE)-LOANWORD >> No-D$^2_{STEM}$. The reversed ranking in (27) explains the examples in (26), as illustrated in (28).

(26) No-D$^2_{STEM}$ Effects on Loanwords with the Plural Morpheme (= (4))
    a. buruusu   'blues'
    b. taigaasu   '(Detroit) Tigers' (an MLB team)
    c. kabusu   '(Chicago) Cubs' (an MLB team)

(27) No-D$^2_{STEM}$ >> IDENT(VOICE)-LOANWORD

(28) Tableau for 'Cubs → kabusu'

kabuzu	No-D$^2_{STEM}$	IDENT(VOICE)-LW
a. kabuzu	*!	
b. ☞ kabusu		*

Second, *NC needs to be ranked higher than No-D$^2_{STEM}$, as in (29). In Itô and Mester (2001a), No-D$^2_{STEM}$ is ranked higher than *NC. But this ranking fails to account for the examples in (30) where the English plural morpheme immediately following a nasal is realized as *zu* despite another voiced obstruent in the stem. The ranking in (29) correctly predicts the optimal output, as illustrated in the tableau (31).

(29) *NC >> No-D$^2_{STEM}$

(30) *NC Effects on Loanwords with the Plural Morpheme (= (14))
    a. jiinzu   *jiinsu   'jeans'
    b. indianzu   *indiansu   '(Cleveland) Indians' (an MLB team)
    c. penginzu   *penginsu   '(Pittsburgh) Penguins' (an NHL team)

(31) Tableau for 'Indians → indianzu'

indianzu	*NC	No-D$^2_{STEM}$
a. ☞ indianzu		*
b. indiansu	*!	

Third, *NC is ranked higher than IDENT(VOICE)-LOANWORD. As shown in (27) and (29), the rankings between No-D$^2_{STEM}$ and IDENT(VOICE)-LOANWORD and *NC and No-D$^2_{STEM}$ are No-D$^2_{STEM}$ >> IDENT(VOICE)-LOANWORD and *NC >> No-D$^2_{STEM}$. This leads to the ranking in (32), because dominance relations in OT are transitive. This ranking contradicts Itô and Mester's ranking IDENT(VOICE)-LOANWORD >> *NC.

(32) *NC >> IDENT(VOICE)-LOANWORD

The three paradoxical cases for the ranking in (18) that Fukazawa and Kitahara claim are summarized as in (33) (cf. Itô and Mester's rankings in (34)).

(33) Partial Rankings for *zu*
    a. No-D$^2_{STEM}$ >> IDENT(VOICE)-LOANWORD
    b. *NC >> No-D$^2_{STEM}$
    c. *NC >> IDENT(VOICE)-LOANWORD

(34) Partial Rankings for Rendaku (Itô and Mester 2001a)
   a. IDENT(VOICE)-LOANWORD >> NO-D$^2_{STEM}$
   b. NO-D$^2_{STEM}$ >> *NC
   c. IDENT(VOICE)-LOANWORD >> *NC

Fukazawa and Kitahara (2005) assume that two of the three paradoxical rankings in (33), i.e. (33a) and (33c), are due to mixing up etymological knowledge with phonological knowledge. Following Fukazawa, Kitahara, Ota (2002), Fukazawa and Kitahara propose a phonology-based categorization of the lexicon, which is independent of etymological information. That is, in lieu of etymology-based categories such as Yamato and Loanword, they employ morphological categories, namely stem and affix. In this model, markedness constraints cannot be relativized while faithfulness constraints can. The ranking in (35) is the constraint ranking Fukazawa and Kitahara develop. In this ranking, Fukazawa and Kitahara adopt NO-D^2 instead of NO-D$^2_{STEM}$, since the relativization of markedness constraints is not allowed in their model. The definitions of these constraints are given in (36)–(41) (cited form Fukazawa and Kitahara (2005)).

(35) Ranking for Consonant Voicing and Devoicing in Japanese

NO-D^2
|
MAX(VOICE)$_{STEM}$
|
UNIFORMITY(VOICE)$_{STEM}$
|
EXPRESSAFFIX
|
IDENT(VOICE)$_{STEM}$
|
*NC
|
UNIFORMITY(VOICE)$_{WORD}$
|
IDENT(VOICE)$_{AFFIX}$
|
MAX(VOICE)$_{AFFIX}$

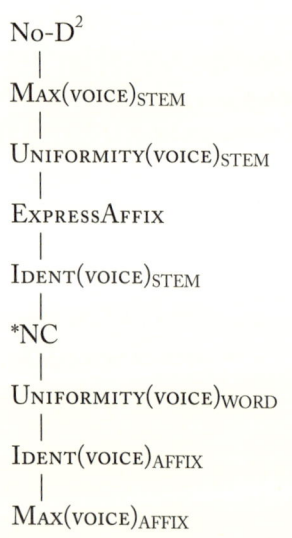

(36) IDENT(VOICE)$_{STEM}$: The correspondent segments in a stem in the input and the output have identical values for the feature [voice].

(37) IDENT(VOICE)$_{\text{AFFIX}}$: The correspondent segments in an affix in the input and the output have identical values for the feature [voice].

(38) UNIFORMITY(VOICE)$_{\text{STEM}}$: No feature in a stem in the output has multiple correspondents in the input (i.e., no coalescence regarding the feature [voice] in a stem).

(39) UNIFORMITY(VOICE)$_{\text{WORD}}$: No feature in a word in the output has multiple correspondents in the input (i.e., no coalescence regarding the feature [voice] in a word).

(40) MAX(VOICE)$_{\text{STEM}}$: Every feature [voice] attached to a segment in a stem in the input has a correspondent in the output.

(41) MAX(VOICE)$_{\text{AFFIX}}$: Every feature [voice] attached to a segment in a affix in the input has a correspondent in the output.

The ranking in (35) accounts for consonant voicing and devoicing in Japanese, i.e. Rendaku and the realization of the English plural morpheme, as illustrated in (42) and (43).[8] In the tableau (42), the plural morpheme does not undergo devoicing because the candidate (42c), which has the devoiced plural morpheme, violates the constraint *NC, and it is fatal. In the tableau (43), Rendaku is considered as the realization of a linking morpheme [+voice] (***R*** in (43)) (see Itô and Mester 2003b: 81–87 for discussion). The candidates (43d) and (43e) lose to the candidate (43c), because Rendaku dose not take place in (43d) and (43e), resulting the violation of EXPRESSAFFIX, which requires the affix ***R*** be realized in the output.

(42) Tableau for 'Indians → indianzu'

indianzu	No-D²	Max_ST	Uni_ST	ExpAff	ID_ST	*NC	Uni_WD	ID_AFF
a. ☞ indianzu \V/ [voi]						*		
b. indianzu | | [voi][voi]	*!							
c. indiansu | [voi]						*!		*
d. intianzu | [voi]		*!			*	*		
e. intian-su		*!			*	**		*

(43) Tableau for 'oyako-genka' (Rendaku)

oyako + **R** + kenka	No-D²	Max_ST	Uni_ST	ExpAff	ID_ST	*NC	Uni_WD	ID_AFF
a. oyako-genga \V/ [voi]_R			*!		**		*	
b. oyako-genga | | [voi]_R [voi]	*!				**			
c. ☞ oyako-genka | [voi]_R						*	*	
d. oyako-kenga | [voi]				*!	*			
e. oyako-kenka				*!		*		

Thus far, I have introduced Fukazawa and Kitahara (2005). Their analysis of the English plural morpheme has two problems. First, as Itô and Mester (2003b: 97–98) point out, their analysis is problematic because it is difficult to reconcile with Richness of the Base, a core tenet of OT. Fukazawa and Kitahara's analysis makes crucial use of Uniformity and accounts for both Rendaku and the realization of the English plural morpheme. But, this model is problematic because the constraint Uniformity cannot rule out input representations as in (44). In (44), the feature [voi] is multiply linked in the input. This is a problem since forms like /buda/ in the output do not violate Uniformity or No-D^2 and it is predicted that they are well-formed Yamato items. As illustrated in (11) (e.g. *buda), however, forms like /buda/ cannot appear as Yamato items in the output. This is a basic problem that any Uniformity-based approach to OCP encounters. This problem occurs because the constraint Uniformity militates against fusion but has nothing to say about input-given multiple linking

(44) [voi]

    b u d a

Second, Fukazawa and Kitahara's analysis dose not account for other affixes in the Japanese lexicon. Fukazawa and Kitahara propose phonology-based categorizations of the lexicon where etymological information plays little role. In this model, the plural morpheme *zu* and other affixes fall into the same category, namely 'affix', regardless of their etymological backgrounds. This model predicts that *zu* (plural) and *zu* (negative) in (45), which is etymologically Yamato, behave phonologically alike. But, the plural morpheme and the negative morpheme behave differently with respect to the constraint No-D^2, as illustrated in (46) and (47).

(45) *zu* (negative) (= (16))
    a. shirazu   'know-not'
    b. kaerazu   'return-not'
    c. yomazu   'read-not'

(46) Lyman's Law Effects on Loanwords with *zu* (plural) (= (4))
    a. buruusu   'blues'
    b. taigaasu   '(Detroit) Tigers' (an MLB team)
    c. kabusu   '(Chicago) Cubs' (an MLB team)

(47) No Lyman's Law Effects on *zu* (negative) (= (17))
    a. tabezu   *tabesu   'eat-not'
    b. shinjizu   *shinjisu 'believe-not'
    c. kangaezu *kangaesu 'think-not'

The affixes *zu* (plural) and *zu* (negative) are both suffixes and phonetically identical. If etymological information is irrelevant as Fukazawa and Kitahara claim, these suffixes should behave alike with regard to No-D^2. Interestingly, however, the constraint No-D^2 applies to *zu* (plural) but not to *zu* (negative). Why does *zu* (plural) behave differently from *zu* (negative)? The only difference between them is etymological background. Then, it is plausible to assume that the etymological categorization is relevant and that the constraint No-D^2 applies only to the items in the Loanword sublexicon. The examples above indicates that the ranking in (35) developed by Fukazawa and Kitahara does not account for the consonant devoicing in Japanese.

5.3.2. Analysis

As discussed above, the previous studies reveal that the English plural morpheme does not fall in the Yamato sublexicon and that morphological categorization is not enough to account for the devoicing of the plural morpheme. In this chapter, therefore, I propose that both etymological information, i.e. Yamato or Loanword, and morphological categorization, i.e. stem or affix, are relevant to the devoicing of the English plural morpheme and that only affixes in the Loanword sublexicon can be devoiced in Japanese. In the following subsection, I will analyze the devoicing, diachronic change, and deletion of the English plural morpheme within the OT framework.

5.3.2.1. The Devoicing of the English Plural Morpheme

Within the OT framework, the devoicing of the English plural morpheme can be explained by the three constraints *NC, No-D^2_{PW}, and IDENT(VOICE)$_{LOANWORD\ STEM}$. These constraints are defined as in (48)–(50).

(48) *NC: Post-nasal obstruents must be voiced. (= (8))

(49) No-D^2_{PW}: No double obstruent voicing in a prosodic word.

(50) IDENT(VOICE)$_{\text{LOANWORD STEM}}$: In a loanword stem, an output segment has the identical feature value for [voice] as its input correspondent.

The constraint IDENT(VOICE)$_{\text{LOANWORD STEM}}$ is the conjunction of the two faithfulness constraints IDENT(VOICE)$_{\text{LOANWORD}}$ and IDENT(VOICE)$_{\text{STEM}}$, whose definitions are given in (51) and (52).

(51) IDENT(VOICE)$_{\text{LOANWORD}}$: In a loanword, an output segment has the identical feature value for [voice] as its input correspondent.

(52) IDENT(VOICE)$_{\text{STEM}}$: In a stem, an output segment has the identical feature value for [voice] as its input correspondent.

The five constraints introduced above are ranked as follows. The conjoined constraint IDENT(VOICE)$_{\text{LOANWORD STEM}}$ outranks the component constraints IDENT(VOICE)$_{\text{LOANWORD}}$ and IDENT(VOICE)$_{\text{STEM}}$. It has been assumed in the literature that a conjoined constraint is universally ranked higher than its component constraints (Smolensky 1993). The ranking between *NC and No-D$^2_{\text{PW}}$ is *NC >> No-D$^2_{\text{PW}}$. As illustrated in (53), this ranking accounts for why the English plural morpheme immediately following a nasal is not devoiced even when the word has another voiced obstruent. The constraint IDENT(VOICE)$_{\text{LOANWORD STEM}}$ is highest-ranked, since phonological changes with respect to the feature [voice] are not observed in loanword stems. The constraint *NC, on the other hand, is ranked lower than IDENT(VOICE)$_{\text{LOANWORD STEM}}$ because, as illustrated in (54), many loanwords violate *NC (Itô and Mester 1999). This leads to the ranking IDENT(VOICE)$_{\text{LOANWORD STEM}}$ >> *NC, which selects the optimal output, as illustrated in (55). The ranking between No-D$^2_{\text{PW}}$ and IDENT(VOICE)$_{\text{LOANWORD}}$ is No-D$^2_{\text{PW}}$ >> IDENT(VOICE)$_{\text{LOANWORD}}$ because the devoicing occurs to avoid the violation of No-D$^2_{\text{PW}}$, as shown in (56).

(53) *NC >> No-D²_PW

Indians	*NC	No-D²_PW
a. ☞ indianzu		*
b. indiansu	*!	

(54) *NC: Ineffective in the Loanword Sublexicon (= (12))
    a. rantan   *randan   'lantern'
    b. atoranta   *atoranda   'Atlanta'
    c. tento   *tendo   'tento'

(55) IDENT(VOICE)_LOANWORD STEM >> *NC

lantern	IDENT(VOICE)_LWST	*NC
a. randan	*!	
b. ☞ rantan		*

(56) No-D²_PW >> IDENT(VOICE)_LOANWORD

(Chicago) Cubs	No-D²_PW	IDENT(VOICE)-LW
a. kabuzu	*!	
b. ☞ kabusu		*

In sum, the constraints introduced above are ranked as in (57).[9] This constraint ranking accounts for the realization of the English plural morpheme, as illustrated in (58)–(60).

(57)

    IDENT(VOICE)_LOANWORD STEM
    |
    *NC
    |
    No-D²_PW
    |
    IDENT(VOICE)_LOANWORD

In (58), the optimal output is the candidate (58a) where no phonological change is observed with respect to the feature [voice]. The candidate (58b), on the other hand, is ruled out due to its violation of IDENT(VOICE)$_{\text{LOANWORD}}$.

(58) [s] → su

socks	ID$_{\text{LWST}}$	*NC	No-D$^2_{\text{PW}}$	ID$_{\text{LW}}$
a. ☞ sokkusu				
b. sokkuzu				*!

In (59), the plural morpheme is not devoiced in the optimal output. The optimal candidate (59c), where no phonological changes with respect to the feature [voice] are observed, violates the constraint No-D$^2_{\text{PW}}$. But that is not fatal. The candidate (59b), where the plural morpheme is devoiced, is not optimal due to its violation of a higher-ranked constraint *NC. The candidate (59a) is not the optimal candidate either, since it violates the highest-ranked constraint IDENT(VOICE)$_{\text{LOANWORD STEM}}$.

(59) [z] → zu

jeans	ID$_{\text{LWST}}$	*NC	No-D$^2_{\text{PW}}$	ID$_{\text{LW}}$
a. siinzu	*!			
b. jiinsu		*!		*
c. ☞ jiinzu			*	

In (60), the plural morpheme in the optimal candidate (60c) is devoiced. The candidate (60b), which is faithful to the input to the Operative Level with respect to the feature [voice], is eliminated due to its violation of the constraint No-D$^2_{\text{PW}}$, while the candidate (60a) is ruled out because of the highest-ranked constraint IDENT(VOICE)$_{\text{LOANWORD STEM}}$.

(60) [z] → su

(Chicago) Cubs	ID$_{\text{LWST}}$	*NC	No-D$^2_{\text{PW}}$	ID$_{\text{LW}}$
a. kafuzu	*!			
b. kabuzu			*!	
c. ☞ kabusu				*

As mentioned above, affixes in the Loanword sublexicon can be devoiced whereas affixes in the other sublexica cannot. This asymmetry can be explained in terms of the constraint ranking between the three constraints IDENT(VOICE), *NC, and No-D$^2_{PW}$. The constraint rankings in (62) and (63) are the rankings for the Yamato and Sino-Japanese sublexica, respectively. Compared with the ranking for the Loanword sublexicon in (61), the constraint IDENT(VOICE) is ranked higher than No-D$^2_{PW}$ in both the Yamato and Sino-Japanese sublexica, which blocks the devoicing (see the tableau (64)). Yamato and Sino-Japanese are different, on the other hand, with respect to the ranking between IDENT(VOICE) and *NC. Post-nasal voiceless obstruents are not allowed in the Yamato, while they are allowed in the Sino-Japanese (Itô and Mester's 1999). This leads to the ranking IDENT(VOICE)$_{S-J}$ >> *NC >> IDENT(VOICE)$_{YAMATO}$. The ranking between *NC and No-D$^2_{PW}$ in the Yamato and Sino-Japanese is *NC >> No-D^2, as in Loanword.

(61) Constraint Ranking for the Loanword Sublexicon (= (57))

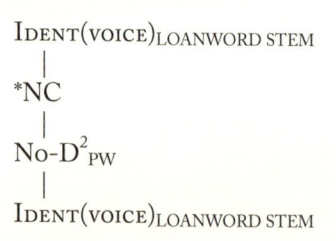

IDENT(VOICE)$_{LOANWORD STEM}$
|
*NC
|
No-D$^2_{PW}$
|
IDENT(VOICE)$_{LOANWORD STEM}$

(62) Constraint Ranking for the Yamato Sublexicon[10]

*NC
|
IDENT(VOICE)$_{YAMATO}$
|
No-D$^2_{PW}$

(63) Constraint Ranking for the Sino-Japanese Sublexicon

IDENT(VOICE)$_{S-J}$
|
*NC
|
No-D$^2_{PW}$

(64) Yamato Sublexicon

tabe-zu 'eat-not'	*NC	ID_YAMATO	No-D²_PW
a. tabesu		*!	
b. ☞ tabezu			*

The rankings in (61)–(63) can be combined as in (65). The ranking in (65) accounts for the devoicing of the English plural morpheme. This ranking seems to conflict with the constraint ranking for Rendaku in (18) (Itô and Mester 2001a). The constraint IDENT(VOICE)_LOANWORD is ranked higher than *NC in Itô and Mester's analysis whereas the ranking between them is reversed in (65). But, the ranking in (65), where IDENT(VOICE)_LOANWORD is divided into two constraints IDENT(VOICE)_LOANWORD and IDENT(VOICE)_LOANWORD STEM and they are ranked as IDENT(VOICE)_LOANWORD STEM >> *NC >> IDENT(VOICE)_LOANWORD, does not affect Itô and Mester's analysis of Rendaku, because Rendaku is a phenomenon observed in the stem of the items in the Yamato sublexicon and Itô and Mester (2001a) focus only on the stem.

(65) Ranking for Devoicing

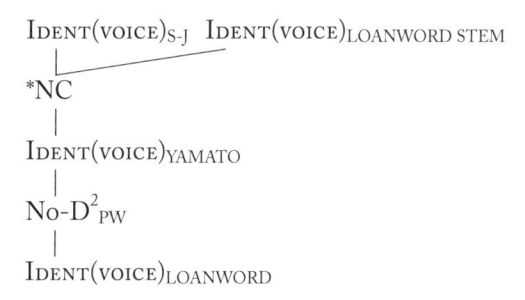

IDENT(VOICE)_S-J   IDENT(VOICE)_LOANWORD STEM
         |
*NC
         |
IDENT(VOICE)_YAMATO
         |
No-D²_PW
         |
IDENT(VOICE)_LOANWORD

I have shown that both etymological information and morphological categorization are relevant to the devoicing of the English plural morpheme. The fact that morphological categorization is relevant to the devoicing indicates that Japanese borrowers have access to the morphological information of English and distinguish the stem and the affix.

5.3.2.2. Diachronic Change in the Realization of the English Plural Morpheme

In the previous subsection, I have discussed the devoicing of the English plural morpheme within the OT framework. In this subsection, I will discuss diachronic change with regard to the realization of the plural morpheme.

As I have shown in the previous subsection, the devoicing of the English plural morpheme is observed in the word whose input has more than one obstruent. The devoicing of the plural morpheme is a phonological phenomenon where the markedness constraints No-D^2_{PW} and *NC play significant roles: the constraint No-D^2_{PW} triggers devoicing while the constraint *NC blocks it.

With respect to the diachronic change in the realization of the English plural morpheme in Japanese, Tateishi (2003) introduces an interesting observation that, in the older generation (the generation of Tateishi's parents) in Japan, the English plural morpheme is always devoiced (e.g. raionsu 'lions', taigaasu 'tigers'), whereas in the younger generation, as discussed in the previous subsection, the plural morpheme can be devoiced only in the word whose input contains more than one voiced obstruent (e.g. raionzu 'lions', taigaasu 'tigers'). Tateishi's observation suggests that the realization of the English plural morpheme in Japanese has been changing.

Why does the generation gap exist with respect to the realization of the English plural morpheme? There are two possible explanations: (i) phonology, i.e. the constraint ranking, has been changing, and (ii) the input to the Operative Level has been changing. But, the explanation that phonology has been changing has a problem. As mentioned above, the constraints No-D^2_{PW} triggers the devoicing of the English plural morpheme. In the case of 'lions', however, No-D^2_{PW} does not trigger devoicing because the word 'lions' does not have more than one voiced obstruent. The fact that the word 'lions' undergoes devoicing in the older generation suggests that there is another constraint that triggers devoicing and that the constraint is ranked higher than *NC, which blocks devoicing, in the phonology of the older generation. The possible constraint that triggers devoicing in the older generation is No-D, the component of the self-conjoined constraint No-D^2_{PW}. But, the ranking No-D >> *NC contradicts the ranking *NC >> (IDENT(VOICE)-YAMATO >>) No-D, which is uncontroversial in the literature (see (18) for example). In fact, there are many Yamato words with a voiced obstruent (e.g. kagi 'key') and those words do not undergo devoicing even in the older generation (e.g. *kaki 'key'). In this chapter, therefore, I take the latter position that the input to the Operative Level has been changing.

Tateishi (2003) mainly analyzes the names of professional sports teams and concludes that the English plural morpheme is always devoiced in the older generation (e.g. raionsu 'lions'). But, there are counterexamples to his analysis, as shown in (66). What distinguishes *raionsu* 'lions' from the counterexamples lies in that, in the case of *raionsu* 'lions', the singular form *raion* 'lion' also exists as a loanword in the Japanese lexicon, whereas the singular forms of the counterexamples do not. This fact suggests that *raionsu* 'lions' and *jiinzu* 'jeans' are borrowed differently, as schematized in (67) and (68): in the case of *raionsu* 'lions', the English plural morpheme is realized as a morpheme in the input to the Operative Level, whereas the word 'jeans' is borrowed as one word, i.e. 'jeans' is not treated as 'jean + s'.

(66) Counterexamples
    a. jeans → jiinzu
    b. shoes → shuuzu

(67) lions → raionsu
    a. lion → raion
    b. raion + the plural morpheme → raionsu

(68) jeans → jiinzu

The example *raionsu* 'lions' reveals two things. First, the plural morpheme in the input to the Operative Level is [s]. The plural morpheme in 'lions' should not be devoiced, because the constraint No-D^2_{PW}, which triggers the devoicing, does not apply to this word. The fact that the plural morpheme is realized as *su* in *raionsu* 'lions' indicates that the realization of the plural morpheme in the output in the older generation is not the result of devoicing but faithful to the input to the Operative Level with respect to the feature [voice]. There are two possible explanations for the [s] in the input to the Operative Level. One explanation is that the plural morpheme in 'lions' in the input to the Operative Level is [s] because the older generation does not have access (or has limited access) to the morpho-phonological information of English. The plural morpheme always appears as '-s' in English orthography irrespective of the pronunciation. In the older generation, the plural morpheme is realized as [s] in the input to the Operative Level probably because they know how it is written in English but they do not know how it is pronounced in English. The other explanation is that the realization of the plural morpheme in the input to the Operative Level is due to the perception. The perceptual ability can be different between generations, since the younger and older generations have different set of phonemes (or possible syllables). For example, the younger generation have the distinctions such as [di] vs. [ji], [ti] vs. [či], and [ɸ] vs. [h], but the older generation do not. That is, the younger generation can have better perceptual ability (including the perceptual ability with regard to the voicing contrast), since they have more phonemes. It is not easy for Japanese speakers to perceive the word-final [z], since the word-final position is less salient position (Jun 1995, Beckman 1998, Lombardi 1999, among others) and coda consonants are highly restricted in Japanese. One of the explanations above or both of them might be relevant to the [s] in the input to the Operative Level.

Second, the constraint *NC does not apply to the plural morpheme in the older generation. As shown in the previous subsection, *NC applies to the items in the Yamato sublexicon (Itô and Mester 1995, 1999, and others) as well as the English plural morpheme in the younger generation. But, *NC does not apply to the plural morpheme in words such as 'lions' in the older generation and the plural morpheme in 'lions' is realized as *su* in the output. As illustrated in (69) and (70), *NC does not apply to voiceless obstruents immediately following a nasal in stems and compounds in the Loanword sublexicon. English loanwords in the older generation such as *raionsu* 'lions' reveal that there is no distinction between the stem and the suffix in the older generation with respect to the application of the constraint *NC and that the application of the constraint *NC has been changing over generations.

(69) *NC: Ineffective in Stems in the Loanword Sublexicon (= (12))
    a. rantan   *randan   'lantern'
    b. atoranta   *atoranda   'Atlanta'
    c. tento   *tendo   'tento'

(70) *NC: Ineffective in Compounds in the Loanword Sublexicon
    a. man-pawaa   *man-bawaa   'man power'
    b. ten-kaunto   *ten-gaunto   'ten count'
    c. griin-kaado   *griin-gaado   'green card'

The next question to be considered is: Why are the older and younger generations different with respect to the realization of the English plural morpheme? That is because they are different with respect to access to the morpho-phonological information of English: the older generation does not have access (or has limited access) to the morpho-phonological information of English, while the younger generation has access to it. In the older generation, as discussed above, the plural morpheme in words such as 'lions' is treated as a suffix, while the plural morpheme in words such as 'shoes' is not treated as a suffix but as a part of a single word in the input to the Operative Level. In the younger generation, on the other hand, the loanwords with the plural morpheme is always treated as 'stem + suffix', as discussed in the previous subsection. The idea that the older and younger generations are different with respect to access to the morpho-phonological information of English might be relevant to the facts that most of the new words in Japanese are English loanwords (Kay 1995) and that those words tend to be used by the younger generation. The diachronic change with regard to the realization of the plural morpheme suggests that the accessibility to the morphological information of English has been changing.

5.3.2.3. The Deletion of the English Plural Morpheme

This subsection discusses the deletion of the English plural morpheme. In the examples in the previous subsections, the English plural morpheme always has a corresponding segment in the output. In examples such as those in (71), however, the plural morpheme does not have a counterpart in the output.

(71) -z → Ø
    a. roodo obu za ringu   'the Lord of the Rings' (movie title)
    b. fiirudo obu doriimu   'Field of Dreams' (movie title)
    c. atakku obu za kiraa tomato 'Attack of the Killer Tomatoes' (movie title)

Why is the plural morpheme deleted in (71)? And what is the difference between the examples in (71) and those in the previous subsections? The examples in (71) have two common features: (i) these are phrases containing function words such as the preposition 'of' or the definite article 'the', and (ii) the plural morpheme is in the phrase-final position. These common features suggest that Japanese borrowers distinguish the word-level and the phrase-level and that the deletion of the morpheme is a phonological phenomenon at the phrase-level. This idea is supported by the examples in (72).

(72) 'rings'
    a. rings → ringusu (*ringu) (word-level)
    b. the Lord of the Rings → roodo obu za ringu (phrase-level)
        (*roodo obu za ringuzu, *roodo obu za ringusu)

In (72a), the plural morpheme in the word 'rings' is devoiced in Japanese. In (72b), on the other hand, the plural morpheme in the phrase 'the Lord of the Rings' does not correspond to *zu* or *su* but it is deleted. Syntactically, the word 'rings' in (72a) can be a phrase by itself. However, the treatment of the plural morpheme in Japanese indicates that Japanese borrowers consider it as not a phrase but a word. The examples above suggest that the function word is the cue to distinguish words and phrases. That is, Japanese borrowers consider English phrases with function words as phrases and the phrases without them as words. The deletion of the plural morpheme at the phrase-level is observed only phrase-finally. As illustrated in (73), the phrase-medial plural morpheme is preserved in the output.

(73) Phrase-Medial Plural Morpheme
    a. deizu obu sandaa   'Days of Thunder' (movie title)
    b. rediisu and jentorumen   'Ladys and Gnetlemen' (song title)

Within the OT framework, the difference between the word-level and the phrase-level with respect to the treatment of the English plural morpheme can be explained by the four faithfulness constraints in (74)–(77): Dep-IO(Ph Aff), Dep-IO, Max-IO, and I-Contig. As illustrated above, both syntactic categorization, i.e. phrase or word, and morphological categorization, i.e. stem or affix, are relevant to the deletion of the English plural morpheme. This suggests that the deletion of the plural morpheme is triggered by Dep-IO(Ph Aff) in (74), which is the conjunction of the constraints Dep-IO(Ph) in (78) and Dep-IO(Aff) in (79). The plural morpheme in the input cannot appear in the output by itself because the coda consonants are highly restricted in Japanese. To preserve the plural morpheme in the input, a vowel needs to be epenthesized. But, since Dep-IO(Ph Aff) prohibits vowel epenthesis in affixes at the phrase-level, the plural morpheme can be deleted at the phrase level.

(74) Dep-IO(Ph Aff): No epenthesis of segments in affixes at the phrase-level.

(75) Dep-IO: No epenthesis.

(76) Max-IO: No deletion.

(77) I-Contig: No word-medial (or phrase-medial) deletion.

(78) Dep-IO(Ph): No epenthesis of segments at the phrase-level.

(79) Dep-IO(Aff): No epenthesis of segments in affixes.

The four constraints in (74)–(77) are ranked as follows. First, the ranking between Max-IO and Dep-IO is Max-IO >> Dep-IO. In Japanese, the sequence of consonants and coda consonants is highly restricted (Itô 1986, 1989, among others). But, consonants in the input are preserved in the output by epenthetic vowels. This indicates that Max-IO outranks Dep-IO. Second, the constraint Dep-IO(Ph Aff) is ranked higher than Max-IO and Dep-IO. In Japanese, as mentioned above, the segments in the input are preserved in the output. But the English plural morpheme in the phrase-final position is an exception. The English plural morpheme, which is an affix, is deleted when it is in the phrase-final position. The constraint Dep-IO(Ph Aff) outranks Max-IO and the deletion of the plural morpheme at the phrase-level is triggered by Dep-IO(Ph Aff). Finally, the constraint I-Contig is ranked higher than Dep-IO(Ph Aff), since no deletion is observed word- or phrase-medially.

In sum, the four constraints are ranked as in (80).[11] This ranking accounts for the difference between the word-level and the phrase-level with respect to the treatment of the plural morpheme, as illustrated in (81) and (82). In the tableau (81), the plural morpheme in the input is preserved in the output because of the constraint Max-IO. In the tableau (82), on the other hand, the plural morpheme in the input is deleted in the output, since Japanese borrowers consider the input 'the Lord of the Rings' as a phrase and the plural morpheme in it cannot have a corresponding segment in the output due to the constraint Dep-IO(Ph Aff).

(80)

>   I-Contig
> |
>   Dep-IO(Ph Aff)
> |
>   Max-IO
> |
>   Dep-IO

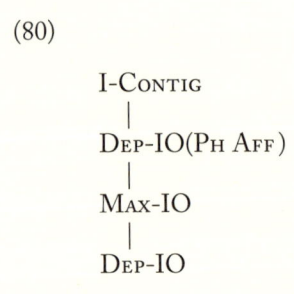

(81) Tableau for 'rings' (word-level)

rings	I-Contig	Dep-IO(Ph Aff)	Max-IO	Dep-IO
a. ringu			*!	*
b. ☞ ringu-su				**

(82) Tableau for 'the Lord of the Rings'[12] (phrase-level)

the Lord of the Rings	I-Contig	Dep-IO(Ph Aff)	Max-IO	Dep-IO
a. ☞ roodo obu za ringu			*	***
b. roodo obu za ringu-su		*!		****

The ranking in (80) also accounts for the realization of the phrase-medial English plural morpheme as illustrated in (83). In the tableau (83), the candidate (83a), where the plural morpheme in the input is preserved, is the optimal candidate, since the candidate (83b), where the plural morpheme is deleted, violates the highest-ranked constraint I-Contig.

(83) Tableau for 'Days of Thunder' (phrase-level)

Days of Thunder	I-Contig	Dep-IO(Ph Aff)	Max-IO	Dep-IO
a. ☞ deizu obu sandaa		*		**
b. dei obu sandaa	*!		*	*

The next question to be considered is: Why is the English plural morpheme deleted at the phrase-level? I believe it is deleted to avoid 'long' phrases. When foreign words are borrowed into the Japanese lexicon, since the sequence of consonants and coda consonants are highly restricted in Japanese, vowels are epenthesized to preserve all segments in the input. But, it is not economical to pronounce prolonged words with epenthetic vowels. As a result, long words tend to be abbreviated at the word-level, as will be discussed in the next chapter. The deletion of the plural morpheme is another example at the phrase level of avoidance of prolonged phrases (and words). The deletion of the plural morpheme at the phrase-level occurs only phrase-finally, because the final position is the least marked position for phonological changes crosslinguistically (e.g. word-final deletion of English /r/ in Japanese discussed in Chapter 4, and word-final devoicing in German and Russian). At the phrase-level, only the phrase-initial definite article and the phrase-final plural morpheme can be deleted. This suggests that only semantically-less-significant items in phrase-edge positions can be deleted.

5.4. Conclusion

This chapter has discussed three phenomena related to the realization of the English plural morpheme in Japanese within the OT framework. This chapter is summarized as follows.

First, the devoicing of the English plural morpheme is a phenomenon within the affixes in the Loanword sublexicon. Previous studies claim that this devoicing is a phenomenon in the Yamato sublexicon or in affixes. However, those studies do not explain why only the English plural morpheme undergoes devoicing in Japanese. Also, since devoicing is highly restricted in Japanese, it is plausible to assume that it occurs in the periphery of the lexicon, i.e. in the Loanword sublexicon, where more constraints can be violated. This chapter revealed that both etymological and morphological categories are relevant to this devoicing and that the devoicing is a phenomenon that can occur only in the affixes in the Loanword sublexicon.

Second, Japanese borrowers have access to the morphological information of English when they borrow English words into the Japanese lexicon. As discussed in this chapter, the devoicing is observed only in the affix, which is a morphological category. This indicates that Japanese borrowers have access to the morphological information of English. This chapter revealed that Japanese borrowers distinguish the English plural morpheme from the stem. But it is not clear yet how they treat other English affixes in borrowing. I leave this question for future research.

Third, the accessibility to the morpho-phonological information of English has been changing over time. The older and younger generations are different with respect to the realization of the English plural morpheme. In the older generation, the English plural morpheme is always devoiced when it is in a word whose singular form also exists as a loanword in the Japanese lexicon. But it is faithful to the input when the English plural morpheme is in a word whose singular form does not exist in the Japanese lexicon. In the younger generation, on the other hand, the plural morpheme can be devoiced only in a word whose input contains more than one voiced obstruent. This chapter revealed that the generation gap with respect to the realization of the English plural morpheme lies in that the older generation does not have access (or has limited access) to the morpho-phonological information of English and the younger generation has access to it. The diachronic change with regard to the realization of the plural morpheme suggests that the accessibility to the morpho-phonological information of English has been changing.

In the older generation, the plural morpheme in words such as 'lions' is realized as [s] in the input to the Operative Level. The plural morpheme in the word 'lions' appears as *su*, although it is not in the position where the constraint No-D^2_{PW} applies. This is because *su* in the output is not the result of devoicing but it is faithful to the input to the Operative Level. Also, the fact that the constraint *NC, which applies to the English plural morpheme but not to stems in the Loanword sublexicon in the younger generation, does not apply to 'lions' in the older generation indicates that there is no distinction between the stem and the suffix in the older generation with respect to the application of *NC and that the application of *NC has been changing over generations

Finally, Japanese borrowers distinguish the word level and the phrase level when they borrow English words into the Japanese lexicon. The plural morpheme does not have a counterpart in Japanese when it is in the phrase-final position in English, while it always has a corresponding segment at the word-level. This suggests Japanese borrowers distinguish the word-level and the phrase-level.[13] The English plural morpheme is deleted at the phrase-level because of the constraint DEP-IO(PH AFF). This chapter focused only on the deletion of the plural morpheme and did not discuss the deletion of other elements such as the definite article, which is also observed at the phrase-level. The phonological differences between the word-level and the phrase-level would be an interesting topic for future study.

Endnotes

* Earlier versions of parts of this chapter appear in Proceedings of the 3rd Seoul International Conference on Phonology and KLS28.

1 There is another consonant devoicing observed in Japanese, which is a phenomenon in the Loanword sublexicon (e.g. beddo→ betto 'bed'). This devoicing occurs to avoid the sequence of voiced obstruents (Nishimura 2001). In this chapter, I will ignore this phenomenon because it is optional and subject to individual differences.

2 English pronunciation in this study is based on Kenyon and Knott (1944).

3 The realization of [ɪz] in Japanese is not shown here, since few English words with it, if any, have been taken into Japanese and I could not find examples of this type.

4 Vowel devoicing in Japanese is not a phonological phenomenon but a phonetic phenomenon because it 'shows properties characteristic of phonetic processes, such as gradualness and optionality' (Itô and Mester 2003b: 276 en. 7).

5 According to Fukazawa and Kitahara, this ranking is from Itô and Mester (2001a). But Itô and Mester (2001a) do not discuss Rendaku and I could not find the constraint ranking for Rendaku in the paper, although I found the ranking similar to this in Itô and Mester (2003b: 152).

6 In Fukazawa and Kitahara (2005), instead of *No-D, No-D^2_{STEM}, IDENT(VOICE)-LOANWORD, and *NC, the constraints *VOIOBS, *VOIOBS$^2_{STEM}$, IDENT(VOICE)-FOREIGN, and *NT are used, respectively. In this chapter, I will use *No-D, No-D^2_{STEM}, IDENT(VOICE)-LOANWORD, and *NC for consistency.

7 No-D^2_{STEM} is the self-conjoined constraint of the markedness constraint *No-D in stem domain.

8 The constraint MAX(VOICE)$_{AFFIX}$ is not included in these tableaux, since it plays little role in selecting the optimal candidate.

9 The constraint IDENT(VOICE)$_{STEM}$ will not be shown in the constraint rankings and tableaux in the rest of this chapter, because it plays little role in selecting the optimal candidate.

10 The constraint No-D^2_{PW} needs to be distinguished from No-D^2_{STEM}. The constraint No-D^2_{PW} accounts for the devoicing of the English plural morpheme, as discussed thus far, but not Lyman's Law effect, because this constraint does not allow more than one voiced obstruent in a compound (e.g. fude + hako → fudebako (*fudehako) 'pencil case'). The constraint No-D^2_{STEM} is the OT version of Lyman's Law and is ranked higher than *NC, as discussed in Itô and Mester (2003b) (see (18)). In the rest of this chapter, I will ignore No-D^2_{STEM}, since it is not relevant to the focus of this study.

11 The constraints DEP-IO(PH) and DEP-IO(AFF) are not shown in the ranking, since they do not play significant roles in selecting the optimal output.

12 The deletion of 'the' is ignored in this tableau. In the phrase 'the Lord of the Rings', the function word 'the' in the phrase-initial position is deleted in the output while 'the' in the phrase-medial position is not. This also might be relevant to the constraint I-CONTIG.

13 The distinction between the word-level and phrase-level phonology, i.e. the distinction between lexical phonology and postlexical phonology, also plays a significant role in Chapter 6.

Chapter 6
English Compound Abbreviation*

6.1. Introduction

This chapter explores English compound abbreviation in Japanese within the framework of Optimality Theory (OT: Prince and Smolensky 1993/2004).[1]

There are three possible ways of abbreviation: (i) the first element is retained as in (1), (ii) the second element is retained as in (2), and (iii) both elements are partially retained as in (3).

(1) a. mini sukaato → mini 'mini skirt'
    b. konbiniensu sutoa → konbini 'convenience store'
    c. shorudaa baggu → shorudaa 'shoulder bag'

(2) a. gooru kiipaa → kiipaa 'goal keeper'
    b. fasshon moderu → moderu 'fashion model'
    c. nyuusu kyasutaa → kyasutaa 'news caster (anchor)'

(3) a. waado purosessaa → waa-puro 'word processor'
    b. dejitaru kamera → deji-kame 'digital camera'
    c. rimooto kontorooru → rimo-kon 'remote control'

Among them, the pattern in (3) is the most productive in Japanese (Nishihara et al. 2001), whereas the pattern in (1) is most productive in languages such as Dutch (Hamans 1997: 1734), English (Szymanek 1989), French (Niikura et al. 1996: 384), and German (Wiese 1996: 62–63). This chapter deals with the pattern in (3) and discusses how abbreviated compounds of this type are formed.

The goals of this chapter are fourfold. First, this chapter explains how trimoraic words can be formed in English compound abbreviation. The most productive abbreviation pattern in Japanese is quadrimoraic consisting of two bimoraic components. But trimoraic words are also possible and there are three types of trimoraic abbreviated compounds. This chapter accounts for them within the OT framework.

The second goal is to argue that abbreviated trimoraic words can appear in the output as a result of assimilation to the core part of the lexicon with respect to the constraint *[a:]]$_{PW}$. A previous study (Nishihara et al. 2001) claims that abbreviated English compounds become trimoraic as a result of the word-final vowel shortening and this is a phenomenon in the Loanword sublexicon. But, based on the result of a dictionary research, this chapter claims that it is due to *[a:]]$_{PW}$, which plays a significant role in the core part of the Japanese lexicon.

Third, this chapter reveals that English compound abbreviation in Japanese involves a case of phonological opacity, which is similar to the opaque case observed in German truncation. This type of compound abbreviation in Japanese has not been discussed in the literature. This chapter accounts for the opaque case within the framework of the Weakly Parallel Model, a subtheory of OT, proposed by Itô and Mester (2001b and 2003a). This model explains the opaque case in English compound abbreviation in Japanese straightforwardly. This chapter shows how successfully the case of phonological opacity observed in English compound abbreviation in Japanese can be explained within the framework of the Weakly Parallel Model.

Finally, this chapter discusses that there are two types of coda conditions in Japanese. In the literature, only one of them has been discussed. But, the opaque case and verb stems reveal that there are actually two types of coda conditions and that the coda condition discussed by Itô (1986) applies only to prosodic words while the other type of coda condition applies to both bound morphemes and prosodic words.

This chapter is organized as follows. After introducing two subtheories of OT, Sympathy Theory (McCarthy 1999) and the Weakly Parallel Model, in section 2, section 3 presents the data. Section 4 overviews three previous studies relevant to English compound abbreviation in Japanese. Then, in section 5, I analyze four patterns of English compound abbreviation within the OT framework. Finally, this chapter concludes in section 6.

6.2. Sympathy Theory vs. Weakly Parallel Model

This section introduces two subtheories of OT, Sympathy Theory (McCarthy

1999) and the Weakly Parallel Model (Itô and Mester 2001b, 2003a), which are proposed to deal with phonological opacity within the framework of OT.

6.2.1. Sympathy Theory

Sympathy Theory (McCarthy 1999) is a subtheory of OT, which is developed to cope with phonological opacity. McCarthy (1999) proposes a new type of correspondence relation: 'sympathy'. Sympathy is a relation between candidates. A candidate can be an optimal output because of the sympathy relation with a particular failed co-candidate, i.e. a candidate that is optimal with respect to a specific lower-ranked constraint. McCarthy (1999) discusses Tiberian Hebrew and develops Sympathy Theory.

Tiberian Hebrew reveals a case of phonological opacity, which is caused by the interaction of *e*-epenthesis and *ʔ*-deletion: a vowel [e] is inserted between the word-final consonants whereas the [ʔ] is deleted in the coda position. In derivational model, the case in Tiberian Hebrew can be explained as in (4). But, as illustrated in (5), this is problematic in the framework of OT, because it is not clear why the vowel [e] is epenthesized in the output form, i.e. it is not followed by a consonant in the output. In the tableau (5), the constraint ranking predicts the wrong winner *deš*.

(4) /dešʔ/ → [deše]

   Input: /dešʔ/
         | *e*-epenthesis
        dešeʔ
         | *ʔ*-deletion
   Output: [deše]

(5) Tableau for /dešʔ/ → [deše] (Wrong Prediction)

Input: /dešʔ/	Coda-Cond	*Complex	Max-C	Dep-V
a. dešʔ	*!	*		
b. dešeʔ	*!			*
c. ☹ deš			*	
d. deše			*	*!

McCarthy (1999) claims that the candidate *deše* is selected as the optimal output because it is in the sympathy relation with the candidate *deše?*, which is the intermediate form in derivational model. The candidate *deše?* cannot be the optimal output because of the violation of CODA-COND. But it serves as the sympathy candidate. The sympathy candidate is selected among the candidates that satisfy the selector constraint MAX-C. In the tableau (5), the possible candidates for the sympathy candidate are (5a) and (5b). The candidate *deše?* in (5b) is selected as the sympathy candidate, since it best satisfies other constraints. Then, the candidate *deše* is selected as the optimal output by the sympathy constraint, i.e. the faithfulness constraint between a candidate and the sympathy candidate. In the tableau (5), the output form *deše* and the sympathy candidate *deše?* have the epenthetic vowel but the others do not. This suggests that the sympathy constraint is MAX-✿O-V, which requires that all vowels in the sympathy candidate be preserved in the output form. This constraint is ranked higher than MAX-C. This constraint ranking selects the optimal output *deše*, as illustrated in (6). In the tableau (6), the candidate (6c), the optimal output in the tableau (5), is ruled out by the sympathy constraint MAX-✿O-V.

(6) Tableau for /deš?/ → [deše]

Input: /deš?/	CODA-COND	*COMPLEX	MAX-✿O-V	MAX-C	DEP-V
a. deš?	*!	*	*		
b. deše?	*!				*
c. deš			*!	*	
d. ☞ deše				*	*!

6.2.2. Weakly Parallel Model

The Weakly Parallel Model (Itô and Mester 2001b, 2003a) is another subtheory of OT to handle phonological opacity. In this model, "the traditional distinction between lexical phonology and postlexical phonology persists as a serial interface between two separate modules of grammar" (Itô and Mester 2003a). Lexical phonology and postlexical phonology are characterized by the three properties in (7) (cited from Itô and Mester (2003a)).

(7) a. The lexical and postlexical modules constitute separate constraint systems.
　　b. They share many (not necessarily all)[2] constraints, but rankings can differ

in limited ways.
c. The two modules interact serially, with the output of the lexical module serving as the input to the postlexical module.

Itô and Mester (2001b and 2003a) argue against Sympathy Theory and develop this alternative model. Their argument against Sympathy Theory is that it is difficult to reconcile with a core tenet of OT, i.e. Richness of the Base, and is problematic for the treatment of phonological opacity. In Itô and Mester (2003a), they argue against Sympathy Theory as follows.

Japanese reveals a case of phonological opacity, which is caused by the interaction of two well-known processes: Rendaku and *g*-weakening. Rendaku is a phonological process observed in compounds that replaces voiceless obstruents with their voiced counterparts at the beginning of second members. But, it is systematically blocked whenever second members already contain a voiced obstruent (e.g. hana + sono → hanazono 'flower garden', furi + sode → furisode (*furizode) 'long-sleeved kimono'). The other process *g*-weakening is an allophonic process where non-initial [g] is replaced by [ŋ] (e.g. /gai/ → [ŋai] in [koku + ŋai] 'abroad', vs. word-initial [gai] in [gai + ǰin] 'foreigner'). The properties of *g*-weakening, i.e. phonetic gradiency, non-contrastiveness, and sociolinguistic variation, suggest that this is a postlexical process. In derivational terms, the interaction of these processes can be shown as in (8): In (8b), these processes are in a counterfeeding relation and the reversed order of application would produce the wrong output *[saka + doŋe].

(8) The Interaction of Rendaku and *g*-weakening

	a. 'folding paper'	b. 'reverse thorn'
	/ori + kami/	/saka + toge/
Rendaku	ori gami	n/a
g-weakening	ori ŋami	saka toŋe
	[ori ŋami]	[saka toŋe]

In OT terms, relevant constraint rankings for these processes are the rankings in (9) and (10): the ranking in (9) is for Rendaku while the ranking in (10) is for *g*-weakening.

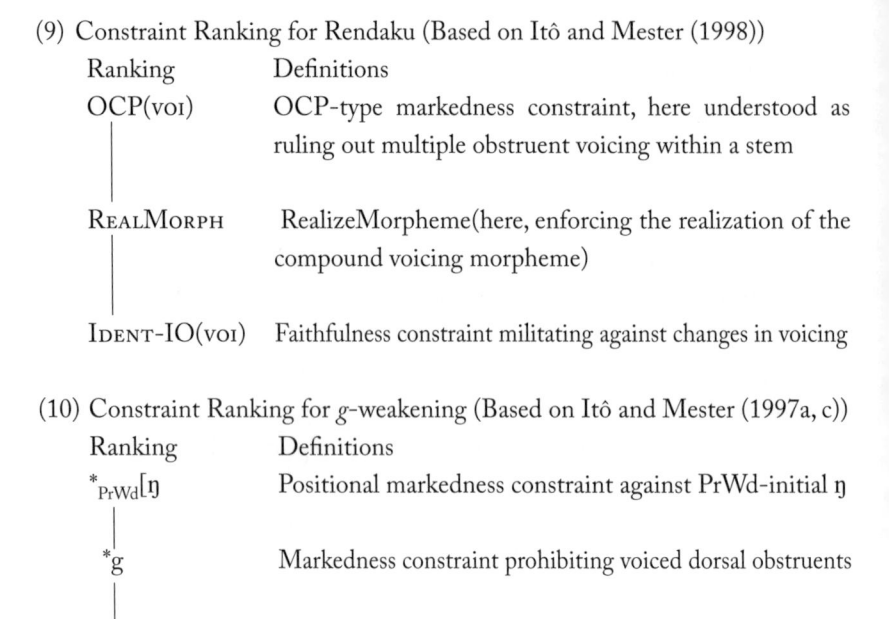

(9) Constraint Ranking for Rendaku (Based on Itô and Mester (1998))

Ranking	Definitions
OCP(voi)	OCP-type markedness constraint, here understood as ruling out multiple obstruent voicing within a stem
RealMorph	RealizeMorpheme(here, enforcing the realization of the compound voicing morpheme)
Ident-IO(voi)	Faithfulness constraint militating against changes in voicing

(10) Constraint Ranking for *g*-weakening (Based on Itô and Mester (1997a, c))

Ranking	Definitions
*$_{PrWd}$[ŋ	Positional markedness constraint against PrWd-initial ŋ
*g	Markedness constraint prohibiting voiced dorsal obstruents
Ident-IO(nas)	Faithfulness constraint against changes in nasality

The constraint ranking in (10) selects the optimal outputs regardless of the input status of /g/, as illustrated in (11) and (12). This will be a significant point in their argument against Sympathy Theory. Richness of the Base should allow either of them as a viable input, because "the two segments do not stand in contrast and their distribution is allophonically determined (Itô and Mester 2003a)."

(11) /g/ as input

/geta/ 'clogs'	*$_{PrWd}$[ŋ	*g	Ident-IO(nas)
a. ☞ geta		*	
b. ŋeta	*!		*
/kagi/ 'key'	*$_{PrWd}$[ŋ	*g	Ident-IO(nas)
a. kagi		*!	
b. ☞ kaŋi			*

(12) /ŋ/ as input

/ŋeta/ 'clogs'	*_PrWd_[ŋ]	*g	Ident-IO(nas)
a. ☞ geta		*	*
b. ŋeta	*!		
/kaɲi/ 'key'	*_PrWd_[ŋ]	*g	Ident-IO(nas)
a. kagi		*!	*
b. ☞ kaɲi			

The constraint rankings in (9) and (10) can be combined as in (13). The ranking in (13) accounts for the phonological process /ori + kami/ → [ori ŋami] 'folding paper' in (8a), but not /saka + toge/ → [saka toŋe] 'reverse thorn', as illustrated in (14) and (15).

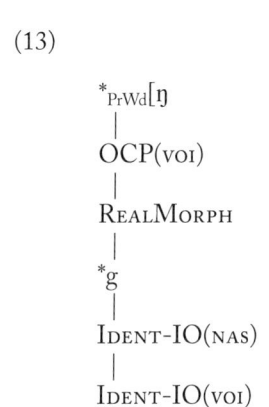

(13)

*_PrWd_[ŋ]
|
OCP(voi)
|
RealMorph
|
*g
|
Ident-IO(nas)
|
Ident-IO(voi)

(14) /ori + kami/ → [ori ŋami] 'folding paper'

/ori-kami/	*_PrWd_[ŋ]	OCP(voi)	Real Morph	*g	Ident-IO (nas)	Ident-IO (voi)
a. ori-kami			*!			
b. ori-gami				*!		*
c. ☞ ori-ŋami					*	*

(15) /saka + toge/ → [saka toŋe] 'reverse thorn' (Wrong Prediction)

/saka-toge/	*PrWd[ŋ	OCP(VOI)	REAL MORPH	*g	IDENT-IO (NAS)	IDENT-IO (VOI)
a. saka-toge			*!	*		
b. saka-doge		*!		*		*
c. saka-toŋe			*!		*	
d. ☹ saka-doŋe					*	*

The ranking in (13) does not account for /saka + toge/ → [saka toŋe], because this is a case of phonological opacity. With the help of the sympathy constraint IDENT-❀O(VOI), which is ranked higher than REALMORPH, the phonological process /saka + toge/ → [saka toŋe] can be explained as in (16) where the selector constraint and the sympathy candidate are marked by "❀".

(16) /saka + toge/ → [saka toŋe] 'reverse thorn'

/saka-toge/	*PrWd[ŋ	OCP (VOI)	❀O-(VOI)	REAL MORPH	*g	IO-(NAS)❀	IO-(VOI)
a. ❀ saka-toge				*	*!		
b. saka-doge		*!	*		*		*
c. ☞ saka-toŋe				*		*	
d. saka-doŋe			*!			*	*

The Sympathy-based analysis in (16) seems to accounts for [saka toŋe] successfully. But, it contains a serious problem. That is, it presupposes that the input is /saka-toge/ but not /saka-toŋe/. As mentioned above (see tableaux (11) and (12)), the surface distribution of [g] and [ŋ] is predicted by the constraint system. That means a core tenet of OT, i.e. Richness of the Base, requires that "the ranking of output constraints alone be responsible for the derivation of the distribution of the two variant" (Itô and Mester 2003a). As illustrated in (17), however, the Sympathy-based analysis does not explain a possible input variant /saka-toŋe/. Based on this, Itô and Mester (2003a) conclude that "Sympathy cannot cope with the rich inputs demanded by Richness of the Base whenever the masking process of an opaque interaction is allophonic" and propose the Weakly Parallel Model to handle phonological opacity.

(17) /saka + toŋe/ → [saka toŋe] 'reverse thorn' (Wrong Prediction)

/saka-toŋe/	*ₚᵣWd[ŋ	OCP (voi)	❀O-(voi)	Real Morph	*g	IO- (nas)❀	IO- (voi)
a. saka-toge			*!	*	*	*	
b. saka-doge		*!			*	*	*
c. saka-toŋe			*!	*			
d. ☹ saka-doŋe							*

In the framework of the Weakly Parallel Model, the case of [saka toŋe] can be accounted for as illustrated in (18) and (19).³ In this model, the lexical and postlexical modules constitute separate constraint systems, where rankings can differ in limited ways, and the two modules interact serially, with the output of the lexical module serving as the input to the postlexical module (see (7)). In (18), the ranking for the lexical module produces *saka-toge*, which is the input to the postlexical modules. Then, in (19), the ranking for the postlexical module selects *saka-toŋe* as the optimal output. In (18) and (19), *VgV, i.e. no intervoalic [g], and IDENT-IO(voi), i.e. no changes in voicing, are the constraints that are ranked differently in the lexical and postlexical modules.

(18) /saka + toŋe/ → [saka toŋe] 'reverse thorn' (lexical)

/saka-toŋe/	*ŋ	OCP (voi)	Real Morph	*VgV	*g	IO- (nas)	IO- (voi)
a. ☞ saka-toge			*	*	*		
b. saka-doge		*!		*	*		*
c. saka-toŋe	*!		*			*	
d. saka-doŋe	*!						*

(19) /saka + toŋe/ → [saka toŋe] 'reverse thorn' (postlexical)

saka-toge	*VgV	IO- (voi)	*ŋ	OCP (voi)	Real Morph	*g	IO- (nas)
a. saka-toge	*!				*	*	
b. saka-doge	*!	*				*	
c. ☞ saka-toŋe			*		*		*
d. saka-doŋe		*!	*				*

6.3. Data

The majority of abbreviated loanword compounds in Japanese are four-mora long, consisting of two bimoraic components (Itô 1990, Nishihara et al. 2001, Labrune 2002), as shown in (20). But, trimoraic words are also possible and have been becoming more common (Nishihara et al. 2001). The trimoraic words fall into three groups ((21)–(23)).

(20) (= (3))
    a. waado purosessaa → waa-puro 'word processor'
    b. dejitaru kamera → deji-kame 'digital camera'
    c. rimooto kontorooru → rimo-kon 'remote control'

(21) a. dansu paatii → dan-pa 'dance party'
    b. furii maaketto → furi-ma 'flea market'
    c. terefon kaado → tere-ka 'telephone card'

(22) a. buraddo pitto → bura-pi 'Brad Pitt'
    b. poteto chippu → pote-chi 'potato chip'
    c. netto sukeepu → ne-suke 'Netscape'

(23) a. purasutikku moderu → pura-mo 'plastic model'
    b. roiyaru hosuto → roi-ho 'Royal Host (a restaurant chain)'
    c. burakku bisuketto → bura-bi 'Black Biscuit (a band name)'

The three types of trimoraic words have the following common features. In

(21), the unabbreviated form of the monomoraic component has a long vowel in the first syllable (e.g. p<u>aa</u>.tii (21a)). In (22), the unabbreviated form of the monomoraic component has a coda consonant in the first syllable (e.g. pi<u>t</u>.to (22a)). In (23), the second syllable of the unabbreviated form of the monomoraic component starts with an obstruent (e.g. mo.<u>d</u>e.ru (23a)).

6.4. Previous Studies

This section overviews three previous studies on abbreviation: Itô (1990), Nishihara et al. (2001), and Itô and Mester (1997b).

6.4.1. Itô (1990)

Itô (1990) is the first comprehensive study about loanword abbreviation in Japanese. This study deals with compound abbreviation, as well as non-compound abbreviation, and reveals that the majority of abbreviated loanword compounds in Japanese are four-mora long, consisting of two bimoraic components, as illustrated in (24).

(24) Typology of Loanword Compound Abbreviation (Itô 1990: 221)

μ-Pattern	Count	Example	
2μ = [1μ + 1μ]	4	be(esu) a(ppu)	'base up, pay raise'
3μ = [2μ + 1μ]	4	dore(su) me(ekaa)	'dressmaker'
4μ = [2μ + 2μ]	134	suke(eto) boo(do)	'skateboard'

Itô claims that individual members of the compound cannot be monomoraic because of Minimal Stem Requirement, which requires that the minimal prosodic stem be bimoraic. But, this study does not explain why trimoraic forms such as *doreme* can be selected over quadrimoraic ones consisting of two bimoraic components, *doremee* for example.

6.4.2. Nishihara et al. (2001)

Nishihara et al. (2001) argue against headedness in compound abbreviation and develop a phonological account for compound abbreviation. Nishihara et al. introduce three types of compound abbreviation in Japanese and show that double truncation is most productive pattern in Japanese. Among the three patterns in (25), Nishihara et al. account for the pattern (25a) within the framework of OT, as shown below.[4]

(25) Nishihara et al. (2001: 308)
    a. double truncation (47%)

maikuro konpyuutaa → mai-kon	'micro computer'
sekusharu harasumento → seku-hara	'sexual harassment'
purofeshonaru resuringu → puro-resu	'professional wrestling'
pawaa sutearingu → pawa-sute	'power steering'
afutaa rekoodingu → afu-reko	'post-recording'

    b. back truncation (39%)

paato taimu → paato	'part-time job'
homo sekusharu → homo	'homosexual'
bideo dekki → bideo	'video deck'
tekisuto bukku → tekisuto	'textbook'
shorudaa bakku → shorudaa	'shoulder bag'

    c. front truncation (14%)

nyuusu kyasutaa → kyasutaa	'news caster'
mootaa baiku → baiku	'motor bike'
fasshon moderu → moderu	'fashion model'
kafe oore → oore	'café au lait'

Most of the double-truncated compounds are four-mora long consisting of two bimoraic components as in (25a). The quadrimoraic form is selected by the constraints in (26)–(28), which are ranked as in (29). The constraint ranking in (29) predicts for the correct output, as illustrated in (30).

(26) MinWd: Truncated outputs are minimal words, i.e. bimoraic.

(27) Parse-PrWd: Even a small fraction of every prosodic word which composes the compound must be parsed into the truncated output.

(28) Leftmost: The leftmost element of constituent is retained in truncation.

(29) Leftmost >> MinWd, Parse-PrWd

6 English Compound Abbreviation 119

(30) Tableau for 'pawaa sutearingu ('power steering') → pawa-sute'

pawaa sutearingu	Leftmost	MinWd	Parse-PrWd
a. ☞ pawa-sute			
b. waa-sute	*!		
c. pawa-su		*!	
d. pawa			*!

Next, Nishihara et al. explain two types of trimoraic abbreviated compounds in (31) and (32) as follows.

(31) a. buraddo pitto → bura-pi 'Brad Pitt'
     b. poteto chippu → pote-chi 'potato chip'

(32) a. furii maaketoo → furi-ma 'flea market'
     b. depaato gaaru → depa-ga 'department store girl'
     c. haiwei kaado → hai-ka 'highway card'
     d. terefon kaado → tere-ka 'telephone card'
     e. misutaa doonatu → misu-do 'Mr. Donuts (a donuts shop chain)'

In (31), the unabbreviated form of the second component has a coda consonant in the first syllable (e.g. pit.to (31a)). But, the coda consonant cannot be retained in the output due to the constraint Coda-Cond in (33) (Itô 1986). A possible repair strategy for the ill form like *pit* is to skip the second mora, which results in *pito*. But this also cannot be the optimal output because of the constraint Contiguity in (34) (McCarthy and Prince 1993a). In (32), the unabbreviated form of the second component has a long vowel in the first syllable (e.g. maa.ket. to (32a)). But the long vowel cannot appear in the output due to the constraint NoFinalLongVowels in (35).

(33) Coda-Cond: *Place]

(34) Contiguity: Segmental material that is contiguous in the input must also be contiguous in the output.

(35) NoFinalLongVowels (NFLV): *VV]$_{\text{Major PrWd}}$ [5]

Nishihara et al. assume that the constraints in (33)–(35) are ranked higher than MinWd and Parse-PrWd and propose the constraint ranking in (36). The constraint ranking in (36) accounts for the trimoraic abbreviated compounds in (31) and (32) as well as the quadrimoraic ones, as illustrated in (37)–(39).

(36) Coda-Cond, Contiguity, NFLV, Leftmost >> MinWd, Parse-PrWd

(37) Tableau for 'buraddo pitto ('Brad Pitt') → bura-pi'

buraddo pitto	CodaCd	Contig	NFLV	L-most	MinWd	Parse
a. ☞ bura-pit	*!					
b. bura-pi					*	
c. bura-pito		*!				

(38) Tableau for 'furii maaketoo ('flea market') → furi-ma'

furii maaketoo	CodaCd	Contig	NFLV	L-most	MinWd	Parse
a. furi-maa			*!			
b. ☞ furi-ma					*	
c. furi-make		*!				

(39) Tableau for 'pawaa sutearingu ('power steering') → pawa-sute'

pawaa sutearingu	CodaCd	Contig	NFLV	L-most	MinWd	Parse
a. ☞ pawa-sute						
b. waa-sute				*!		
c. pawa-su					*!	
d. pawa						*!

Nishihara et al. introduce the third pattern of trimoraic abbreviated compounds such as those in (23) (repeated in (40)). But they ignore this pattern because "there is no phonological reason to avoid [quadrimoraic forms]" (Nishihara et al. (2001: 311)).

(40) (= (23))

   a. purasutikku moderu → pura-mo 'plastic model'

b. roiyaru hosuto → roi-ho 'Royal Host (a restaurant chain)'
c. burakku bisuketto → bura-bi 'Black Biscuit (a band name)'

6.4.3. Itô and Mester (1997b)

Itô and Mester (1997b) adopt Sympathy Theory (McCarthy 1999) to deal with German truncations within the OT framework.

Itô and Mester introduce a productive pattern of truncation deriving hypocoristics and other kinds of shortenings in (41) and draw the general form of German truncation in (42), i.e. the whole first syllable and the first onset consonant of the second syllable of the base word followed by the suffix -i.

(41) a. Personal Names
  Gàbriéle   Gábi
  Éva   Évi
  Wáldemàr   Wáldi
 b. Surnames
  Górbatschòw Górbi
  Klínsmànn   Klínsi
  Wásmèier   Wási
 c. Common Nouns (mostly denoting persons)
  Àlkohóliker Àlki
  Pròletárier Pròli
  Érdkùnde   Érdi

(42) The General Form of German Truncations

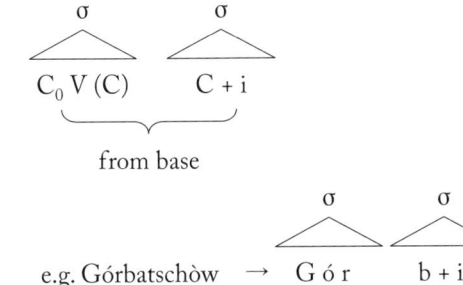

$$\underbrace{C_0\ V\ (C)}_{\text{from base}}\ \ C + i$$

e.g. Górbatschòw → Gór b + i

In this study, Itô and Mester adopt the model of truncation in (43), which is a modified version of Benua's (1995). This model of truncation accounts for examples like *Górbatschòw* → *Górbi*, as illustrated in (44). Constraints in (44) are defined as in (45)–(48).[6]

(43) Itô and Mester's Model of Truncation

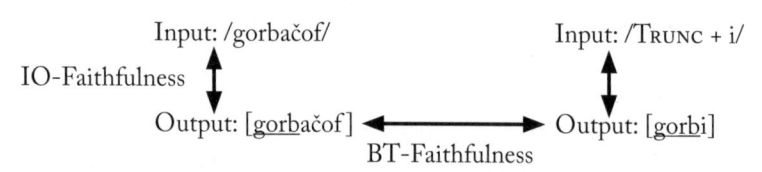

               Input: /gorbačof/   Input: /TRUNC + i/

IO-Faithfulness   ↕   ↕

            Output: [gorbačof] ←————→ Output: [gorbi]
                             BT-Faithfulness

(44) Tableau for 'Górbatschòw → Górbi'

Base: [(.gór.ba).(čòw.)] Input: /TRUNC + i/	MAX-IO	ALL-FT-LEFT	PARSE-σ	MAX-BT
a. (.gór.ba).(čòf-i.)		*!		
b. (.gór.ba).č-i.			*!	of
c. ☞ (.gór.b-i)				ačòf
d. (.gó.r-i.)				bačòf!
e. (.gór.ba.)	i!			čòf
f. (.górb.)	i!			ačòf
g. (.gór.)	i!			bačòf

(45) MAX-IO: Every element in the input has a correspondent in the output. ('No deletion')

(46) ALL-FT-LEFT: Every foot stands at the left edge of the PrWd.

(47) PARSE-σ: Syllables are parsed by feet.

(48) MAX-BT: Every element in B has a correspondent in T. ('No truncation')

The constraint ranking in (44) explains examples like *Górbatschòw* → *Górbi* but not examples such as *Gàbriéle* → *Gábi*. As illustrated in (49), the constraint ranking predicts the wrong winner *Gábri*. This problem occurs due to the constraint MAX-BT. MAX-BT has the effect of maximally preserving elements in the base. This constraint copes with the word with a simplex onset in the second syllable of the base such as *Górbatschòw* but not with the word with a complex onset in the second syllable of the base like *Gàbriéle*.

(49) Tableau for 'Gàbriéle → Gábi' (Wrong Prediction)

Base: [(.gà.bri).(é.le.)] Input: /Trunc + i/	Max-IO	All-Ft- Left	Parse-σ	Max-BT
a. (.gà.bri).(é.le.)-i.		*!	*	
b. (.gà.bri).(é.l-i.)		*!		e
c. ☹ (.gà.br-i.)				iéle
d. (.gà.b-i.)				riéle!
e. (.gàb.)	i!			riéle

Górbatschòw and *Gàbriéle* are truncated as *Górbi* and *Gábi*, respectively. Two generalizations can be drawn from these truncated words: (i) the bare truncatum, i.e. the truncated form without the suffix -*i*, is a possible syllable of German (see (50)) and (ii) the truncatum is the maximal syllable abstracted from the base (see (51)).

(50)

Górbatschòw → Górbi	✓σ △ .górb. <ačòw>	
Gàbriéle → Gábi	✓σ △ .gàb. <riéle>	*σ △ .gàbr. <iéle>

(51)

Górbatschòw → Górbi	σ △ ✓.górb. <ačòw> (Górb-i) *.gór. <bačòw> (*Gór-i)
Gàbriéle → Gábi	σ △ ✓.gàb. <riéle> (Gáb-i) *.gà. <briéle> (*Gá-i)

What is significant here is that the syllables [.górb.] and [.gàb.] are not found anywhere in the input or the output in spite of the fact that they play significant roles in selecting the optimal output. In that sense, this is a case of phonological opacity. Itô and Mester (1997b) account for the case of phonological opacity by adopting the expanded Sympathy Theory. Itô and Mester expand Sympathy Theory by removing the stipulation made by McCarthy (1999) that the constraint that selects the sympathy candidate must be a faithfulness constraint.

In Itô and Mester (2001b and 2003a)[7], however, they argue against Sympathy Theory and propose the Weakly Parallel Model, since Sympathy Theory is difficult to reconcile with a core tenet of OT, i.e. Richness of the Base, and is problematic for the treatment of phonological opacity, as illustrated in 6.2.2. As will be revealed in the following section, English compound abbreviation in Japanese has a case of phonological opacity that is similar to the case of German truncation introduced above. I will account for English compound abbreviation in Japanese within the framework of the Weakly Parallel Model.

6.5. Analysis

As introduced in 6.3., abbreviated English compounds in Japanese are trimoraic or quadrimoraic. Among them, quadrimoraic words (e.g. (52)) are the most common, and trimoraic words are further divided intro three subgroups as in (53)–(55).

(52) (= (3))
    a. waado purosessaa → waa-puro 'word processor'
    b. dejitaru kamera → deji-kame 'digital camera'
    c. rimooto kontorooru → rimo-kon 'remote control'

(53) (= (21))
    a. dansu paatii → dan-pa 'dance party'
    b. furii maaketto → furi-ma 'flea market'
    c. terefon kaado → tere-ka 'telephone card'

(54) (= (22))
    a. buraddo pitto → bura-pi 'Brad Pitt'

| | b. poteto chippu | → | pote-chi | 'potato chip' |
| | c. netto sukeepu | → | ne-suke | 'Netscape' |

(55) (= (23))
	a. purasutikku moderu	→	pura-mo	'plastic model'
	b. roiyaru hosuto	→	roi-ho	'Royal Host (a restaurant chain)'
	c. burakku bisuketto	→	bura-bi	'Black Biscuit (a band name)'

The four constraints in (56)–(59), i.e. TRUNC=F, CONTIGUITY, ANCHOR-L-BT, and MAX-μ-BT, are relevant to the quadrimoraic abbreviated compounds in (52).[8]

(56) TRUNC=F: Truncated form must be a foot, i.e. bimoraic.

(57) CONTIGUITY: Segmental material that is contiguous in the input must also be contiguous in the output.

(58) ANCHOR-L-BT: The left peripheral element of the truncated form corresponds to the left peripheral element of the base.

(59) MAX-μ-BT: Every mora in the base has a correspondent in the truncated form.

TRUNC=F in (56) is a markedness constraint that requires the truncated form be a foot, i.e. bimoraic. Due to this constraint, the output form consists of bimoraic components. CONTIGUITY in (57) (McCarthy and Prince 1993a) and ANCHOR-L-BT in (58), which is a member of the constraint family ANCHORING (McCarthy and Prince 1995), are faithfulness constraints. CONTIGUITY prohibits intrusion or skipping while ANCHOR-L-BT prohibits deletion or epenthesis at the left edge. The first two morae of the base are preserved in the truncated form because of these constraints. MAX-μ-BT in (59), which is a member of the constraint family MAX (McCarthy and Prince 1995), militates against truncation.

These four constraints, which are ranked as in (60), accounts for the quadrimoraic abbreviated compounds in (52), as illustrated in (61). The candidate (61a), where the first and third morae of the first component of the base compound is preserved in the output, cannot be the optimal candidate due to the constraint

CONTIGUITY. The candidate (61b), where the second and third morae of the second component of the base compound is preserved in the output, is not optimal either, because of ANCHOR-L-BT. The candidate (61c) is ruled out since it violates TRUNC=F. The candidate (61d) is the optimal candidate because it satisfies all the highest-ranked constraints. The candidates (61a)–(61d) violate MAX-BT. But it does not affect the selection of the optimal candidate because it is ranked lowest. Finally, the candidate (61e), which is maximally faithful to the input, is ruled out by TRUNC=F, one of the highest ranked constraints.

(60) Constraint Ranking I

CONTIGUITY ANCHOR-L-BT TRUNC=F

MAX-BT

(61) Tableau for 'waado purosessaa ('word processor') + T → waa-puro'

Input: waado purosessaa + T [9] Base: waado purosessaa	CONTIG	ANCHOR-L	TRUNC=F	MAX-BT
a. wado puro	*!			*,****
b. waa rose		*!		*,****
c. waa pu			*!	*,*****
d. ☞ waa puro				*,****
e. waado purosessaa			*!*	

Next consider the trimoraic abbreviated compounds in (53). In (53), the base form of the monomoraic component has a long vowel [aː] in the first syllable (e.g. p<u>aa</u>.tii (53a)). The examples in (53) cannot be quadrimoraic due to the constraint *[aː]]$_{PW}$ in (62). *[aː]]$_{PW}$ is ranked higher than TRUNC=F, as illustrated in (63). Based on this, the constraint ranking in (60) can be modified as in (64). The modified constraint ranking accounts for the examples in (53) as well as those in (52), as illustrated in (65) and (66).

(62) *[a:]]$_{PW}$: No word-final long vowel [a:].

(63) *[a:]]$_{PW}$ >> TRUNC=F

Input: dansu paatii + T Base: dansu paatii	*[a:]]$_{PW}$	TRUNC=F
a. dan paa	*!	
b. ☞ dan pa		*

(64) Constraint Ranking II

CONTIGUITY   ANCHOR-L-BT   *[a:]]$_{PW}$
       |
    TRUNC=F
       |
    MAX-BT

(65) Tableau for 'dansu paatii ('dance party') + T → dan pa'

Input: dansu paatii + T Base: dansu paatii	CONTIG	ANCHOR-L	*[a:]]$_{PW}$	TRUNC=F	MAX-BT
a. dan pati	*!				*,**
b. dan tii		*!			*,**
c. dan paa			*!		*,**
d. ☞ dan pa				*	*,***
e. dansu paatii				*!*	

(66) Tableau for 'waado purosessaa ('word processor') + T → waa-puro'

Input: waado purosessaa + T Base: waado purosessaa	CONTIG	AN- CHOR-L	*[a:]]$_{PW}$	TRUNC=F	MAX-BT
a. wado puro	*!				*,****
b. waa rose		*!			*,****
c. waa pu				*!	*,*****
d. ☞ waa puro					*,****
e. waado purosessaa			*!	**	

In (65), the candidates (65a) and (65b) are ruled out by the highest-ranked constraints Contiguity and Anchor-L-BT, respectively. The candidate (65c) has the most common structure, i.e. quadrimoraic consisting of two bimoraic components, but cannot be the optimal because it violates a higher-ranked constraint *[a:]]$_{PW}$. The candidate (65d) is not quadrimoraic. But it is selected as the optimal candidate since its violation of Trunc=F is not fatal. The candidate (65e), which is maximally faithful to the input, is not optimal due to its doubly violation of Trunc=F. In (66), on the other hand, the candidate (66d) is still the optimal candidate, because the constraint *[a:]]$_{PW}$ does not affect the selection of the optimal output.

The constraint ranking in (64) accounts for most of the trimoraic abbreviated compounds of this type. But, there is one type of counterexamples, which is shown in (67).[10] In counterexamples in (67), the long vowel [a:] in the second component never appears as [a]. The common feature counterexamples share is that the second component is short, i.e. bimoraic. This common feature indicates that the truncation morpheme does not apply to bimoraic words.[11] The basic motivation for abbreviation is to make words shorter, and a bimoraic form is the favored abbreviated form. The second component of the counterexamples in (67) is not truncated because it is short by itself.

(67) a. patorooru kaa → pato-kaa (*pato-ka) '*lit.* patrol car' ('police car')
     b. gei baa   → *gei-ba   'gay bar'

As introduced above, Nishihara et al. (2001) adopt the constraint NFLV in (68) to explain the vowel shortening in examples in (69). But, this constraint is too strong for two reasons. First, the vowel that undergoes shortening is the long vowel [a:] in most cases and many of other long vowels resist shortening, as Nishihara et al. (2001) notice (see (70)).[12] In Nishihara et al. (2001), *misu-do* in (69e) is the only example of the shortening of a long vowel other than [a:]. This shortening might occur due to the analogy to *makudo* (makudonarudo → makudo 'Mcdonald's') because they are both fast food chains selling American food.

(68) NoFinalLongVowels (NFLV): *VV]$_{\text{Major PrWd}}$ (= (35))

(69) (= (32))
- a. furii maaketoo → furi-ma 'flea market'
- b. depaato gaaru → depa-ga 'department store girl'
- c. haiwei kaado → hai-ka 'highway card'
- d. terefon kaado → tere-ka 'telephone card'
- e. misutaa doonatu → misu-do 'Mr. Donuts (a donuts shop chain)'

(70)
- a. sukeeto boodo → suke-boo (*suke-bo) 'skateboard'
- b. rondon buutu → ron-buu (*ron-bu) 'London Boots (comic duo)'
- c. bataa piinattu → bata-pii (*bata-pi) 'buttered peanut'

Second, Nishihara et al. (2001) assume that the vowel shortening in (69) is a phenomenon in the Loanword sublexicon. But this is not correct. As illustrated in (71), the word-final long vowel [a:] is highly restricted in the core sublexicon of the Japanese lexicon, but not in the Loanword sublexicon. In this book, therefore, I propose that the long vowel shortening observed in English compound abbreviation is a phenomenon in the core sublexicon of the Japanese lexicon triggered by the constraint $^{*}[a:]]_{PW}$.

(71) The Number of the Words with Word-final [a:] (the result of a dictionary research)

Total #	# of Loanwords	# of Non-loanwords
1426	1382 (96.9%)	44 (3.1%)

(The majority of non-loanwords are interjections, onomatopoeia, non-standard words, etc.)

Next, let us consider the trimoraic abbreviated compounds in (54). In (54), the unabbreviated form of the monomoraic component has a coda consonant in the first syllable (e.g. pit.to (54a)). In these words, the coda consonant cannot be preserved in the output because of a highest-ranked constraint CODA-COND in (72) (Itô 1986). There are two possible ways to avoid the ill form like *pit* and maintain the quadrimoraic form consisting of two bimoraic components: (i) skipping the second mora or (ii) vowel epenthesis. But neither of them works, because the former is blocked by the constraint CONTIGUITY while the latter by the constraint DEP-BT in (73), which is a member of the constraint family DEP (McCarthy and Prince 1995), as illustrated in (74). In (74), 'o_i' and 'o_j' indicate non-epenthetic and epenthetic vowels respectively.

(72) Coda-Cond: *Place]

(73) Dep-BT: Every element in the truncated form has a correspondent in the base.

(74) Contiguity, Coda-Cond, Dep-BT >> Trunc=F

Input: buraddo pitto$_i$ + T Base: buraddo pitto$_i$		Contig	Coda-Cond	Dep-BT	Trunc=F
a.	bura pito$_i$	*!			
b.	bura pito$_j$			*!	
c.	bura pit		*!		
d.	bura pii			*!	
e. ☞	bura pi				*

Based on the tableau (74), the constraint ranking in (64) can be modified as in (75). The modified constraint ranking accounts for the examples in (54) as well as those in (52) and (53), as illustrated in (76)–(78).

(75) Constraint Ranking III

    Contiguity Anchor-L-BT *[a:]]$_{PW}$ Coda-Cond Dep-BT

    Trunc=F

    Max-BT

(76) Tableau for 'buraddo pitto ('Brad Pitt') + T → bura pi'

Input: buraddo pitto$_i$ + T Base: buraddo pitto$_i$		Contig	Anchor-L	Coda-Cond	Dep-BT	*[a:]]$_{pw}$	Trunc=F	Max-BT
a.	bura pito$_i$	*!						**,*
b.	bura pito$_j$				*!			**,*
c.	bura pit			*!				**,*
d.	bura pii				*!			**,**
e. ☞	bura pi						*	**,**
f.	buraddo pitto$_i$						*!*	

In (76), the quadrimoraic candidates consisting of two bimoraic components (76a)–(76d) are ruled out by Contiguity, Dep-BT, and Coda-Cond. The candidate (76e), which is not quadrimoraic but trimoraic, is selected as the optimal candidate since its violation of Trunc=F is not fatal. The candidate (76f) is the most faithful to the input but cannot be optimal due to its doubly violation of Trunc=F. In (77) and (78), on the other hand, the constraints Contiguity, Coda-Cond, and Dep-BT do not affect the selection of the optimal candidate and the candidates (77d) and (78d) are selected as the optimal outputs.

(77) Tableau for 'dansu paatii ('dance party') + T → dan pa'

Input: dansu paatii + T Base: dansu paatii	Contig	Anchor-L	Coda-Cond	Dep-BT	*[aː]]pw	Trunc=F	Max-BT
a. dan pati	*!						*,**
b. dan tii		*!					*,**
c. dan paa					*!		*,**
d. ☞ dan pa						*	*,***
e. dansu paatii						*!*	

(78) Tableau for 'waado purosessaa ('word processor') + T → waa-puro'

Input: word processor Base: waado purosessaa	Contig	Anchor-L	Coda-Cond	Dep-BT	*[aː]]pw	Trunc=F	Max-BT
a. wado puro	*!						*,****
b. waa rose		*!					*,****
c. waa pu						*!	*,*****
d. ☞ waa puro							*,****
e. waado purosessaa						*!*	

Finally, consider the examples in (55). In (55), the second syllable of the unabbreviated form of the monomoraic component starts with an obstruent (e.g. mo.de.ru (55a)). In these examples, the first syllable of the base form of the monomoraic component does not have a long vowel [aː] as in (53) (e.g. paa.tii (53a)) or a coda consonant as in (54) (e.g. pit.to (54a)). In other words, there seems no motivation for monomoraicity. But, as illustrated in (55), the abbreviated form is trimoraic consisting of one bimoraic component and one monomoraic component. Why are the abbreviated forms in (55) not quadrimoraic? As will be shown below, this is a case of phonological opacity.

The English compound *purasutikku moderu* 'plastic model' is abbreviated as *pura-mo* (*pura-mode). The output form suggests that the monomoraic candidate *mo* satisfies the constraint ranking better than the bimoraic candidate *mode* does, although, as mentioned above, there seems no motivation for the monomoraicity. Why is the bimoraic candidate *mode* not selected as the optimal candidate? I assume that is because the bimoraic candidate *mode* is worse than another bimoraic candidate *mod* in terms of the number of syllable. The basic motivation for abbreviation is to make words shorter. In that sense, the disyllabic candidate *mode* is worse than the monosyllabic candidate *mod*. The monosyllabic candidate *mod*, however, cannot be the optimal output, either, since it violates the constraint CODA-COND. As a result, the monomoraic candidate *mo* can be the optimal candidate. In derivational model, this process can be shown as in (79).

(79) 'moderu ('model') → mo'

    Input: mo.de.ru.
                | resyllabification, TRUNC=F
              mod.
                | CODA-COND
    Output: mo.

In (79), the intermediate form *mod* plays a significant role in determining the output form. The truncation *moderu* → *mo* is a case of phonological opacity in the sense that the truncated form *mod* is not found anywhere in the input or the output but plays a significant role in selecting the optimal output. The case of phonological opacity at hand is similar to the one in German truncation discussed by Itô and Mester (1997b) in the sense that the resyllabified form plays a significant role in determining the output form.[13] In this chapter, I will account for the case of phonological opacity at hand within the framework of the Weakly Parallel Model (Itô and Mester 2001b, 2003a). In this model, the abbreviation *purasutikku moderu* → *pura-mo* can be explained as follows.

As mentioned above, the bimoraic form *mod* seems to play a significant role in determining the output form. This is because the bimoraic form *mod* is the output of the lexical module (and the input to the postlexical module). The constraint ranking developed thus far is the one for postlexical phonology. This ranking predicts the correct output, as illustrated in (80). In (80), the bimoraic candidate *mo.de* in (80a) is ruled out by DEP-BT, while the candidate *mod.* in (80c), which is faithful to the input, is ruled out by CODA-COND.

(80) Tableau for 'purasutikku moderu ('plastic model') T → pura mo' (postlexical)

Input: purasutikku moderu + T Base: pu.ra. mod.	CONTIG	ANCHOR	CODA-COND	DEP-BT	*[aː]Pw	TRUNC=F	MAX-BT
a. pu.ra. mo.de.				*!			
b. pu.ra. mod.e.			*!	*		*	
c. pu.ra. mod.			*!				
d. ☞ pu.ra. mo.						*	*
e. pur. mo.			*!			*	**

The next question to be considered is: How is the bimoraic form *mod* selected by the lexical module? In lexical phonology, resyllabificaton occurs when truncated (mo.de.ru. → mod.). This resyllabificaton is triggered by the constraint ALL-σ-LEFT in (81), which is a version of ALL-FT-LEFT by McCarthy and Prince (1993a). This constraint explains why the bimoraic candidate *mode* is worse than the candidate *mod*.

(81) ALL-σ-LEFT: Every syllable stands at the left edge of the truncated form.

There is one more issue we need to consider. That is the treatment of coda consonants. In Japanese, obstruents without independent place of articulation, as well as the placeless nasal, can be in the coda position.[14] In lexical phonology, the optimal output *mod* has a coda consonant [d]. But this coda consonant seems illegitimate, since it has independent place of articulation. Why is the [d] with independent place of articulation possible in the form *mod*? That is because *mod* is a bound morpheme. Itô (1990) discusses the phonological difference between prosodic words and bound morphemes in compound loanword abbreviation in Japanese. For example, consider *dansu paatii* → *dan-pa*. The abbreviated component *dan* is a well-formed component but it cannot occur in isolation. This suggests that different set of constraints apply to bound morphemes.

In this book, I propose that there are actually two types of Coda-Cond in Japanese: (i) only nasals and obstruents can be in the coda position (Coda-Cond$_{BM}$ in (82))[15], and (ii) they cannot have independent place of articulation (henceforth Coda-Cond$_{PW}$ in (83)). The constraint Coda-Cond$_{BM}$ plays an active role in both lexical phonology and postlexical phonology and applies to bound morphemes as well as prosodic words, whereas Coda-Cond$_{PW}$ plays an active role only in postlexical phonology and applies only to prosodic words. That is, Coda-Cond$_{PW}$ is the constraint that needs to be ranked differently in lexical phonology and postlexical phonology.

(82) Coda-Cond$_{BM}$: Coda consonants are obstruents or nasals.

(83) Coda-Cond$_{PW}$: *Place]

The idea that Coda-Cond$_{PW}$ plays an active role only in postlexical phonology and applies only to prosodic words is supported by verb stems, which are also bound morphemes. As illustrated in (84), verb stems in Japanese can have coda consonants with independent place of articulation, although the output forms, i.e. the outputs of postlexical phonology, never have coda consonants with independent place of articulation.[16]

(84) Verb Stems (Coda Consonants with Independent Place of Articulation)
	Stem	Past	Causative	
a.	mat	mat.ta.	ma.ta.se.ru.	'to wait'
b.	kat	kat.ta.	ka.ta.se.ru.	'to win'
c.	yom	yon.da.	yo.ma.se.ru.	'to read'

The constraint Coda-Cond$_{BM}$ is a highest-ranked constraint and prohibits coda consonants other than obstruents or nasals. This constraint accounts for why the second component of the examples in (85), which has an approximant [r] in the onset of the second syllable, never appears as the monomoraic form in compound abbreviation.

(85) a. sarada doressingu → sara-dore (*sara-do) 'salad dressing'
     b. pari korekushon → pari-kore (*pari-ko) 'Paris collection'
     c. imeeji toreeningu → ime-tore (*ime-to) 'image training'
     d. intaa karezzi → in-kare (*in-ka) 'lit. intercollege'
                                                ('intercollegiate game')

Now, let us get back to the main point: How is the monosyllabic and bimoraic form *mod* selected by the lexical module? The constraint rankings in (86) and (87) are the rankings for English compound abbreviation in Japanese, where the constraint CODA-COND$_{PW}$ is ranked differently. These rankings explain why *model* is truncated as *mo* and why *doressingu* cannot be *do*, as illustrated in (88)–(91).

(86) Constraint Ranking for English Compound Abbreviation (Lexical Phonology)

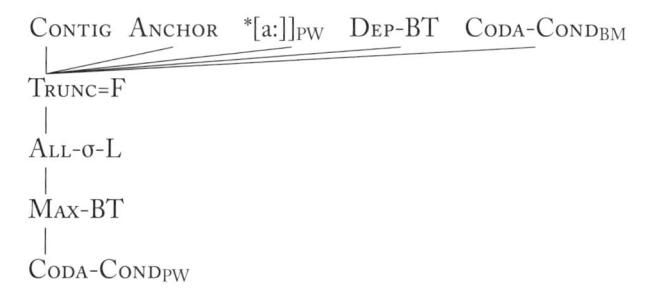

CONTIG ANCHOR *[a:]]$_{PW}$ DEP-BT CODA-COND$_{BM}$
|
TRUNC=F
|
ALL-σ-L
|
MAX-BT
|
CODA-COND$_{PW}$

(87) Constraint Ranking for English Compound Abbreviation (Postlexical Phonology)

CONTIG ANCHOR *[a:]]$_{PW}$ DEP-BT CODA-COND$_{PW}$ CODA-COND$_{BM}$
|
TRUNC=F
|
ALL-σ-L
|
MAX-BT

(88) Tableau for 'purasutikku moderu ('plastic model') T → pura mo' (lexical)[17]

Input: purasutikku moderu + T Base: purasutikku moderu	Contig	Anchor	Coda-Cond_{BM}	Dep-BT	*[a:]]_{pw}	Trunc=F	All-σ-L	Max-BT	Coda-Cond_{PW}
a. pu.ra. mo.de.						*,*!	**** ,*		
b. pu.ra. mod.e.					*!	*,*	****	*	
c. ☞ pu.ra. mod.						*	****,*	*	
d. pu.ra. mo.					*!	*	****,**		
e. pur. mo.			*!			*	****,**	*	

(89) Tableau for 'purasutikku moderu ('plastic model') T → pura mo' (postlexical)

Input: purasutikku moderu + T Base: pu.ra. mod.	Contig	Anchor	Coda-Cond_{PW}	Coda-Cond_{BM}	Dep-BT	*[a:]]_{pw}	Trunc=F	All-σ-L	Max-BT
a. pu.ra. mo.de.					*!			*,*	
b. pu.ra. mod.e.		*!			*		*	*,*	
c. pu.ra. mod.		*!						*	
d. ☞ pu.ra. mo.							*	*	*
e. pur. mo.			*!		*		*		*,*

In the case of *purasutikku moderu*, the candidate *pura-mode* loses to *pura-mod* in the lexical module due to the constraint All-σ-Left, and the candidate *pura-mo* is the optimal candidate in the postlexical module because the candidate *pura-mod* is ruled out due to its violation of Coda-Cond_{PW}. In the case of *sarada doressingu*, on the other hand, the candidate *sara-dore* is the optimal in both lexical and postlexical modules, since the candidates *sara-dor* and *sara-do* violate Coda-Cond (both Coda-Cond_{PW} and Coda-Cond_{BM}) and Trunc=F, respectively.

(90) Tableau for 'sarada doressingu ('salad dressing') T → sara dore' (lexical)

Input: sarada doressingu + T Base: sarada doressingu	Contig	Anchor	Coda-Condbm	Coda- Condpw	Dep-BT	*[aː]]pw	Trunc=F	All-σ-L	Max-BT	Coda-Condpw
a. ☞ sa.ra.do.re.								**	*,***	
b. sa.ra.dor.		*!						*	*,***	*
c. sa.ra.do.						*!		*	*,****	

(91) Tableau for 'sarada doressingu ('salad dressing') T → sara dore' (postlexical)

Input: sarada doressingu + T Base: sa.ra.do.re.	Contig	Anchor	Coda-Condpw	Coda- Condbm	Dep-BT	*[aː]]pw	Trunc=F	All-σ-L	Max-BT
a. ☞ sa.ra.do.re.								*,*	
b. sa.ra.dor.			*!	*				*	*
c. sa.ra.do.							*!	*	*

The constraint rankings in (86) and (87) account for the other types of compound abbreviation in (52)–(54) as well, as illustrated in (92)–(97).

(92) Tableau for 'buraddo pitto ('Brad Pitt') + T → bura pi' (lexical)

Input: buraddo pitto$_i$ + T Base: buraddo pitto$_i$	Contig	Anchor	Coda- Condbm	Coda-	Dep-BT	*[aː]]pw	Trunc=F	All-σ-L	Max-BT	Coda-Condpw
a. bu.ra.pi.to$_i$.	*!							**	**,*	
b. bu.ra.pi.to$_j$.					*!			**	**,*	
c. ☞ bu.ra.pit.								*	**,*	*
d. bu.ra.pi.						*!		*	**,**	
e. bur.pi.		*!						*	**,**	*

(93) Tableau for 'buraddo pitto ('Brad Pitt') + T → bura pi' (postslexical)

Input: buraddo pitto$_i$ + T Base: bu.ra. pit.	Contig	Anchor	Coda-Cond$_{PW}$	Coda-Cond$_{BM}$	Dep-BT	*[aː]]$_{PW}$	Trunc=F	All-σ-L	Max-BT
a. bu.ra. pi.to.					*!			**,	
b. bu.ra. pit.			*!					*	
c. ☞ bu.ra. pi.							*	*	*
d. bur. pi.			*!	*			*		**,

In the case of *buraddo pitto*, the candidate *bura-pit* is selected by the lexical module because the quadrimoraic candidates (92a) and (92b) violate the highest-ranked constraints Contiguity and Dep-BT, respectively. In the postlexical module, on the other hand, the candidate *bura-pit* loses to the candidate *bura-pi* because of the violation of Coda-Cond$_{PW}$.

(94) Tableau for 'dansu paatii ('dance party') + T → dan pa' (lexical)

Input: dansu paatii + T Base: dansu paatii	Contig	Anchor	Coda-Cond$_{BM}$	Dep-BT	*[aː]]$_{PW}$	Trunc=F	All-σ-L	Max-BT	Coda-Cond$_{PW}$
a. dan. pa.ti.	*!						*	**,**	
b. dan. tii.		*!						**,**	
c. dan. paa.					*!			**,**	
d. ☞ dan. pa.							*	***,**	

(95) Tableau for 'dansu paatii ('dance party') + T → dan pa' (postslexical)

Input: dansu paatii + T Base: dan. pa.	Contig	Anchor	Coda-Cond$_{PW}$	Coda-Cond$_{BM}$	Dep-BT	*[aː]]$_{PW}$	Trunc=F	All-σ-L	Max-BT
a. dan. pa.ti.					*!			*	
b. dan. paa.					*!	*			
c. ☞ dan. pa.							*		

In the case of *dansu paatii*, the trimoraic candidate *dan-pa* is selected by the lexical module because the quadrimoraic candidate (94c) violates the highest-ranked constraint *[a:]]$_{PW}$, which is fatal. In the postlexical module, the candidate *dan-pa* is selected again as the optimal output, since the other candidates violate the highest-ranked constraints.

(96) Tableau for 'waado purosessaa ('word processor') + T → waa-puro' (lexical)

Input: waado purosessaa + T Base: waado purosessaa	CONTIG	ANCHOR	CODA- CONDBM	CODA-	DEP-BT	*[a:]]$_{PW}$	TRUNC=F	ALL-σ-L	MAX-BT	CODA- CONDPW
a. wa.do. pu.ro.	*!						**	*	****	
b. waa. ro.se.		*!						*	****	
c. waa. pu.							*!	*	*****	
d. ☞ waa. pu.ro.								*	****	
e. waa. pur.					*!			*	****	*

(97) Tableau for 'waado purosessaa ('word processor') + T → waa-puro' (postslexical)

Input: waado purosessaa + T Base: waa. pu.ro.	CONTIG	ANCHOR	CODA- CONDPW	CODA- CONDBM	CODA-	DEP-BT	*[a:]]$_{PW}$	TRUNC=F	ALL-σ-L	MAX-BT
a. waa. pu.								*!		*
b. ☞ waa. pu.ro.									*	
c. waa. pur.					*!			*		*

In the case of *waado purosessaa*, the quadrimoraic candidate *waa-puro* is selected by both the lexical and postlexical modules because the trimoraic candidates *waa-pu* violates the constraint TRUNC=F and it is fatal.

There is one more issue we need to consider. That is asymmetric word structures. As introduced above, there are three types of trimoraic abbreviated compounds. Among them, almost all of them have the structure like *pura-mo*, where the first component is truncated as a bimoraic form and the second as a monomoraic form, i.e. [μμ$_{BM}$ + μ$_{BM}$]. But, the structure like *ne-suke* in (98), where the first component is truncated as a monomoraic form and the second as a bimoraic form, i.e. [μ$_{BM}$ + μμ$_{BM}$], is quite uncommon.[18] Among the three types of trimoraic abbreviated compounds discussed thus far, one type is triggered by the constraint *[a:]]$_{PW}$ whereas the others by two types of CODA-COND, i.e. CODA-COND$_{PW}$ and CODA-COND$_{BM}$. The trimoraic words triggered by *[a:]]$_{PW}$ do not have the structure [μ$_{BM}$ + μμ$_{BM}$], since the constraint applies only to prosodic word-finally. But, the other two types such as those in (99) should be able to have the structure [μ$_{BM}$ + μμ$_{BM}$], because CODA-COND is a positional constraint for the coda, but not for the prosodic word-final position. Why is the structure [μ$_{BM}$ + μμ$_{BM}$] disfavored? That is because the Light-Heavy structure is marked in Japanese, as shown below.

(98) netto sukeepu   →   ne-suke   'Netscape'

(99) a. dejitaru kamera   →   deji-kame (*de-kame) 'digital camera'
     b. poteto sarada   →   pote-sara (*po-sara) 'potato salad'
     c. sutaatingu menbaa →   suta-men   (*su-men)   '*lit.* starting member'
                                                     ('starting lineup')

Kubozono (1988) discusses the dispreference for the Light-Heavy structure at the prosodic word level (see also Kubozono 2003). Kubozono (1988) analyzes the structure of Japanese compound nouns and finds that the left-branching structure is more common than the right-branching structure. In other words, the left-branching component tends to be heavier than the right-branching component, as schematized in (100). The morphological asymmetry in (100) is reflected in the prosodic asymmetry. The right-branching structure is generally realized as two prosodic words, i.e. the output has two accented morae, whereas the left-branching structure is realized as one word, i.e. the output has only one accented mora, as illustrated in (101).

(100)   [[AB][C]] > [[A][BC]]

(101)   (Kubozono 2003: 117)
     a. [[AB][C]] → {ABC}
        [[[do´itu][bu´ngaku]][kyookai] → {doitu-bungaku-kyo´okai}
        'Germany-literature-association'   'Association of German literature'
     b. [[A][BC]] → {A}{BC}
        [[do´itu][[bu´ngaku][kyookai]]] → {do´itu}{ bungaku-kyo´okai}
        'Germany-literature-association'   'German Association of literature'

Itô (1990) discusses the avoidance of the Light-Heavy structure at the syllable level. Itô (1990) studies non-compound loanword abbreviation in Japanese and finds the truncation patterns in (102) (Itô 1990:217, see also Labrune 2002). As illustrated in (102), where nonproductive abbreviation patterns are marked by the symbol "#", the sequence of [σ$_\mu$ σ$_{\mu\mu}$] in the word-initial position is highly disfavored in Japanese.

(102) μ-Pattern σ-Pattern Example
  1μ   # [σ$_\mu$]
  2μ   [σ$_\mu$ σ$_\mu$]   choko(reeto)   'chocolate'
        # [σ$_{\mu\mu}$]
  3μ   [σ$_{\mu\mu}$ σ$_\mu$]   saike(derikku)   'psychedelic'
        [σ$_\mu$ σ$_\mu$ σ$_\mu$] anime(eshon)   'animation'
        # [σ$_\mu$ σ$_{\mu\mu}$]
  4μ   [σ$_{\mu\mu}$ σ$_{\mu\mu}$]   baaten(daa)   'bartender'
        [σ$_{\mu\mu}$ σ$_\mu$ σ$_\mu$]   intoro(dakushon)   'introduction'
        [σ$_\mu$ σ$_\mu$ σ$_{\mu\mu}$]   eakon(dishonaa)   'airconditioner'
        [σ$_\mu$ σ$_\mu$ σ$_\mu$ σ$_\mu$] furasuto(reeshon)   'frustration'
        # [σ$_\mu$ σ$_{\mu\mu}$ σ$_\mu$]

The avoidance of the word-initial [σ$_\mu$ σ$_{\mu\mu}$] has been explained in terms of foot parsing. Itô (1990) claims that this is due to Left Edge Requirement (the interaction of Align-L(Pw, Ft) (Every foot stands at the left edge of the prosodic words.) and Parse-HeavySyl (Heavy syllables are properly parsed by feet.) in OT terms), which requires the left edge of a prosodic word matches the left edge of a foot (see also Kubozono 2003). In other words, Itô (1990) claims that the word-initial [σ$_\mu$ σ$_{\mu\mu}$] is not allowed because the possible foot pursing ([(σ$_\mu$ σ$_\mu$)μ] or [σ$_\mu$ (σ$_{\mu\mu}$)]) violates one of the higher-ranked constraints Align-L(Pw, Ft) and Parse-HeavySyl.

The dispreference for [μ$_{BM}$ + μμ$_{BM}$] observed in English compound abbreviation is another example of avoidance of the Light-Heavy structure, i.e. the avoidance of the Light-Heavy structure at the mora level. The structure [μ$_{BM}$ + μμ$_{BM}$] is disfavored because it is prosodically worse than [μμ$_{BM}$ + μ$_{BM}$]. The avoidance of [μ$_{BM}$ + μμ$_{BM}$] can be explained in terms of foot parsing. As mentioned above, Itô (1990) claims that the avoidance of Light-Heavy structure is due to Left Edge Requirement (the interaction of Align-L(Pw, Ft) and Parse-HeavySyl in OT terms). But, if this is the correct analysis, the words in (99) should be able to have the structure [$\mu_{BM} + \mu\mu_{BM}$] because the constraints ALIGN-L(Pw, FT) and PARSE-HEAVYSYL do not prohibit the foot parsing [($\mu_{BM} + \mu$) μ_{BM}]. The fact that the foot parsing such as [($\mu_{BM} + \mu$) μ_{BM}] is not allowed suggests that the foot parsing across stem boundaries is not allowed in Japanese. In other words, the morphological structure plays a significant role in foot parsing. As mentioned above, Kubozono (1988) finds that the morphological asymmetry is reflected in the prosodic asymmetry. But the prosodic asymmetry pointed out in Kubozono (1988) is not relevant to the asymmetric word structures observed in English compound abbreviation, since the examples in this chapter do not have more than one accented mora in the abbreviated form. In other words, the abbreviated words are all single prosodic words.

In sum, the avoidance of the structure [$\mu_{BM} + \mu\mu_{BM}$] is not a sporadic phenomenon in Japanese. But, it is a part of the systematic dispreference for the Light-Heavy structure observed at the levels of the prosodic hierarchy in (103).[19]

(103) Prosodic Hierarchy

Prosodic Word
|
Foot
|
Syllable
|
Mora

6.6. Conclusion

This chapter has discussed English compound abbreviation in Japanese within the OT framework. This chapter is summarized as follows.

The majority of abbreviated loanword compounds in Japanese are quadrimoraic consisting of two bimoraic components. But, trimoraic words are also possible and can be divided into three groups. The trimoraic words can be explained as follows.

The first type of the trimoraic words are triggered by the constraint *[a:]]$_{PW}$. In those words, the unabbreviated form of the monomoraic component has a long vowel in the first syllable. Nishihara et al. (2001) claim that they are trimoraic due to the constraint NoFinalLongVowels and this is a phenomenon in the Loanword sublexicon. But, this chapter revealed that it is only the long vowel [aː] that undergoes shortening and that the constraint *[aː]]$_{PW}$ triggers it. As discussed in Chapter 4, this constraint plays a significant role in the core part of the Japanese lexicon. It suggests that the shortening of [aː] observed in English compound abbreviation is a phenomenon in the core part of the lexicon and the trimoraic words of this type are assimilated to the core part of the Japanese lexicon with respect to the constraint *[aː]]$_{PW}$.

The second type of the trimoraic words are triggered by the constraint Coda-Cond$_{PW}$. In those words, the unabbreviated form of the monomoraic component has a coda consonant in the first syllable. But the coda consonant cannot appear in the output because the coda consonant with independent place of articulation is not allowed in the output.

The third type of the trimoraic words are a case of phonological opacity. In those words, the second syllable of the unabbreviated form of the monomoraic component starts with an obstruent. This type of compound abbreviation has not been discussed in the literature. This chapter revealed that this is a case of phonological opacity where the constraint All-σ-Left plays a significant role. In this chapter, I have accounted for the opaque case within the framework of the Weakly Parallel Model. I have argued that there are actually two types of Coda-Cond, i.e. Coda-Cond$_{PW}$ and Coda-Cond$_{BM}$, and that Coda-Cond$_{PW}$ plays an active role only in postlexical phonology. This idea is supported by verb stems in Japanese. The Weakly Parallel Model accounts for the opaque case observed in English compound abbreviation straightforwardly, since it handles the coda consonants in the opaque case and those in verb stems in a unified manner: they are both bound morphemes and are allowed in lexical phonology. The asymmetries between the coda consonants in the opaque case and those in verb stems were introduced but not discussed in detail. That needs to be further studied in future research.

This chapter has provided supporting evidence for the Weakly Parallel Model, a subtheory of OT. Phonological opacity is problematic for OT, because markedness constraints apply only to surface representations of candidates and the surface representations do not show the motivation for opaque phonological processes, and OT has not resolved it successfully. But, the Weakly Parallel Model accounts for it successfully by adopting the traditional distinction between lexical phonology and postlexical phonology. This chapter has shown how the case of phonological opacity observed in English compound abbreviation in Japanese can be explained within the framework of OT.

Also, the Weakly Parallel Model gives a straightforward explanation for the difference between the two types of CODA-COND, i.e. CODA-COND$_{BM}$ and CODA-COND$_{PW}$. In this chapter, I have argued that CODA-COND$_{BM}$ applies to both bound morphemes and prosodic words whereas CODA-COND$_{PW}$ applies only to prosodic words. The difference between these two constraints can be explained straightforwardly within the framework of the Weakly Parallel Model, since the lexical and postlexical modules can have separate constraint systems in this framework.

Finally, this chapter has revealed that Japanese disfavors the Light-Heavy structure systematically. When English compounds are abbreviated into trimoraic forms, almost all the abbreviated forms have the structure [μμ$_{BM}$ + μ$_{BM}$]. This is because of the dispreference for the Light-Heavy structure. Previous studies discussed avoidance of the Light-Heavy structure at the syllable and prosodic word levels. But they have not shown that it is a general characteristic of Japanese. This chapter has revealed that avoidance of the Light-Heavy structure is observed at any level of the prosodic hierarchy and it is a general characteristic of Japanese.

Endnotes

* An earlier version of this chapter appears in Proceedings of the 4th International Conference on Phonology and Morphology.
1 Compound abbreviation in Japanese is different from non-compound abbreviation. Labrune (2002) studies the abbreviation of non-compound loanwords in Japanese and finds that apocope and aphaeresis generally occurs just before the accented mora of a base. As will be shown in this chapter, however, this is not the case for English compound abbreviation in Japanese.
2 "Thus it is at least conceivable that certain types of phonetic constraints, calling for quantitative modes of evaluation, are literally not part of the lexical module (Itô and Mester 2003a)." Itô and Mester (2003a) further comment on (7b): "[W]e also do not exclude the possibility that the postlexical system might be quite different in character from the lexical one...For example, only the latter might turn out to be a strict OT-system, whereas the former might be a more broadly optimization-based quantitative system." Many questions regarding the nature and structure of the lexical module have not been answered. In this book, however, I will ignore them and leave them for future research.
3 Itô and Mester (2003a) employ the constraints *ŋ and *VgV instead of *PrWd[ŋ, which is

adopted in their earlier study.

4   Nishihara et al. ignore front truncation because the abbreviated loanwords of this type "make up only a small percentage of the total number of truncated forms" and "seem less central to a prosodic account" (Nishihara et al. (2001: 310)). Nishihara et al. do not explain explicitly why back-truncated forms such as *paato* can be selected over double-truncated forms such as *paa-tai*. But it seems that they assume the preference for back truncation over double truncation is lexically determined.

5   Nishihara et al. assume that abbreviated compounds in Japanese take the following structure. They call the word-level PrWd, i.e. PrWd1 and PrWd2, as minor PrWd and the compound-level PrWd as major PrWd.
    [[PrWd$_1$] [PrWd$_2$]]PrWd (both PrWd$_1$ and PrWd$_2$ consist of two morae)

6   Itô and Mester do not define those constraints in their study. The definitions in (29)–(32) are from Kager (1999).

7   These studies deal with dorsal fricative assimilation and allophonic r-vocalization in German and the interaction of g-weakening with compound voicing in Japanese, respectively.

8   The constraint MinWd in (26) and Leftmost in (28), which are adopted by Nishihara et al. (2001), might work in the case at hand. Instead of them, however, the present study adopts Trunc=F and Anchor-L-BT, since they are more commonly used in recent studies in the literature.

9   Following Itô and Mester (1997b), I assume that truncation is triggered by the truncation morpheme (T in the tableau). See also Itô and Mester's (2003b: Ch 4) argument that Rendaku is triggered by a morpheme.

10 The examples *kaa* 'car' and *baa* 'bar' in (67) are the only counterexamples I found.

11 As mentioned in Chapter 3 (p.26), monomoraic loanword does not exist in the Japanese lexicon.

12 Nishihara et al. (2001) refer to the examples in (70) in the endnote as exceptions to their analysis.

13 As Itô and Mester (1997b) point out, this type of phonological opacity is "detached from the rule interactionist thinking of traditional rule-based phonology ("feeding, bleeding, counterfeeding, counterbleeding"; "opaque vs. transparent rule interaction") … This case at hand arises in the midst of prosodic morphology, where phenomena of this kind were treated procedurally by means of Posodic Circumscription (McCarthy and Prince 1990)" (Itô and Mester 1997b: 9).

14 In Japanese, the nasal in coda is considered as the placeless nasal (Yip 1991). The placeless nasal assimilates in place when followed by a consonant (e.g. ni[ŋ].ki. 'popularity'), while it appears as [N] when followed by a vowel (e.g. ni[N].i. 'optional') or in word-final position (e.g. ho[N]. 'book').

15 Although this constraint applies to both obstruents and nasals, nasals in the onset position of the second syllable of the unabbreviated form seem to resist resyllabification in lexical phonology (e.g. dejitaru kamera → deji-kame (*deji-kan, *deji-ka)). This suggests a possibility that Coda-Cond$_{BM}$ needs to be further divided into two subconstraints, i.e. one applies to obstruents and the other to nasals, and that they are ranked differently. In this book, however, I will leave this question for future study for two reasons: (i) it is not

clear whether nasals in the onset position of the second syllable of the unabbreviated form never undergo resyllabification, since we do not have enough data on the realization of onset nasals, and (ii) the nature of the truncation morpheme that triggers truncation has not been fully explained, i.e. English compound abbreviation in Japanese is productive but not observed in all the words that share properties.

16   There are asymmetries between verb stems and the truncated forms such as *mod*. First, [d] and [z] never appear stem-finally while they do in the coda position of truncated forms (e.g. mo.de.ru. → mo<u>d</u>.). Avoidance of [d] and [z] in the stem-final position may be relevant to the fact that voiced obstruents are marked in Japanese. Second, truncated forms never have approximants, i.e. [r], [w], and [y], in the coda position, whereas verb stems can have [r] in coda. (Some verb stems seem to have [w] in coda (e.g. *wa.ra, wa.rat.ta., wa.ra.<u>wa</u>.se.ru.* 'to laugh' (cf. (84))). But it is not considered as a coda consonant in Modern Japanese because this is the result of phonological changes ([p] → [ɸ] → [w] → Ø) (McCawley 1968: 82, Vance 1987: 182, among others).) The coda [r] is unique in Japanese in the sense that (i) it is the only approximant that can appear in the coda position and (ii) it is the only voiced coda consonant that does not trigger voicing assimilation (e.g. *kar-u* → *kat-<u>t</u>a* 'cut-past' (cf. *ton-<u>d</u>a* 'fly-past', *mat-<u>t</u>a* 'wait-past')) (McCawley 1968: 96). The peculiarity of coda [r] suggests that it needs to be treated differently from the other coda consonants in lexical phonology, although it does not need to be treated differently in postlexical phonology, because no consonants including [r] can appear in the coda position in postlexical phonology. One possible explanation I have for the peculiarity of coda [r] in verb stems is that the stem-final [r] in verb stems is not in the coda position but in the nucleus position. The asymmetry between the coda consonant of verb stems and that of truncated forms is interesting in its own right, but it is beyond the focus of this book. I will leave it for future research.

17   In traditional lexical phonology model, it has been assumed that the outputs of lexical phonology are prosodic words. In this book, however, following Itô and Mester (2001b, 2003a), I assume that this does not apply in the Weakly Parallel Model.

18   *ne-suke* 'Netscape' and *me(ru)-ado* 'email address' are the only examples I found. The abbreviation process of 'email address' has two steps: *iimeeru adoresu* 'email address' → *meeru adoresu* → *me(ru)-ado*.

19   The avoidance of the Light-Heavy structure is not observed at the foot level probably because degenerate feet are not allowed in Japanese.

Chapter 7
Conclusion

In this book, I have discussed issues surrounding the phonology of English loanwords in Japanese within the framework of OT. OT can account for dialect differences (see Chapter 3) and diachronic changes (see Chapter 4 and 5) in terms of different rankings of universal constraints. Furthermore, OT can deal with phonological opacity by weakening one of the core tenets of OT, i.e. no intermediate levels, and by adopting the traditional distinction between lexical and postlexical phonology (see Chapter 6). To close this book, I will summarize the major findings below. The major findings of this book can be categorized into two groups: findings regarding the nature of inputs to loanword adaptation and findings regarding Japanese phonology including the structure of the Loanword sublexicon.

7.1. The Nature of Inputs

With respect to the nature of inputs to loanword adaptation, the present study reached three major findings. First, this study revealed that the inputs to phonological processes in loanword adaptation are the perceived segments. In the previous studies, Silverman (1992) and Peperkamp and Dupoux (2003) claim that the input is based on the phonetic representation of the source language while Paradis and LaCharité (1997) and LaCharité and Paradis (2005) claim that it is based on the phonological representation. Based on the realization of English /r/ in Japanese (Chapter 4), this study argued that the input to phonological processes in loanword adaptation is not the phonetic or phonemic representation of the source language but it is based on the perception. The present study supports Silverman's (1992) idea that the phonetic representation of the source language and the input to loanword adaptation are different and need to be distinguished. Also, I argued that the different realization of the onset /r/ and the coda /r/ in Japanese is due to the perception and that an input segment can be perceived differently at the Perceptual Level based on the location it appears.

Second, this book argued that Japanese borrowers have access to the information on the locus of English stress and English morphology. It has not been fully discussed in the literature what information is included in the input. With regard to the phonological information of the source language, Silverman (1992) and Peperkamp and Dupoux (2003) claim that the speakers of the host language cannot have access to it while Paradis and LaCharité (1997) and LaCharité and Paradis (2005) claim that they can. The four phonological phenomena analyzed in this study did not give any evidence directly supporting the claim that the speakers of the host language have access to the phonological representation of the source language. But, the accentuation of English loanwords (Chapter 3) and the realization of the English plural morpheme (Chapter 5) showed that the information on the locus of English stress and English morphology is included in the input.

Third, in this book, I claimed that English loanwords in Japanese are introduced by limited bilinguals, i.e. Japanese-English bilinguals with the knowledge of English morphology but not necessarily with the knowledge of English phonology. Paradis and LaCharité (1997) and LaCharité and Paradis (2005) claim that loanwords are borrowed by bilinguals and that the speakers of the host language have access to the phonological representation of the source language. As mentioned above, however, the four phonological phenomena analyzed in this book did not give evidence supporting their claim that the phonological representation of the source language is accessible, although the realization of the English plural morpheme (Chapter 5) indicates that morphological information is accessible. Based on this, I elaborated Paradis and LaCharité's claim and claimed that English loanwords in Japanese are introduced by limited bilinguals. This claim is supported by the facts that all the Japanese people study English at secondary school and that they have some knowledge of English.[1]

With regard to the accessibility to the morpho-phonological information of English, the present study revealed that there is a difference between generations (Chapter 5). The English plural morpheme is treated differently in the older generation and the younger generation. In this book, I argued that the generation gap with respect to the realization of the English plural morpheme is due to the difference in the accessibility to the morpho-phonological information of English. That is, the older generation does not have access (or has limited access) to the morpho-phonological information of English, whereas the younger generation has access to the morpho-phonological information of English.

7.2. Japanese Phonology

With regard to Japanese phonology including the structure of the Loanword sublexicon, this book reached four major findings. First, the present study revealed that Japanese disfavors the Light-Heavy structure systematically (Chapter 6). Itô (1990) and Kubozono (1988) introduce the dispreference for the Light-Heavy structure at the syllable and prosodic word levels, respectively. But they do not show that it is a general characteristic of Japanese. Discussing the dispreference for the Light-Heavy structure at the mora level, this book showed that avoidance of the Light-Heavy structure is observed at any level of the prosodic hierarchy and that it is a general characteristic of Japanese.

Second, this study argued that there are actually two types of CODA-COND, i.e. CODA-COND$_{PW}$ and CODA-COND$_{BM}$ in Japanese (Chapter 6). English compound abbreviation in Japanese reveals a case of phonological opacity. Adopting the Weakly Parallel Model (Itô and Mester 2001b, 2003a), this study discussed the opaque case and argued that CODA-COND$_{BM}$ plays an active role in both lexical and postlexical phonology and applies to bound morphemes as well as prosodic words, whereas CODA-COND$_{PW}$ plays an active role only in postlexical phonology and applies only to prosodic words. This idea is supported by verb stems in Japanese.

Third, this book showed that the word-initial pitch of English loanwords in Kansai Japanese is predictable (Chapter 3). Pierrehumbert and Beckman (1988: 214) claim that the word-initial pitch of non-loanwords in Kansai Japanese is unpredictable. The present study revealed that the word-initial high pitch is more common and that the word-initial low pitch of English loanwords in Kansai Japanese is triggered by the accent on the second mora. This study also showed that Kansai Japanese and Tokyo Japanese are the same with respect to accent assignment and that the English accent is preserved in both dialects.

Finally, this book discussed the assimilation to the core part of the Japanese lexicon. Among the four phonological phenomena analyzed in this study, two phenomena, i.e. the realization of English /r/ (Chapter 4) and English compound abbreviation (Chapter 6), showed the assimilation to the core part of the Japanese lexicon with regard to the constraint *[a:]]$_{PW}$. Itô and Mester (1995) claim that recent loanwords violate more constraints and are less assimilated. The realization of English /r/ in Japanese, however, revealed that this is not always the case, since less recent English loanwords with the word-final coda /r/ violate this constraint but recent ones do not.

7.3. Future Research

Regarding the findings of this study, the following research needs to be done in the future. First, this book discussed the assimilation to the core part of the Japanese lexicon with regard to the constraints *[a:]]$_{PW}$ (Chapter 4 and 6) and *HL (Chapter 3). But it is not clear yet what aspect of the word tends to undergo the assimilation in Japanese and crosslinguistically. The assimilation phenomena discussed in this book suggest that prosodic features are assimilated to the core part of the Japanese lexicon more easily. But it is not clear whether this is the case crosslinguistically. This question needs to be further studied.

Second, this study theoretically accounted for how the Japanese borrowers perceived English sounds, especially English /r/ (Chapter 4), and what is included in the input. But, the claims developed in this book lack empirical support through experimental studies. Experimental studies regarding the claims developed in this book need to be conducted in the future.

Endnotes

1 This does not necessarily mean that the Japanese people are fully competent in English. On the contrary, most of the Japanese people do not have phonological competence of English, since what they learn is mostly English grammar but not English conversation.

Appendix

The complete list of 1090 English loanwords in Kansai Japanese is given below, comparing accentuation in Kansai Japanese with that in Tokyo Japanese. The list is divided into three types, six groups, and entries are listed in Japanese alphabetical order. Asterisks indicate words whose accentuation is different in Kansai Japanese and Tokyo Japanese.

English Type H (460 Words)

Kansai Japanese		Tokyo Japanese		Gloss
a´acherii	HLLLL	a´acherii	HLLLL	"archery"
a´atisuto	HLLLL	a´atisuto	HLLLL	"artists"
a´amondo	HLLLL	a´amondo	HLLLL	"almond"
a´itemu	HLLL	a´itemu	HLLL	"item"
a´idoru	HLLL	a´idoru	HLLL	"idol"
a´iborii	HLLLL	a´iborii	HLLLL	"ivory"
a´irisu	HLLL	a´irisu	HLLL	"iris"
a´kusidento	HLLLLL	a´kusidento	HLLLLL	"accident"
a´kushon	HLLL	a´kushon	HLLL	"action"
a´kusesu	HLLL	a´kusesu	HLLL	"access"
a´kusento	HLLLL	a´kusento	HLLLL	"accent"
a´kutaa	HLLL	a´kutaa	HLLL	"actor"
a´kutoresu	HLLLL	a´kutoresu	HLLLL	"actress"
a´ppuru	HLLL	a´ppuru	HLLL	"apple"
adobe´nchaa	HHHLLL	adobe´nchaa	LHHLLL	"adventure"
a´tomu	HLL	a´tomu	HLL	"atom"
a´nimaru	HLLL	a´nimaru	HLLL	"animal"
a´bereeji	HLLLL	a´bereeji	HLLLL	"average"
amari´risu	HHHLL	amari´risu	LHHLL	"amaryllis"
a´nkaa	HLLL	a´nkaa	HLLL	"anchor"
a´nguru	HLLL	a´nguru	HLLL	"angle"
i´iguru	HLLL	i´iguru	HLLL	"eagle"
i´isutaa	HLLLL	i´isutaa	HLLLL	"Easter"
i´buningu	HLLLL	i´buningu	HLLLL	"evening"
imite´eshon	HHHLLL	imite´eshon	LHHLLL	"imitation"

151

i´yaringu	HLLLL	i´yaringu	HLLLL	"earring"
irumine´eshon	HHHHLLL	irumine´eshon	LHHHLLL	"illumination"
i´ngurando	HLLLLL	i´ngurando	HLLLLL	"England"
i´ngurisshu	HLLLLL	i´ngurisshu	HLLLLL	"English"
i´ntabyuu	HLLLL	i´ntabyuu	HLLLL	"interval"
i´npakuto	HLLLL	i´npakuto	HLLLL	"impact"
we´eruzu	HLLL	we´eruzu	HLLL	"Wales"
we´dingu	HLLL	we´dingu	HLLL	"wedding"
ekijibi´jon	HHHHLL	ekijibi´jon	LHHHLL	"exhibition"
e´kusasaizu	HLLLLL	e´kusasaizu	HLLLLL	"exercise"
ekusupu´resu	HHHHLL	ekusupu´resu	LHHHLL	"express"
e´ssee	HLLL	e´ssee	HLLL	"essay"
e´ssensu	HLLLL	e´ssensu	HLLLL	"essence"
e´pisoodo	HLLLL	e´pisoodo	HLLLL	"episode"
e´puron	HLLL	e´puron	HLLL	"apron"
e´raa	HLL	e´raa	HLL	"error"
e´ria	HLL	e´ria	HLL	"area"
e´remento	HLLLL	e´remento	HLLLL	"element"
e´njin	HLLL	e´njin	HLLL	"engine"
e´nzeru	HLLL	e´nzeru	HLLL	"angel"
entaate´imento	HHHHHLLLL	entaate´imento	LHHHHLLLL	"entertainment"
e´ntorii	HLLLL	e´ntorii	HLLLL	"entry"
e´nburemu	HLLLL	e´nburemu	HLLLL	"emblem"
o´iru	HLL	o´iru	HLL	"oil"
*o´ogasuta	HLLLL	ooga´suta	LHHLL	"Augusta"
o´okushon	HLLLL	o´okushon	HLLLL	"auction"
*o´okurando	HLLLLL	ooku´rando	LHHLLL	"Oakland"
o´osutin	HLLLL	o´osutin	HLLLL	"Austin"
o´odaa	HLLL	o´odaa	HLLL	"order"
ootome´eshon	HHHHLLL	ootome´eshon	LHHHLLL	"automation"
o´onaa	HLLL	o´onaa	HLLL	"owner"
o´obun	HLLL	o´obun	HLLL	"oven"
o´zon	HLL	o´zon	HLL	"ozone"
o´nion	HLLL	o´nion	HLLL	"onion"
o´fisu	HLL	o´fisu	HLL	"office"
o´pushon	HLLL	o´pushon	HLLL	"option"
oriente´eshon	HHHHLLL	oriente´eshon	LHHHLLL	"orientation"
orijina´ritii	HHHHLLL	orijina´ritii	LHHHLLL	"originality"
o´regon	HLLL	o´regon	HLLL	"Oregon"
ka´aten	HLLL	ka´aten	HLLL	"curtain"
ga´aden	HLLL	ga´aden	HLLL	"garden"
ka´atorijji	HLLLLL	ka´atorijji	HLLLLL	"cartridge"
ka´aton	HLLL	ka´aton	HLLL	"carton"
ka´anibaru	HLLLL	ka´anibaru	HLLLL	"carnival"

kaane´eshon	HHHLLL	kaane´eshon	LHHLLL	"carnation"
ka´apetto	HLLLL	ka´apetto	HLLLL	"carpet"
ka´abon	HLLL	ka´abon	HLLL	"carbon"
ga´arikku	HLLLL	ga´arikku	HLLLL	"garlic"
ga´ido	HLL	ga´ido	HLL	"guide"
ka´kuteru	HLLL	ka´kuteru	HLLL	"cocktail"
ka´sutamu	HLLL	ka´sutamu	HLLL	"custom"
ka´ttaa	HLLL	ka´ttaa	HLLL	"cutter"
ka´ppuru	HLLL	ka´ppuru	HLLL	"couple"
ka´baa	HLL	ka´baa	HLL	"cover"
ka´bareeji	HLLLL	ka´bareeji	HLLLL	"coverage"
ka´husu	HLL	ka´husu	HLL	"cuffs"
ka´ruchaa	HLLL	ka´ruchaa	HLLL	"culture"
ka´ruto	HLL	ka´ruto	HLL	"cult"
ka´rejji	HLLL	ka´rejji	HLLL	"college"
ka´rotin	HLLL	ka´rotin	HLLL	"carotene"
ga´ron	HLL	ga´ron	HLL	"gallon"
ka´nzasu	HLLL	ka´nzasu	HLLL	"Kansas"
ka´ntorii	HLLLL	ka´ntorii	HLLLL	"country"
ka´npanii	HLLLL	ka´npanii	HLLLL	"company"
ki´ipaa	HLLL	ki´ipaa	HLLL	"keeper"
ki´ttin	HLLL	ki´ttin	HLLL	"kitchen"
gi´huto	HLL	gi´huto	HLL	"gift"
kya´sutaa	HLLL	kya´sutaa	HLLL	"caster"
kya´suto	HLL	kya´suto	HLL	"cast"
kya´cchaa	HLLL	kya´cchaa	HLLL	"catcher"
kya´dii	HLL	kya´dii	HLL	"caddy"
kya´pitaru	HLLL	kya´pitaru	HLLL	"capital"
kya´binetto	HLLLL	kya´binetto	HLLLL	"cabinet"
kya´bin	HLL	kya´bin	HLL	"cabin"
kya´pushon	HLLL	kya´pushon	HLLL	"caption"
kya´puten	HLLL	kya´puten	HLLL	"captain"
kya´betu	HLL	kya´betu	HLL	"cabbage"
kya´raban	HLLL	kya´raban	HLLL	"caravan"
gya´rarii	HLLL	gya´rarii	HLLL	"gallery"
gya´roppu	HLLL	gya´roppu	HLLL	"gallop"
kya´nseru	HLLL	kya´nseru	HLLL	"cancel"
kya´ndii	HLLL	kya´ndii	HLLL	"candy"
kya´ndoru	HLLL	kya´ndoru	HLLL	"candle"
kya´nbasu	HLLL	kya´nbasu	HLLL	"canvas"
kya´npasu	HLLL	kya´npasu	HLLL	"campus"
gya´nburaa	HLLLL	gya´nburaa	HLLLL	"gambler"
gya´nburu	HLLL	gya´nburu	HLLL	"gamble"
kyu´upiddo	HLLLL	kyu´upiddo	HLLLL	"cupid"

gi´rudo	HLL	gi´rudo	HLL		"guild"
ku´uraa	HLLL	ku´uraa	HLLL		"cooler"
ku´kkii	HLLL	ku´kkii	HLLL		"cookie"
ku´kkingu	HLLLL	ku´kkingu	HLLLL		"cooking"
ku´sshon	HLLL	ku´sshon	HLLL		"cushion"
gu´ppii	HLLL	gu´ppii	HLLL		"guppy"
kurarin´etto	HHHHLL	kurarin´etto	LHHHLL		"clarinet"
ge´suto	HLL	ge´suto	HLL		"guest"
kenta´kkii	HHHLLL	kenta´kkii	LHHLLL		"Kentucky"
ko´iru	HLL	ko´iru	HLL		"coil"
ko´in	HLL	ko´in	HLL		"coin"
ko´osutaa	HLLLL	ko´osutaa	HLLLL		"coaster"
go´osuto	HLLL	go´osuto	HLLL		"ghost"
koopore´eshon	HHHHLLL	koopore´eshon	LHHHLLL		"cooperation"
ko´orasu	HLLL	ko´orasu	HLLL		"chorus"
ko´suchuumu	HLLLL	ko´suchuumu	HLLLL		"costume"
ko´suto	HLL	ko´suto	HLL		"cost"
ko´sumosu	HLLL	ko´sumosu	HLLL		"cosmos"
kosumopo´ritan	HHHHLLL	kosumopo´ritan	LHHHLLL		"cosmopolitan"
ko´tton	HLLL	ko´tton	HLLL		"cotton"
ko´teeji	HLLL	ko´teeji	HLLL		"cottage"
ko´pii	HLL	ko´pii	HLL		"copy"
ko´bura	HLL	ko´bura	HLL		"cobra"
ko´mikku	HLLL	ko´mikku	HLLL		"comic"
ko´medii	HLLL	ko´medii	HLLL		"comedy"
ko´ramu	HLL	ko´ramu	HLL		"column"
go´ruhu	HLL	go´ruhu	HLL		"golf"
ko´ronii	HLLL	ko´ronii	HLLL		"colony"
ko´nsaato	HLLLL	ko´nsaato	HLLLL		"concert"
ko´nseputo	HLLLL	ko´nseputo	HLLLL		"concept"
konse´nsasu	HHHLLL	konse´nsasu	LHHLLL		"consensus"
ko´ntakuto	HLLLL	ko´ntakuto	HLLLL		"contact"
ko´ntesuto	HLLLL	ko´ntesuto	HLLLL		"contest"
kondomi´niamu	HHHHLLL	kondomi´niamu	LHHHLLL		"condominium"
ko´ntorasuto	HLLLLL	ko´ntorasuto	HLLLLL		"contrast"
ko´npakuto	HLLLL	ko´npakuto	HLLLL		"compact"
sa´akasu	HLLL	sa´akasu	HLLL		"circus"
sa´akitto	HLLLL	sa´akitto	HLLLL		"circuit"
sa´abisu	HLLL	sa´abisu	HLLL		"service"
sa´afaa	HLLL	sa´afaa	HLLL		"surfer"
sa´afin	HLLL	sa´afin	HLLL		"surfing"
sa´amon	HLLL	sa´amon	HLLL		"salmon"
sa´iensu	HLLLL	sa´iensu	HLLLL		"science"
sa´ikuringu	HLLLLL	sa´ikuringu	HLLLLL		"cycling"

Appendix 155

sa´ikuru	HLLL	sa´ikuru	HLLL	"cycle"
sa´ikuron	HLLLL	sa´ikuron	HLLLL	"cyclone"
sa´izu	HLL	sa´izu	HLL	"size"
sa´ihon	HLLL	sa´ihon	HLLL	"siphon"
sa´iren	HLLL	sa´iren	HLLL	"siren"
sa´in	HLL	sa´in	HLL	"sign"
sakurame´nto	HHHHLL	sakurame´nto	LHHHLL	"Sacramento"
sa´supensu	HLLLL	sa´supensu	HLLLL	"suspense"
sa´kkaa	HLLL	sa´kkaa	HLLL	"soccer"
sa´maa	HLL	sa´maa	HLL	"summer"
sa´rada	HLL	sa´rada	HLL	"salad"
sa´rarii	HLLL	sa´rarii	HLLL	"salary"
sa´ndee	HLLL	sa´ndee	HLLL	"sundae"
sa´npuru	HLLL	sa´npuru	HLLL	"sample"
si´ataa	HLLL	si´ataa	HLLL	"theater"
si´ikuretto	HLLLLL	si´ikuretto	HLLLLL	"secret"
si´izun	HLLL	si´izun	HLLL	"season"
si´isoo	HLLL	si´isoo	HLLL	"seesaw"
she´ebaa	HLLL	she´ebaa	HLLL	"shaver"
je´suchaa	HLLL	je´suchaa	HLLL	"gesture"
je´rasii	HLLL	je´rasii	HLLL	"jealousy"
she´rutaa	HLLL	she´rutaa	HLLL	"shelter"
je´ndaa	HLLL	je´ndaa	HLLL	"gender"
si´sutemu	HLLL	si´sutemu	HLLL	"system"
si´huto	HLL	si´huto	HLL	"shift"
sha´abetto	HLLLL	sha´abetto	HLLLL	"sherbet"
ja´gaa	HLL	ja´gaa	HLL	"jaguar"
ja´ketto	HLLL	ja´ketto	HLLL	"jacket"
sha´ttaa	HLLL	sha´ttaa	HLLL	"shutter"
sha´beru	HLL	sha´beru	HLL	"shovel"
sha´waa	HLL	sha´waa	HLL	"shower"
ja´nguru	HLLL	ja´nguru	HLLL	"jungle"
jo´okaa	HLLL	jo´okaa	HLLL	"joker"
jo´ojia	HLLL	jo´ojia	HLLL	"Georgia"
sho´kkingu	HLLLL	sho´kkingu	HLLLL	"shocking"
sho´ppingu	HLLLL	sho´ppingu	HLLLL	"shopping"
sho´rudaa	HLLL	sho´rudaa	HLLL	"shoulder"
si´riaru	HLLL	si´riaru	HLLL	"cereal"
si´rikon	HLLL	si´rikon	HLLL	"silicon"
si´ruku	HLL	si´ruku	HLL	"silk"
si´nguru	HLLL	si´nguru	HLLL	"single"
si´nfonii	HLLLL	si´nfonii	HLLLL	"symphony"
si´nboru	HLLL	si´nboru	HLLL	"symbol"
se´etaa	HLLL	se´etaa	HLLL	"sweater"

se´orii	HLLL	se´orii	HLLL		"theory"
se´kushon	HLLL	se´kushon	HLLL		"section"
se´kutaa	HLLL	se´kutaa	HLLL		"sector"
se´kkusu	HLLL	se´kkusu	HLLL		"sex"
se´ssion	HLLL	se´ssion	HLLL		"session"
se´rapii	HLLL	se´rapii	HLLL		"therapy"
se´remonii	HLLLL	se´remonii	HLLLL		"ceremony"
se´rohan	HLLL	se´rohan	HLLL		"cellophane"
sense´eshon	HHHLLL	sense´eshon	LHHLLL		"sensation"
se´nsaa	HLLL	se´nsaa	HLLL		"sensor"
se´ntaa	HLLL	se´ntaa	HLLL		"center"
se´ntensu	HLLLL	se´ntensu	HLLLL		"sentence"
so´kkusu	HLLL	so´kkusu	HLLL		"socks"
so´faa	HLL	so´faa	HLL		"sofa"
ta´agetto	HLLLL	ta´agetto	HLLLL		"target"
ta´abin	HLLL	ta´abin	HLLL		"turbine"
da´ietto	HLLLL	da´ietto	HLLLL		"diet"
ta´itoru	HLLL	ta´itoru	HLLL		"title"
da´ibingu	HLLLL	da´ibingu	HLLLL		"diving"
ta´imaa	HLLL	ta´imaa	HLLL		"timer"
ta´imu	HLL	ta´imu	HLL		"time"
*ta´iya	HLL	taiya	LHH		"tire"
ta´iru	HLL	ta´iru	HLL		"tile"
ta´kusii	HLLL	ta´kusii	HLLL		"taxi"
da´kuto	HLL	da´kuto	HLL		"duct"
da´suto	HLL	da´suto	HLL		"dust"
ta´buretto	HLLLL	ta´buretto	HLLLL		"tablet"
*ta´pesutorii	HLLLLL	tape´sutorii	LHLLLL		"tapestry"
da´rasu	HLL	da´rasu	HLL		"Dallas"
ta´waa	HLL	ta´waa	HLL		"tower"
ta´nkaa	HLLL	ta´nkaa	HLLL		"tanker"
che´rii	HLL	che´rii	HLL		"cherry"
ti´kin	HLL	ti´kin	HLL		"chicken"
cha´imu	HLL	cha´imu	HLL		"chime"
cha´peru	HLL	cha´peru	HLL		"chapel"
cha´ritii	HLLL	cha´ritii	HLLL		"charity"
cha´npion	HLLLL	cha´npion	HLLLL		"champion"
chu´urippu	HLLLL	chu´urippu	HLLLL		"tulip"
tu´aa	HLL	tu´aa	HLL		"tour"
tu´urisuto	HLLLL	tu´urisuto	HLLLL		"tourist"
di´suku	HLL	di´suku	HLL		"disc"
di´supuree	HLLLL	di´supuree	HLLLL		"display"
te´kisasu	HLLL	te´kisasu	HLLL		"Texas"
te´kisuto	HLLL	te´kisuto	HLLL		"text"

de´suku	HLL	de´suku	HLL	"desk"
te´suto	HLL	te´suto	HLL	"test"
te´nisu	HLL	te´nisu	HLL	"tennis"
de´nimu	HLL	de´nimu	HLL	"denim"
te´rasu	HLL	te´rasu	HLL	"terrace"
te´nshon	HLLL	te´nshon	HLLL	"tension"
de´nbaa	HLLL	de´nbaa	HLLL	"Denver"
to´osutaa	HLLLL	to´osutaa	HLLLL	"toaster"
toosuto	HLLL	toosuto	HLLL	"toast"
do´onatu	HLLL	do´onatu	HLLL	"doughnut"
to´onamento	HLLLLL	to´onamento	HLLLLL	"tournament"
do´kyumento	HLLLL	do´kyumento	HLLLL	"document"
do´kutaa	HLLL	do´kutaa	HLLL	"doctor"
do´naa	HLL	do´naa	HLL	"donor"
to´nikku	HLLL	to´nikku	HLLL	"tonic"
to´pikku	HLLL	to´pikku	HLLL	"topic"
do´mino	HLL	do´mino	HLL	"domino"
toransi´ibaa	HHHHLLL	toransi´ibaa	LHHHLLL	"transeiver"
toransure´eshon	HHHHHLLL	toransure´eshon	LHHHHLLL	"translation"
toronbo´on	HHHHLL	toronbo´on	LHHHLL	"trombone"
*to´nneru	HLLL	tonneru	LHHH	"tunnel"
na´iron	HLLL	na´iron	HLLL	"nylon"
na´pukin	HLLL	na´pukin	HLLL	"napkin"
na´nbaa	HLLL	na´nbaa	HLLL	"number"
nu´udoru	HLLL	nu´udoru	HLLL	"noodle"
ne´on	HLL	ne´on	HLL	"neon"
ne´kutai	HLLL	ne´kutai	HLLL	"necktie"
ne´kkuresu	HLLLL	ne´kkuresu	HLLLL	"necklace"
no´zuru	HLL	no´zuru	HLL	"nozzle"
paaka´sshon	HHHLLL	paaka´sshon	LHHLLL	"percussion"
ba´agen	HLLL	ba´agen	HLLL	"bargain"
ba´ajin	HLLL	ba´ajin	HLLL	"virgin"
ba´asudee	HLLLL	ba´asudee	HLLLL	"birthday"
paase´nto	HHHLL	paase´nto	LHHLL	"percent"
paasona´ritii	HHHHLLL	paasona´ritii	LHHHLLL	"personality"
pa´atii	HLLL	pa´atii	HLLL	"party"
pa´atonaa	HLLLL	pa´atonaa	HLLLL	"partner"
ba´anaa	HLLL	ba´anaa	HLLL	"burner"
ba´abaa	HLLL	ba´abaa	HLLL	"barber"
ha´amonii	HLLLL	ha´amonii	HLLLL	"harmony"
pa´araa	HLLL	pa´araa	HLLL	"parlor"
ha´ikingu	HLLLL	ha´ikingu	HLLLL	"hiking"
ba´ison	HLLL	ba´ison	HLLL	"bison"
haibi´sukasu	HHHLLL	haibi´sukasu	LHHLLL	"hibiscus"

*pa´irotto	HLLLL	pairo´tto	LHHLL	"pilot"
ha´usu	HLL	ha´usu	HLL	"house"
pa´udaa	HLLL	pa´udaa	HLLL	"powder"
ba´suto	HLL	ba´suto	HLL	"bust"
ha´zubando	HLLLL	ha´zubando	HLLLL	"husband"
pa´zuru	HLL	pa´zuru	HLL	"puzzle"
ba´taa	HLL	ba´taa	HLL	"butter"
pa´taa	HLL	pa´taa	HLL	"putter"
ba´tahurai	HLLLL	ba´tahurai	HLLLL	"butterfly"
pa`kkeeji	HLLLL	pa`kkeeji	HLLLL	"package"
pa´sshon	HLLL	pa´sshon	HLLL	"passion"
pa´neru	HLL	pa´neru	HLL	"panel"
ha´puningu	HLLLL	ha´puningu	HLLLL	"happening"
ba´buru	HLL	ba´buru	HLL	"bubble"
pa´radaisu	HLLLL	pa´radaisu	HLLLL	"paradise"
ba´ria	HLL	ba´ria	HLL	"barrier"
pa´resu	HLL	pa´resu	HLL	"palace"
pa´rodii	HLLL	pa´rodii	HLLL	"parody"
pa´waa	HLL	pa´waa	HLL	"power"
ha´ngaa	HLLL	ha´ngaa	HLLL	"hunger"
ha´ntaa	HLLL	ha´ntaa	HLLL	"hunter"
ha´ntingu	HLLLL	ha´ntingu	HLLLL	"hunting"
*ha´ndoru	HLLL	handoru	LHHH	"handle"
ba´npaa	HLLL	ba´npaa	HLLL	"bumper"
pa´npukin	HLLLL	pa´npukin	HLLLL	"pumpkin"
pa´nhuretto	HLLLLL	pa´nhuretto	HLLLLL	"pamphlet"
ha´nmaa	HLLL	ha´nmaa	HLLL	"hammer"
hi´itaa	HLLL	hi´itaa	HLLL	"heater"
pi´inattu	HLLLL	pi´inattu	HLLLL	"peanut"
hi´iroo	HLLL	hi´iroo	HLLL	"hero"
pi´kunikku	HLLLL	pi´kunikku	HLLLL	"picnic"
pi´kurusu	HLLL	pi´kurusu	HLLL	"pickles"
bi´jinesu	HLLL	bi´jinesu	HLLL	"business"
bi´jon	HLL	bi´jon	HLL	"vision"
pi´suton	HLLL	pi´suton	HLLL	"piston"
bi´deo	HLL	bi´deo	HLL	"video"
hyu´usuton	HLLLL	hyu´usuton	HLLLL	"Huston"
pi´riodo	HLLL	pi´riodo	HLLL	"period"
bi´rudingu	HLLLL	bi´rudingu	HLLLL	"building"
fa´itaa	HLLL	fa´itaa	HLLL	"fighter"
fa´inansu	HLLLL	fa´inansu	HLLLL	"finance"
fa´iru	HLL	fa´iru	HLL	"file"
fa´kutaa	HLLL	fa´kutaa	HLLL	"factor"
fa´sunaa	HLLL	fa´sunaa	HLLL	"fastener"

Appendix 159

fa′kkusu	HLLL	fa′kkusu	HLLL	"fax"
fa′sshon	HLLL	fa′sshon	HLLL	"fashion"
fa′mirii	HLLL	fa′mirii	HLLL	"family"
fa′ntajii	HLLLL	fa′ntajii	HLLLL	"fantasy"
fi′ibaa	HLLL	fi′ibaa	HLLL	"fever"
fi′gyua	HLL	fi′gyua	HLL	"figure"
fi′kushon	HLLL	fi′kushon	HLLL	"fiction"
fi′ssingu	HLLLL	fi′ssingu	HLLLL	"fishing"
fe′sutibaru	HLLLL	fe′sutibaru	HLLLL	"festival"
fe′rii	HLL	fe′rii	HLL	"ferry"
fe′romon	HLLL	fe′romon	HLLL	"pheromone"
pensiruba′nia	HHHHHLL	pensiruba′nia	LHHHHLL	"Pennsylvania"
fe′nsingu	HLLLL	fe′nsingu	HLLLL	"fencing"
fo′omatto	HLLLL	fo′omatto	HLLLL	"format"
foome′eshon	HHHLLL	foome′eshon	LHHLLL	"formation"
hurasutore′eshon	HHHHHLLL	hurasutore′eshon	LHHHHLLL	"frustration"
purante′eshon	HHHHLLL	purante′eshon	LHHHLLL	"plantation"
puroje′kutaa	HHHLLL	puroje′kutaa	LHHLLL	"projector"
puroda′kushon	HHHLLL	puroda′kushon	LHHLLL	"production"
purodu′usaa	HHHLLL	purodu′usaa	LHHLLL	"producer"
puropo′oshon	HHHLLL	puropo′oshon	LHHLLL	"proportion"
puromo′oshon	HHHLLL	puromo′oshon	LHHLLL	"promotion"
be′ekarii	HLLLL	be′ekarii	HLLLL	"bakery"
be′suto	HLL	be′suto	HLL	"vest"
pe′ndanto	HLLLL	pe′ndanto	HLLLL	"pendant"
ho′iru	HLL	ho′iru	HLL	"foil"
po′emu	HLL	po′emu	HLL	"poem"
po′okaa	HLLL	po′okaa	HLLL	"poker"
bo′onasu	HLLL	bo′onasu	HLLL	"bonus"
bo′kusingu	HLLLL	bo′kusingu	HLLLL	"boxing"
po′sutaa	HLLL	po′sutaa	HLLL	"poster"
ho′sutesu	HLLL	ho′sutesu	HLLL	"hostess"
ho′suto	HLL	ho′suto	HLL	"host"
po′suto	HLL	po′suto	HLL	"post"
bo′suton	HLLL	bo′suton	HLLL	"Boston"
ho′raa	HLL	ho′raa	HLL	"horror"
po′risii	HLLL	po′risii	HLLL	"policy"
ho′ridee	HLLL	ho′ridee	HLLL	"holiday"
ma′agarin	HLLLL	ma′agarin	HLLLL	"margarine"
ma′aketto	HLLLL	ma′aketto	HLLLL	"market"
ma′gajin	HLLL	ma′gajin	HLLL	"magazine"
ma′suku	HLL	ma′suku	HLL	"mask"
ma′sutaa	HLLL	ma′sutaa	HLLL	"master"
ma′ttoresu	HLLLL	ma′ttoresu	HLLLL	"mattress"

ma´nia	HLL	ma´nia	HLL	"mania"
ma´huraa	HLLL	ma´huraa	HLLL	"maffler"
ma´nshon	HLLL	ma´nshon	HLLL	"mansion"
ma´nmosu	HLLL	ma´nmosu	HLLL	"mammoth"
mi´kisaa	HLLL	mi´kisaa	HLLL	"mixer"
mi´sigan	HLLL	mi´sigan	HLLL	"Michigan"
misisi´ppii	HHHLLL	misisi´ppii	LHHLLL	"Mississippi"
mi´suterii	HLLLL	mi´suterii	HLLLL	"mystery"
mi´neraru	HLLL	mi´neraru	HLLL	"mineral"
myu´ujiamu	HLLLL	myu´ujiamu	HLLLL	"museum"
myu´ujikaru	HLLLL	myu´ujikaru	HLLLL	"musical"
myu´ujikku	HLLLL	myu´ujikku	HLLLL	"music"
mi´raa	HLL	mi´raa	HLL	"mirror"
mi´rakuru	HLLL	mi´rakuru	HLLL	"miracle"
mi´rion	HLLL	mi´rion	HLLL	"million"
miruwo´okii	HHHLLL	miruwo´okii	LHHLLL	"Milwaukee"
mi´ruku	HLL	mi´ruku	HLL	"milk"
mu´ubii	HLLL	mu´ubii	HLLL	"movie"
mu´ubumento	HLLLLL	mu´ubumento	HLLLLL	"movement"
me´ekaa	HLLL	me´ekaa	HLLL	"maker"
me´gahon	HLLL	me´gahon	HLLL	"megaphone"
me´jaa	HLL	me´jaa	HLL	"measure"
*me´daru	HLL	medaru	LHH	"medal"
me´sseeji	HLLLL	me´sseeji	HLLLL	"message"
me´dia	HLL	me´dia	HLL	"media"
me´doree	HLLL	me´doree	HLLL	"medley"
me´nyuu	HLL	me´nyuu	HLL	"menu"
me´ritto	HLLL	me´ritto	HLLL	"merit"
me´rodii	HLLL	me´rodii	HLLL	"melody"
me´ntenansu	HLLLLL	me´ntenansu	HLLLLL	"maintenance"
mo´oshon	HLLL	mo´oshon	HLLL	"motion"
mo´otaa	HLLL	mo´otaa	HLLL	"motor"
mo´deru	HLL	mo´deru	HLL	"model"
mo´nitaa	HLLL	mo´nitaa	HLLL	"monitor"
mo´nyumento	HLLLL	mo´nyumento	HLLLL	"monument"
morato´riamu	HHHLLL	morato´riamu	LHHLLL	"moratorium"
mo´raru	HLL	mo´raru	HLL	"moraru"
mo´nkii	HLLL	mo´nkii	HLLL	"monkey"
mo´nsutaa	HLLLL	mo´nsutaa	HLLLL	"monster"
yu´uzaa	HLLL	yu´uzaa	HLLL	"user"
yu´umoa	HLLL	yu´umoa	HLLL	"humor"
yu´nion	HLLL	yu´nion	HLLL	"union"
yu´nifoomu	HLLLL	yu´nifoomu	HLLLL	"uniform"
*ra´ion	HLLL	raion	LHHH	"lion"

ra´isensu	HLLLL	ra´isensu	HLLLL	"license"
ra´itaa	HLLL	ra´itaa	HLLL	"lighter"
ra´idaa	HLLL	ra´idaa	HLLL	"rider"
ra´ito	HLL	ra´ito	HLL	"light"
ra´ihu	HLL	ra´ihu	HLL	"life"
ra´iburarii	HLLLLL	ra´iburarii	HLLLLL	"library"
ra´kkaa	HLLL	ra´kkaa	HLLL	"lacquer"
ra´beru	HLL	ra´beru	HLL	"label"
ra´ndorii	HLLLL	ra´ndorii	HLLLL	"laundry"
ri´idaa	HLLL	ri´idaa	HLLL	"leader"
rikue´suto	HHHLL	rikue´suto	LHHLL	"request"
ri´suku	HLL	ri´suku	HLL	"risk"
ri´bon	HLL	ri´bon	HLL	"ribbon"
ru´aa	HLL	ru´aa	HLL	"lure"
ru´bii	HLL	ru´bii	HLL	"ruby"
re´esaa	HLLL	re´esaa	HLLL	"racer"
re´edaa	HLLL	re´edaa	HLLL	"radar"
re´kuchaa	HLLL	re´kuchaa	HLLL	"lecture"
re´zaa	HLL	re´zaa	HLL	"leather"
re´sipi	HLL	re´sipi	HLL	"recipe"
re´jaa	HLL	re´jaa	HLL	"leisure"
re´suraa	HLLL	re´suraa	HLLL	"wrestler"
re´suringu	HLLLL	re´suringu	HLLLL	"wrestling"
re´tasu	HLL	re´tasu	HLL	"lettuce"
re´dii	HLL	re´dii	HLL	"lady"
re´baa	HLL	re´baa	HLL	"lever"
re´beru	HLL	re´beru	HLL	"level"
ro´oshon	HLLL	ro´oshon	HLLL	"lotion"
roote´eshon	HHHLLL	roote´eshon	LHHLLL	"rotation"
ro´oraa	HLLL	ro´oraa	HLLL	"roller"
ro´jikku	HLLL	ro´jikku	HLLL	"logic"
ro´kkaa	HLLL	ro´kkaa	HLLL	"locker"
ro´bii	HLL	ro´bii	HLL	"lobby"
wa´ipaa	HLLL	wa´ipaa	HLLL	"wiper"
wa´ihu	HLL	wa´ihu	HLL	"wife"
wa´iya	HLL	wa´iya	HLL	"wire"
wa´in	HLL	wa´in	HLL	"wine"
wa´kkusu	HLLL	wa´kkusu	HLLL	"wax"
wa´hhuru	HLLL	wa´hhuru	HLLL	"waffle"

English Type L (272 Words)

Kansai Japanese		Tokyo Japanese		Gloss
*aide´a	LLHL	a´idea	HLLL	"idea"

aide´ntitii	LLHLLLL	aide´ntitii	LHHLLLL	"identity"
asi´sutanto	LHLLLL	asi´sutanto	LHLLLL	"assistant"
ase´sumento	LHLLLL	ase´sumento	LHLLLL	"assessment"
ata´kku	LHLL	ata´kku	LHLL	"attack"
ada´putaa	LHLLL	ada´putaa	LHLLL	"adopter"
ada´ruto	LHLL	ada´ruto	LHLL	"adult"
atora´kushon	LLHLLL	atora´kushon	LHHLLL	"attraction"
atora´nta	LLHLL	atora´nta	LHHLL	"Atlanta"
anime´eshon	LLHLLL	anime´eshon	LHHLLL	"animation"
ahutanu´un	LLLHLL	ahutanu´un	LHHHLL	"afternoon"
apurike´eshon	LLLHLLL	apurike´eshon	LHHHLLL	"application"
apuro´oti	LLHLL	apuro´oti	LHHLL	"approach"
amyu´uzumento	LHLLLLL	amyu´uzumento	LHLLLLL	"amusement"
ame´nitii	LHLLL	ame´nitii	LHLLL	"amenity"
ara´amu	LHLL	ara´amu	LHLL	"alarm"
ari´ina	LHLL	ari´ina	LHLL	"arena"
ie´roo	LHLL	ie´roo	LHLL	"yellow"
imajine´eshon	LLLHLLL	imajine´eshon	LHHHLLL	"imagination"
insutora´kutaa	LLLLHLLL	insutora´kutaa	LHHHHLLL	"instructor"
insupire´eshon	LLLLHLLL	insupire´eshon	LHHHHLLL	"instruction"
intone´eshon	LLLHLLL	intone´eshon	LHHHLLL	"intonation"
infome´eshon	LLLHLLL	infome´eshon	LHHHLLL	"information"
inhure´eshon	LLLHLLL	inhure´eshon	LHHHLLL	"inflation"
inpure´sshon	LLLHLLL	inpure´sshon	LHHHLLL	"impression"
inbe´edaa	LLHLLL	inbe´edaa	LHHLLL	"invader"
*ui´sukii	LHLLL	uisu´kii	LHHLL	"whisky"
wisuko´nsin	LLHLLL	wisuko´nsin	LHHLLL	"Wisconsin"
ui´nku	LHLL	ui´nku	LHLL	"wink"
ui´nti	LHLL	ui´nti	LHLL	"winch"
ue´itaa	LHLL	ue´itaa	LHLL	"waiter"
ue´itoresu	LHLLLL	ue´itoresu	LHLLLL	"waitress"
*ue´suto	LHLL	uesuto	LHHH	"waist"
eko´nomii	LHLLL	eko´nomii	LHLLL	"economy"
eko´rojii	LHLLL	eko´rojii	LHLLL	"ecology"
ooso´ritii	LLHLLL	ooso´ritii	LHHLLL	"authority"
oha´io	LHLL	oha´io	LHLL	"Ohio"
obuza´abaa	LLHLLL	obuza´abaa	LHHLLL	"observer"
opere´eshon	LLHLLL	opere´eshon	LHHLLL	"operation"
kau´nseraa	LHLLLL	kau´nseraa	LHLLLL	"counselor"
*kaka´o	LHL	ka´kao	HLL	"cacao"
kase´tto	LHLL	kase´tto	LHLL	"cassette"
kafete´ria	LLHLL	kafete´ria	LHHLL	"cafeteria"
gare´eji	LHLL	gare´eji	LHLL	"garage"
kyapa´sitii	LHLLL	kyapa´sitii	LHLLL	"capacity"

Appendix 163

kyanpe´en	LLHLL	kyanpe´en	LHHLL	"campaign"
kui´in	LHLL	kui´in	LHLL	"queen"
kuo´ritii	LHLLL	kuo´ritii	LHLLL	"quality"
gura´idaa	LHLLL	gura´idaa	LHLLL	"glider"
kura´imingu	LHLLLL	kura´imingu	LHLLLL	"climbing"
kura`kkaa	LHLLL	kura`kkaa	LHLLL	"cracker"
kura´tti	LHLL	kura´tti	LHLL	"clutch"
*kura`bu	LHL	ku´rabu	HLL	"club"
gura´maa	LHLL	gura´maa	LHLL	"grammar"
kuri´iku	LHLL	kuri´iku	LHLL	"creek"
kuri´imu	LHLL	kuri´imu	LHLL	"cream"
guri´in	LHLL	guri´in	LHLL	"green"
kurie´etaa	LLHLLL	kurie´etaa	LhHLLL	"creator"
kuri´sutaru	LHLLLL	kuri´sutaru	LHLLLL	"crystal"
kuri´suchan	LHLLL	kuri´suchan	LHLLL	"Christian"
kuri´ppu	LHLL	kuri´ppu	LHLL	"clip"
guri´ppu	LHLL	guri´ppu	LHLL	"grip"
kuri´nti	LHLL	kuri´nti	LHLL	"clinch"
kuru´u	LHL	kuru´u	LHL	"crew"
guru´upu	LHLL	guru´upu	LHLL	"group"
kure´e	LHL	kure´e	LHL	"clay"
gure´e	LHL	gure´e	LHL	"gray"
kure´en	LHLL	kure´en	LHLL	"crane"
kure`jitto	LHLLL	kure`jitto	LHLLL	"credit"
kure´nzaa	LHLLL	kure´nzaa	LHLLL	"cleanser"
kuro´ozetto	LHLLLL	kuro´ozetto	LHLLLL	"closet"
kuro´obaa	LHLLL	kuro´obaa	LHLLL	"clover"
guro´obu	LHLL	guro´obu	LHLL	"glove"
kuro´oru	LHLL	kuro´oru	LHLL	"crawl"
kuro´on	LHLL	kuro´on	LHLL	"clone"
koka´in	LHLL	koka´in	LHLL	"cocaine"
*koma´ndo	LHLL	komando	LHHH	"command"
komi´sshon	LHLL	komi´sshon	LHLL	"commission"
komyunike´eshon	LLLHLLL	komyunike´eshon	LHHHLLL	"communication"
komyu´nitii	LHLLL	komyu´nitii	LHLLL	"community"
kome´dian	LHLLL	kome´dian	LHLLL	"comedian"
kore`kushon	LHLLL	kore`kushon	LHLLL	"collection"
*kore`kutaa	LHLLL	korekutaa	LHHHH	"collector"
konsa´rutanto	LLHLLLL	konsa´rutanto	LHHLLLL	"consultant"
konsa´rutingu	LLHLLLL	konsa´rutingu	LHHLLLL	"consulting"
konda`kutaa	LLHLLL	konda`kutaa	LHHLLL	"conductor"
kondi´shon	LLHLL	kondi´shon	LHHLL	"condition"
*konte´na	LLHL	ko´ntena	HLLL	"container"
konde´nsaa	LLHLLL	konde´nsaa	LHHLLL	"condenser"

kontoro´oru	LLLHLL	kontoro´oru	LHHHLL	"control"
konpa´nion	LLHLLL	konpa´nion	LHHLLL	"companion"
konbine´eshon	LLLHLLL	konbine´eshon	LHHHLLL	"combination"
konpyu´utaa	LLHLLL	konpyu´utaa	LHHLLL	"computer"
konpure´ssaa	LLLHLLL	konpure´ssaa	LHHHLLL	"compressor"
konbe´yaa	LLHL	konbe´yaa	LHHL	"conveyer"
saba´ibaru	LHLLL	saba´ibaru	LHLLL	"survival"
saba´nna	LHLL	saba´nna	LHLL	"savanna"
sapo´otaa	LHLLL	sapo´otaa	LHLLL	"supporter"
jenere´eshon	LLHLLL	jenere´eshon	LHHLLL	"generation"
sika´go	LHL	sika´go	LHL	"Chicago"
simyure´eshon	LLHLLL	simyure´eshon	LHHLLL	"simulation"
jire´nma	LHLL	jire´nma	LHLL	"dilemma"
sui´tti	LHLL	sui´tti	LHLL	"switch"
sui´mingu	LHLLL	sui´mingu	LHLLL	"swimming"
suka´ato	LHLL	suka´ato	LHLL	"skirt"
suka´afu	LHLL	suka´afu	LHLL	"scarf"
suka´uto	LHLL	suka´uto	LHLL	"scout"
suka´nku	LHLL	suka´nku	LHLL	"skunk"
suki´ppu	LHLL	suki´ppu	LHLL	"skip"
sukya´naa	LHLL	sukya´naa	LHLL	"scanner"
suku´upu	LHLL	suku´upu	LHLL	"scoop"
suku´uru	LHLL	suku´uru	LHLL	"school"
sukura´ppu	LLHLL	sukura´ppu	LHHLL	"scrap"
sukuri´in	LLHLL	sukuri´in	LHHLL	"screen"
*suke´eto	LHLL	sukeeto	LHHH	"skate"
suke´eru	LHLL	suke´eru	LHLL	"scale"
suke´tti	LHLL	suke´tti	LHLL	"sketch"
suko´a	LHL	suko´a	LHL	"score"
suta´a	LHL	suta´a	LHL	"star"
suta´ato	LHLL	suta´ato	LHLL	"start"
suta´iru	LHLL	suta´iru	LHLL	"style"
suta´jiamu	LHLLL	suta´jiamu	LHLLL	"stadium"
suta´hhu	LHLL	suta´hhu	LHLL	"staff"
suta´nsu	LHLL	suta´nsu	LHLL	"stance"
suta´npu	LHLL	suta´npu	LHLL	"stamp"
suti´imu	LHLL	suti´imu	LHLL	"steam"
sute´eki	LHLL	sute´eki	LHLL	"steak"
sute´eji	LHLL	sute´eji	LHLL	"stage"
sute´eshon	LHLLL	sute´eshon	LHLLL	"station"
sute´etasu	LHLLL	sute´etasu	LHLLL	"status"
sute´kki	LHLL	sute´kki	LHLL	"stick"
sute´ppu	LHLL	sute´ppu	LHLL	"step"
suto´a	LHL	suto´a	LHL	"store"

suto´obu	LHLL	suto´obu	LHLL		"stove"
suto´orii	LHLLL	suto´orii	LHLLL		"story"
suto´kku	LHLL	suto´kku	LHLL		"stock"
sutora´iki	LLHLL	sutora´iki	LHHLL		"strike"
sutora´ipu	LLHLL	sutora´ipu	LHHLL		"stripe"
sutori´ito	LLHLL	sutori´ito	LHHLL		"street"
suna´kku	LHLL	suna´kku	LHLL		"snack"
supa´i	LHL	supa´i	LHL		"spy"
supa´isu	LHLL	supa´isu	LHLL		"spice"
supa´na	LHL	supa´na	LHL		"spanner"
supa´n	LHL	supa´n	LHL		"span"
supi´ikaa	LHLLL	supi´ikaa	LHLLL		"speaker"
supi´iti	LHLL	supi´iti	LHLL		"speech"
supi´ido	LHLL	supi´ido	LHLL		"speed"
supi´ritto	LHLLL	supi´ritto	LHLLL		"spirit"
supu´un	LHLL	supu´un	LHLL		"spoon"
supuri´nkuraa	LLHLLLL	supuri´nkuraa	LHHLLLL		"sprinkler"
supuri´ntaa	LLHLLL	supuri´ntaa	LHHLLL		"sprinter"
supe´a	LHL	supe´a	LHL		"spare"
supe´esu	LHLL	supe´esu	LHLL		"space"
supe´ringu	LHLLL	supe´ringu	LHLLL		"spelling"
supo´oku	LHLL	supo´oku	LHLL		"spoke"
supo´otu	LHLL	supo´otu	LHLL		"sports"
supo´nsaa	LHLLL	supo´nsaa	LHLLL		"sponsor"
suma´iru	LHLL	suma´iru	LHLL		"smile"
sumo´oku	LHLL	sumo´oku	LHLL		"smoke"
sumo´ggu	LHLL	sumo´ggu	LHLL		"smog"
sura´ngu	LHLL	sura´ngu	LHLL		"slang"
sura´npu	LHLL	sura´npu	LHLL		"slump"
*suri´ppa	LHLL	su´rippa	HLLL		"slipper"
suro´ogan	LHLLL	suro´ogan	LHLLL		"slogan"
suro´opu	LHLL	suro´opu	LHLL		"slope"
sere´kushon	LHLLL	sere´kushon	LHLLL		"selection"
turi´i	LHL	turi´i	LHL		"tree"
disuka´unto	LLHLLL	disuka´unto	LHHLLL		"discount"
disuka´sshon	LLHLLL	disuka´sshon	LHHLLL		"discussion"
dire´kutaa	LHLLL	dire´kutaa	LHLLL		"director"
tekuno´rojii	LLHLLL	tekuno´rojii	LHHLLL		"technology"
dekore´eshon	LLHLLL	dekore´eshon	LHHLLL		"decoration"
deza´ato	LHLL	deza´ato	LHLL		"dessert"
deza´inaa	LHLLL	deza´inaa	LHLLL		"designer"
deza´in	LHLL	deza´in	LHLL		"design"
detoro´ito	LHHLL	detoro´ito	LHHLL		"Detroit"
deme´ritto	LHLLL	deme´ritto	LHLLL		"demerit"

*toma´to	LHL	to´mato	HLL	"tomato"
*dora´ibaa	LHLLL	doraibaa	LHHHH	"driver"
dora´ibu	LHLL	dora´ibu	LHLL	"drive"
*dora´iyaa	LHLLL	doraiyaa	LHHHH	"dryer"
tora´kutaa	LHLLL	tora´kutaa	LHLLL	"tractor"
tora´kku	LHLL	tora´kku	LHLL	"truck"
dora´ggu	LHLL	dora´ggu	LHLL	"drug"
tora´ppu	LHLL	tora´ppu	LHLL	"trap"
toradi´shon	LLHLL	toradi´shon	LHHLL	"tradition"
tora´buru	LHLL	tora´buru	LHLL	"trouble"
tora´nku	LHLL	tora´nku	LHLL	"trunk"
tora´nporin	LHLLL	tora´nporin	LHLLL	"trampoline"
tori´itomento	LHLLLL	tori´itomento	LHLLLL	"treatment"
dori´imu	LHLL	dori´imu	LHLL	"dream"
tori´kku	LHLL	tori´kku	LHLL	"trick"
tori´ppu	LHLL	tori´ppu	LHLL	"trip"
dori´ppu	LHLL	dori´ppu	LHLL	"drip"
dori´buru	LHLL	dori´buru	LHLL	"dribble"
*dori´ru	LHL	do´riru	HLL	"drill"
dori´nku	LHLL	dori´nku	LHLL	"drink"
tore´esu	LHLL	tore´esu	LHLL	"trace"
tore´enaa	LHLLL	tore´enaa	LHLLL	"trainer"
tore´eningu	LHLLLL	tore´eningu	LHLLL	"training"
tore´eraa	LHLLL	tore´eraa	LHLLL	"trailer"
tore´ndo	LHLL	tore´ndo	LHLL	"trend"
toro´oti	LHLL	toro´oti	LHLL	"troche"
nare´eshon	LHLLL	nare´eshon	LHLLL	"narration"
nebura´suka	LLHLL	nebura´suka	LHHLL	"Nebraska"
baibure´eshon	LLLHLL	baibure´eshon	LHHHLLL	"vibration"
bairi´ngaru	LLHLLL	bairi´ngaru	LHHLLL	"bilingual"
bake´eshon	LHLLL	bake´eshon	LHLLL	"vacation"
patoro´oru	LLHLL	patoro´oru	LHHLL	"patrol"
*bana´na	LHL	ba´nana	HLL	"banana"
pafo´omansu	LHLLL	pafo´omansu	LHLLL	"performance"
barie´eshon	LLHLLL	barie´eshon	LHHLLL	"variation"
baru´un	LHLL	baru´un	LHLL	"balloon"
pare´edo	LHLL	pare´edo	LHLL	"parade"
*hawa´i	LHL	ha´wai	HLL	"Hawaii"
*bigi´naa	LHLL	bi´ginaa	HLLL	"beginner"
hui´rumu	LHLL	hui´rumu	LHLL	"film"
pura´isu	LHLL	pura´isu	LHLL	"price"
pura´ibasii	LHLLL	pura´ibasii	LHLLL	"privacy"
bura´usu	LHLL	bura´usu	LHLL	"blouse"
bura´un	LHLL	bura´un	LHLL	"brown"

Appendix 167

hura´sshu	LHLL	hura´sshu	LHLL	"flash"
hurami´ngo	LLHLL	hurami´ngo	LHHLL	"flamingo"
hura´waa	LHLL	hura´waa	LHLL	"flower"
bura´nku	LHLL	bura´nku	LHLL	"blank"
*pura´nkuton	LHLLLL	puranku´ton	LHHHLL	"plankton"
huri´izaa	LHLLL	huri´izaa	LHLLL	"freezer"
buri´jji	LHLL	buri´jji	LHLL	"bridge"
puri´nsu	LHLL	puri´nsu	LHLL	"prince"
puri´nsuton	LHLLL	puri´nsuton	LHLLL	"Princeton"
puri´nsesu	LHLLL	puri´nsesu	LHLLL	"princess"
buru´u	LHL	buru´u	LHL	"blue"
buru´usu	LHLL	buru´usu	LHLL	"blues"
huru´utu	LHLL	huru´utu	LHLL	"fruits"
huru´uto	LHLL	huru´uto	LHLL	"flute"
puru´un	LHLL	puru´un	LHLL	"prune"
bure´in	LHLL	bure´in	LHLL	"brain"
pure´e	LHL	pure´e	LHL	"play"
bure´eki	LHLL	bure´eki	LHLL	"break"
pure´eyaa	LHLLL	pure´eyaa	LHLLL	"player"
bure´zaa	LHLL	bure´zaa	LHLL	"blazer"
pure´jidento	LHLLLL	pure´jidento	LHLLLL	"president"
bure´suretto	LHLLLL	bure´suretto	LHLLLL	"bracelet"
purezente´eshon	LLLLHLLL	purezente´eshon	LHHHHLLL	"presentation"
pure´zento	LHLLL	pure´zento	LHLLL	"present"
pure´sshaa	LHLLL	pure´sshaa	LHLLL	"pressure"
huro´a	LHL	huro´a	LHL	"floor"
buro´iraa	LHLLL	buro´iraa	LHLLL	"broiler"
buro´oti	LHLL	buro´oti	LHLL	"brooch"
puro´jekuto	LHLLL	puro´jekuto	LHLLL	"project"
puro´sesu	LHLL	puro´sesu	LHLL	"process"
buro´kku	LHLL	buro´kku	LHLL	"block"
*pote´to	LHL	po´teto	HLL	"potate"
masi´in	LHLL	masi´in	LHLL	"machine"
maji´shan	LHLL	maji´shan	LHLL	"magician"
massa´aji	LLHLL	massa´aji	LHHLL	"massage"
mari´ina	LHLL	mari´ina	LHLL	"marina"
mizu´uri	LHLL	mizu´uri	LHLL	"Missouri"
myuuji´shan	LLHLL	myuuji´shan	LHHLL	"musician"
moza´iku	LHLL	moza´iku	LHLL	"mosaic"
*motibe´eshon	LLHLLL	motibeeshon	LHHHH	"motivation"
ria´ritii	LHLLL	ria´ritii	LHLLL	"reality"
risa´ati	LHLL	risa´ati	LHLL	"research"
rizo´oto	LHLL	rizo´oto	LHLL	"resort"
riha´asaru	LHLLL	riha´asaru	LHLLL	"rehearsal"

Kansai Japanese		Tokyo Japanese		Gloss
rifo´omu	LHLL	rifo´omu	LHLL	"reform"
rekurie´eshon	LLLHLLL	rekurie´eshon	LHHHLLL	"recreation"
resi´ito	LHLL	resi´ito	LHLL	"receipt"
rese´pushon	LHLLL	rese´pushon	LHLLL	"reception"
repo´oto	LHLL	repo´oto	LHLL	"report"
reri´ihu	LHLL	reri´ihu	LHLL	"relief"
roke´eshon	LHLLL	roke´eshon	LHLLL	"location"

Non-English Type H (150 Words)

Kansai Japanese		Tokyo Japanese		Gloss
aaka´nsoo	HHHLLL	aaka´nsoo	LHHLLL	"Arkansas"
a´akeedo	HLLLL	a´akeedo	HLLLL	"arcade"
aari´nton	HHHLLL	aari´nton	LHHLLL	"Arlington"
a´kusesarii	HLLLLL	a´kusesarii	HLLLLL	"accessory"
akuroba´tto	HHHHLL	akuroba´tto	LHHHLL	"acrobat"
ajite´etaa	HHHLLL	ajite´etaa	LHHLLL	"agitator"
asupara´gasu	HHHHLL	asupara´gasu	LHHHLL	"asparagus"
asufa´ruto	HHHLL	asufa´ruto	LHHLL	"asphalt"
a´dobaisu	HLLLL	a´dobaisu	HLLLL	"advice"
adobante´eji	HHHHHLL	adobante´eji	LHHHHLL	"advantage"
anau´nsaa	HHHLLL	anau´nsaa	LHHLLL	"announcer"
anari´suto	HHHLL	anari´suto	LHHLL	"analyst"
apuriko´tto	HHHHLL	apuriko´tto	LHHHLL	"apricot"
arige´etaa	HHHLLL	arige´etaa	LHHLLL	"alligator"
arumini´umu	HHHHLL	arumini´umu	LHHHLL	"aluminum"
anka´rejji	HHHLLL	anka´rejji	LHHLLL	"Anchorage"
anpa´ia	HHHLL	anpa´ia	LHHLL	"umpire"
inisia´tibu	HHHHLL	inisia´tibu	LHHHLL	"initiative"
i´nisharu	HLLL	i´nisharu	HLLL	"initial"
irasutore´etaa	HHHHHLLL	irasutore´etaa	LHHHHLLL	"illustrator"
indianapo´risu	HHHHHHLL	indianapo´risu	LHHHHHLL	"Indianapolis"
inde´kkusu	HHHLLL	inde´kkusu	LHHLLL	"index"
winbu´rudon	HHHHLLL	winbu´rudon	LHHHLLL	"Wimbledon"
earobi´kusu	HHHHLL	earobi´kusu	LHHHLL	"aerobics"
ekisu´tora	HHHLL	ekisu´tora	LHHLL	"extra"
ekisupa´ato	HHHHLL	ekisupa´ato	LHHHLL	"expert"
egoi´suto	HHHLL	egoi´suto	LHHLL	"egoist"
esukare´etaa	HHHHLLL	esukare´etaa	LHHHLLL	"escalator"
epiro´ogu	HHHLL	epiro´ogu	LHHLL	"epilogue"
emera´rudo	HHHLL	emera´rudo	LHHLL	"emerald"
erekutoroni´kusu	HHHHHHLL	erekutoroni´kusu	LHHHHHLL	"electronics"
erebe´etaa	HHHLLL	erebe´etaa	LHHLLL	"elevator"
o´asisu	HLLL	o´asisu	HLLL	"oasis"

*ookesu´tora	HHHHLL	ooke´sutora	LHHLLL	"orchestra"
okura´homa	HHHLL	okura´homa	LHHLL	"Oklahoma"
okkusufo´odo	HHHHHLL	okkusufo´odo	LHHHHLL	"Oxford"
oputimi´suto	HHHHLL	oputimi´suto	LHHHLL	"optimist"
omuni´basu	HHHLL	omuni´basu	LHHLL	"omnibus"
kaaba´ido	HHHLL	kaaba´ido	LHHLL	"carbide"
kasuta´ado	HHHLL	kasuta´ado	LHHLL	"casterd"
katapa´ruto	HHHLL	katapa´ruto	LHHLL	"catapult"
ka´nuu	HLL	ka´nuu	HLL	"canoe"
*karikyu´ramu	HHHLL	ka´rikyuramu	HLLLL	"curriculum"
karihura´waa	HHHHLL	karihura´waa	LHHHLL	"cauliflower"
kya´ria	HLL	kya´ria	HLL	"career"
kuraima´kkusu	HHHHLLL	kuraima´kkusu	LHHHLLL	"climax"
ku´rasu	HLL	ku´rasu	HLL	"class"
gu´rasu	HLL	gu´rasu	HLL	"glass"
gu´rahu	HLL	gu´rahu	HLL	"graph"
gu´rabu	HLL	gu´rabu	HLL	"grab"
kurike´tto	HHHLL	kurike´tto	LHHLL	"cricket"
kurisu´masu	HHHLL	kurisu´masu	LHHLL	"Christmas"
gu´riru	HLL	gu´riru	HLL	"grill"
ku´rosu	HLL	ku´rosu	HLL	"cross"
koodine´etaa	HHHHLLL	koodine´etaa	LHHHLLL	"coordinator"
konetika´tto	HHHHLL	konetika´tto	LHHHLL	"Connecticut"
koresutero´oru	HHHHHLL	koresutero´oru	LHHHHLL	"cholesterol"
ko´rona	HLL	ko´rona	HLL	"corona"
konko´osu	HHHLL	konko´osu	LHHLL	"concourse"
ko´nsento	HLLLL	ko´nsento	HLLLL	"consent"
kondo´omu	HHHLL	kondo´omu	LHHLL	"condom"
saaro´in	HHHLL	saaro´in	LHHLL	"sirloin"
saikuroto´ron	HHHHHLL	saikuroto´ron	LHHHHLL	"cyclotron"
saibo´ogu	HHHLL	saibo´ogu	LHHLL	"cyborg"
satera´ito	HHHLL	satera´ito	LHHLL	"satellite"
sa´fari	HLL	sa´fari	HLL	"safari"
sandoi´tti	HHHHLL	sandoi´tti	LHHHLL	"sandwich"
jaanari´suto	HHHHLL	jaanari´suto	LHHHLL	"journalist"
jaanari´zumu	HHHHLL	jaanari´zumu	LHHHLL	"journalism"
shande´ria	HHHLL	shande´ria	LHHLL	"shandelier"
sha´npuu	HLLL	sha´npuu	HLLL	"shampoo"
*si´atoru	HLLL	sia´toru	LHLL	"Seattle"
sinsi´nati	HHHLL	sinsi´nati	LHHLL	"Cincinnati"
sinme´torii	HHHLLL	sinme´torii	LHHLLL	"symmetry"
sukottora´ndo	HHHHHLL	sukottora´ndo	LHHHHLL	"Scotland"
sutairi´suto	HHHHLL	sutairi´suto	LHHHLL	"stylist"
sutanda´ado	HHHHLL	sutanda´ado	LHHHLL	"standard"

su´riraa	HLLL	su´riraa	HLLL	"thriller"
se´dan	HLL	se´dan	HLL	"sedan"
*soose´eji	HHHLL	so´oseeji	HLLLL	"sausage"
dainama´ito	HHHHLL	dainama´ito	LHHHLL	"dynamite"
daiyamo´ndo	HHHHLL	daiyamo´ndo	LHHHLL	"diamond"
ta´nbarin	HLLLL	ta´nbarin	HLLLL	"tambourine"
tinpa´njii	HHHLLL	tinpa´njii	LHHLLL	"chimpanzee"
te´kunikku	HLLLL	te´kunikku	HLLLL	"technique"
te´nesii	HLLL	te´nesii	HLLL	"Tennessee"
demonsutore´eshon	HHHHHHLLL	demonsutore´eshon	LHHHHHLLL	"demonstration"
derawe´a	HHHL	derawe´a	LHHL	"Delaware"
terori´suto	HHHLL	terori´suto	LHHLL	"terrorist"
terori´zumu	HHHLL	terori´zumu	LHHLL	"terrorism"
do´rama	HLL	do´rama	HLL	"drama"
do´ramu	HLL	do´ramu	HLL	"drum"
toranpe´tto	HHHHLL	toranpe´tto	LHHHLL	"trumpet"
do´resu	HLL	do´resu	HLL	"dress"
to´rofii	HLLL	to´rofii	HLLL	"trophy"
nashonari´zumu	HHHHLL	nashonari´zumu	LHHHLL	"nationalism"
narusi´suto	HHHLL	narusi´suto	LHHLL	"narcissist"
ne´bada	HLL	ne´bada	HLL	"Nevada"
paakore´etaa	HHHHLLL	paakore´etaa	LHHHLLL	"percolator"
baate´ndaa	HHHLLL	baate´ndaa	LHHLLL	"bartender"
baabe´kyuu	HHHLL	baabe´kyuu	LHHLL	"barbecue"
*ba´amonto	HLLLL	baamo´nto	LHHLL	"Vermont"
haija´kku	HHHLL	haija´kku	LHHLL	"hijack"
basuke´tto	HHHLL	basuke´tto	LHHLL	"basket"
pasupo´oto	HHHLL	pasupo´oto	LHHLL	"passport"
*ba´ton	HLL	baton	LHH	"baton"
ba´nira	HLL	ba´nira	HLL	"vanilla"
hanemu´un	HHHLL	hanemu´un	LHHLL	"honeymoon"
parashu´uto	HHHLL	parashu´uto	LHHLL	"parachute"
barike´edo	HHHLL	barike´edo	LHHLL	"barricade"
harike´en	HHHLL	harike´en	LHHLL	"hurricane"
baruko´nii	HHHLL	baruko´nii	LHHLL	"balcony"
hanba´agaa	HHHLLL	hanba´agaa	LHHLLL	"hamburger"
hanmo´kku	HHHLL	hanmo´kku	LHHLL	"hammock"
piani´suto	HHHLL	piani´suto	LHHLL	"pianist"
bisuke´tto	HHHLL	bisuke´tto	LHHLL	"biscuit"
hittiha´iku	HHHHLL	hittiha´iku	LHHHLL	"hitchhike"
pittuba´agu	HHHHLL	pittuba´agu	LHHHLL	"Pittsburg"
hiyasi´nsu	HHHLL	hiyasi´nsu	LHHLL	"hyacinth"
*firaderu´fia	HHHHLL	firaderufi´a	LHHHHL	"Philadelphia"
pirami´ddo	HHHLL	pirami´ddo	LHHLL	"pyramid"

Kansai Japanese		Tokyo Japanese		Gloss
biriya´ado	HHHLL	biriya´ado	LHHLL	"billiards"
femini´zumu	HHHLL	femini´zumu	LHHLL	"feminism"
puraka´ado	HHHLL	puraka´ado	LHHLL	"placard"
purasuti´kku	HHHHLL	purasuti´kku	LHHHLL	"plastic"
purattoho´omu	HHHHHLL	purattoho´omu	LHHHHLL	"platform"
hurancha´izu	HHHHLL	hurancha´izu	LHHHLL	"franchise"
purogu´ramaa	HHHLLL	purogu´ramaa	LHHLLL	"programmer"
purogu´ramu	HHHLL	purogu´ramu	LHHLL	"program"
puroro´ogu	HHHLL	puroro´ogu	LHHLL	"prologue"
heriko´putaa	HHHLLL	heriko´putaa	LHHLLL	"helicopter"
*herume´tto	HHHLL	he´rumetto	HLLLL	"helmet"
borute´eji	HHHLL	borute´eji	LHHLL	"voltage"
ma´agaretto	HLLLLL	ma´agaretto	HLLLLL	"marguerite"
maamare´edo	HHHHLL	maamare´edo	LHHHLL	"marmalade"
maame´ido	HHHLL	maame´ido	LHHLL	"mermaid"
magune´tto	HHHLL	magune´tto	LHHLL	"magnet"
masachuuse´ttu	HHHHHLL	masachuuse´ttu	LHHHHLL	"Massachusetts"
masuka´tto	HHHLL	masuka´tto	LHHLL	"muscat"
masuko´tto	HHHLL	masuko´tto	LHHLL	"mascot"
masuta´ado	HHHLL	masuta´ado	LHHLL	"mustard"
masshuru´umu	HHHHLL	masshuru´umu	LHHHLL	"mushroom"
mekani´zumu	HHHLL	mekani´zumu	LHHLL	"mechanism"
medari´suto	HHHLL	medari´suto	LHHLL	"medalist"
meriigo´orando	HHHHLLLL	meriigo´orando	LHHHLLLL	"merry-go-around"
meriira´ndo	HHHHLL	meriira´ndo	LHHHLL	"Maryland"
monokuro´omu	HHHHLL	monokuro´omu	LHHHLL	"monochrome"
monoto´on	HHHLL	monoto´on	LHHLL	"monotone"
re´ferii	HLLL	re´ferii	HLLL	"referee"
ro´mansu	HLLL	ro´mansu	HLLL	"romance"

Non-English Type L (65 Words)

Kansai Japanese		Tokyo Japanese		Gloss
*ai´su	LHL	a´isu	HLL	"ice"
*akoodi´on	LLLHLL	ako´odion	LHLLLL	"accordion"
anbu´rera	LLHLL	anbu´rera	LHHL	"umbrella"
ime´eji	LHLL	ime´eji	LHLL	"image"
*insuta´nto	LLLHLL	i´nsutanto	HLLLLL	"instant"
inta´abaru	LLHLL	inta´abaru	LHHLL	"interval"
inta´an	LLHLL	inta´an	LHHLL	"intern"
inte´ria	LLHLL	inte´ria	LHHLL	"interior"
edi´nbara	LHLLL	edi´nbara	LHLLL	"Edinburgh"
enji´nia	LLHLL	enji´nia	LHHLL	"engineer"
opere´etaa	LLHLLL	opere´etaa	LHHLLL	"operator"

ori´ibu	LHLL	ori´ibu	LHLL	"olive"
ore´nji	LHLL	ore´nji	LHLL	"orange"
*gau´n	LHL	ga´un	HLL	"gown"
*gaso´rin	LHLL	gasorin	LHHH	"gasoline"
*kame´ra	LHL	ka´mera	HLL	"camera"
kamere´on	LLHLL	kamere´on	LHHLL	"chameleon"
kare´ndaa	LHLLL	kare´ndaa	LHLLL	"calendar"
*kyara´kutaa	LHLLL	kya´rakutaa	HLLLL	"character"
*kui´zu	LHL	ku´izu	HLL	"quiz"
*kuriini´ngu	LLLHLL	kuri´iningu	LHLLLL	"cleaning"
*koko´a	LHL	ko´koa	HLL	"cocoa"
konkuri´ito	LLLHLL	konkuri´ito	LHHHLL	"concrete"
konba´in	LLHLL	konba´in	LHHLL	"combine"
konpa´undo	LLHLLL	konpa´undo	LHHLLL	"compound"
konpure´kkusu	LLLHLLL	konpure´kkusu	LHHHLLL	"complex"
safa´ia	LHLL	safa´ia	LHLL	"sapphire"
*siri´izu	LHLL	si´riizu	HLLL	"series"
suku´ramu	LHLL	suku´ramu	LHLL	"scrum"
suku´ryuu	LHLL	suku´ryuu	LHLL	"screw"
suchuwa´aadesu	LLHLLL	suchuwa´aadesu	LHHLLL	"stewardess"
suchuwa´ado	LLHLL	suchuwa´ado	LHHLL	"steward"
suto´resu	LHLL	suto´resu	LHLL	"stress"
suto´roo	LHLL	suto´roo	LHLL	"straw"
sutorobe´rii	LLLHLL	sutorobe´rii	LHHHLL	"strawberry"
supu´ree	LHLL	supu´ree	LHLL	"spray"
supeshari´suto	LLLHLL	supeshari´suto	LHHHLL	"specialist"
*sero´ri	LHL	se´rori	HLL	"celery"
dame´eji	LHLL	dame´eji	LHLL	"damage"
chokore´eto	LLHLL	chokore´eto	LHHLL	"chocolate"
*teku´nishan	LHLLL	tekuni´shan	LHHLL	"technician"
debero´ppaa	LLHLLL	debero´ppaa	LHHLLL	"developer"
deri´kasii	LHLLL	deri´kasii	LHLLL	"delicacy"
topa´azu	LHLL	topa´azu	HLLL	"topaz"
*bake´tu	LHL	baketu	LHH	"bucket"
*pase´ri	LHL	pa´seri	HLL	"persley"
pata´an	LHLL	pata´an	LHLL	"pattern"
hiro´ine	LHLL	hiro´ine	LHLL	"heroine"
pena´rutii	LHLLL	pena´rutii	LHLLL	"penalty"
hero´in	LHLL	hero´in	LHLL	"heroin"
poke´tto	LHLL	poke´tto	LHLL	"pocket"
bora´ntia	LHLLL	bora´ntia	LHLLL	"volunteer"
*maji´kku	LHLL	ma´jikku	HLLL	"magic"
mane´ejaa	LHLLL	mane´ejaa	LHLLL	"manager"
misa´iru	LHLL	misa´iru	LHLL	"missile"

moju´uru	LHLL	moju´uru	LHLL		"module"
yoogu´ruto	LLHLL	yoogu´ruto	LHHLL		"yoghurt"
rake´tto	LHLL	rake´tto	LHLL		"racket"
rajie´etaa	LLHLLL	rajie´etaa	LHHLLL		"radiator"
*raji´o	LHL	ra´jio	HLL		"radio"
reko´odo	LHLL	reko´odo	LHLL		"record"
repu´rika	LHLL	repu´rika	LHLL		"replica"
roke´tto	LHLL	roke´tto	LHLL		"rocket"
*robo´tto	LHLL	ro´botto	HLLL		"robot"
wasi´nton	LHLLL	wasi´nton	LHLLL		"Washington"

Unaccented Type H (134 Words)

Kansai Japanese		Tokyo Japanese		Gloss
aiowa	HHHH	aiowa	LHHH	"Iowa"
aikon	HHHH	aikon	LHHH	"icon"
aidaho	HHHH	aidaho	LHHH	"Idaho"
airon	HHHH	airon	LHHH	"iron"
*adobaizaa	HHHHHH	adoba´izaa	LHHLLL	"adviser"
*adoresu	HHHH	a´doresu	HLLL	"address"
anarogu	HHHH	anarogu	LHHH	"analogue"
*aparatia	HHHHH	apara´tia	LHHLL	"Appalachian"
*apareru	HHHH	a´pareru	HLLL	"apparel"
abogado	HHHH	abogado	LHHH	"avocado"
amachua	HHHH	amachua	LHHH	"amateur"
amerika	HHHH	amerika	LHHH	"America"
arasuka	HHHH	arasuka	LHHH	"Alaska"
arabama	HHHH	arabama	LHHH	"Alabama"
arizona	HHHH	arizona	LHHH	"Arizona"
aribai	HHHH	aribai	LHHH	"alibi"
arubamu	HHHH	arubamu	LHHH	"album"
antena	HHHH	antena	LHHH	"antenna"
iguana	HHHH	iguana	LHHH	"iguana"
ibento	HHHH	ibento	LHHH	"event"
irinoi	HHHH	irinoi	LHHH	"Illinois"
inshurin	HHHHH	inshurin	LHHHH	"insulin"
*indiana	HHHHH	indi´ana	LHHLL	"Indiana"
ettingu	HHHHH	ettingu	LHHHH	"etching"
endingu	HHHHH	endingu	LHHHH	"ending"
oodio	HHHH	oodio	LHHH	"audio"
oorora	HHHH	oorora	LHHH	"aurora"
kaasoru	HHHH	kaasoru	LHHH	"cursor"
gaadoru	HHHH	gaadoru	LHHH	"girdle"
kauntaa	HHHHH	kauntaa	LHHHH	"counter"

kaunto	HHHH	kaunto	LHHH	"count"
katarogu	HHHH	katarogu	LHHH	"catalog"
katuretu	HHHH	katuretu	LHHH	"cutlet"
kariforunia	HHHHHH	kariforunia	LHHHHH	"California"
kanningu	HHHHH	kanningu	LHHHH	"cunning"
kyasutingu	HHHHH	kyasutingu	LHHHH	"casting"
kyarameru	HHHH	kyarameru	LHHH	"caramel"
*kirutingu	HHHHH	ki´rutingu	HLLLL	"quilting"
guraindaa	HHHHHH	guraindaa	LHHHHH	"grinder"
guraundo	HHHHH	guraundo	LHHHH	"ground"
gurabia	HHHH	gurabia	LHHH	"gravure"
guriserin	HHHHH	guriserin	LHHHH	"glycerin"
*kuruuzaa	HHHHH	kuru´uzaa	LHLLL	"cruiser"
*kuruujingu	HHHHHH	kuru´ujingu	LHLLLL	"cruising"
*kureetaa	HHHHH	kure´etaa	LHLLL	"crater"
gureedo	HHHH	gureedo	LHHH	"grade"
kureemu	HHHH	kureemu	LHHH	"claim"
*keeburu	HHHH	ke´eburu	HLLL	"cable"
kootingu	HHHHH	kootingu	LHHHH	"coating"
komento	HHHH	komento	LHHH	"comment"
kororado	HHHH	kororado	LHHH	"Colorado"
*saakuru	HHHH	sa´akuru	HLLL	"circle"
saundo	HHHH	saundo	LHHH	"sound"
*jaanaru	HHHH	ja´anaru	HLLL	"journal"
sutajio	HHHH	sutajio	LHHH	"studio"
sutamina	HHHH	sutamina	LHHH	"stamina"
sutando	HHHH	sutando	LHHH	"stand"
sutereo	HHHH	sutereo	LHHH	"stereo"
supuringu	HHHHH	supuringu	LHHHH	"spring"
supeedo	HHHH	supeedo	LHHH	"spade"
suponji	HHHH	suponji	LHHH	"sponge"
settingu	HHHHH	settingu	LHHHH	"setting"
*seminaa	HHHH	se´minaa	HLLL	"seminar"
semento	HHHH	semento	LHHH	"cement"
*soketto	HHHH	soke´tto	LHLL	"socket"
taimingu	HHHHH	taimingu	LHHHH	"timing"
daiyaru	HHHH	daiyaru	LHHH	"dial"
dabingu	HHHH	dabingu	LHHH	"dubbing"
*tarento	HHHH	ta´rento	HLLL	"talent"
*tiketto	HHHH	tike´tto	LHLL	"ticket"
channeru	HHHH	channeru	LHHH	"channel"
*chuunaa	HHHH	chu´unaa	HLLL	"tuner"
tuuriingu	HHHHH	tuuriingu	LHHHH	"touring"
*diiraa	HHHH	di´iraa	HLLL	"dealer"

Appendix 175

teeburu	HHHH	teeburu	LHHH	"table"
tenanto	HHHH	tenanto	LHHH	"tenant"
toppingu	HHHHH	toppingu	LHHHH	"topping"
torooringu	HHHHHH	torooringu	LHHHHH	"trolling"
naiagara	HHHHH	naiagara	LHHHH	"Niagara"
neemingu	HHHHH	neemingu	LHHHH	"naming"
*paakingu	HHHHH	pa´akingu	HLLLL	"parking"
*baajinia	HHHHH	baaji´nia	LHHLL	"Virginia"
*baajon	HHHH	ba´ajon	HLLL	"version"
haadoru	HHHH	haadoru	LHHH	"hurdle"
baaberu	HHHH	baaberu	LHHH	"barbell"
haamonika	HHHHH	haamonika	LHHH	"harmonica"
haiena	HHHH	haiena	LHH	"hyena"
baiorin	HHHHH	baiorin	LHHHH	"violin"
baindaa	HHHHH	baindaa	LHHHH	"binder"
bakuteria	HHHHH	bakuteria	LHHHH	"bacteria"
pakkingu	HHHHH	pakkingu	LHHHH	"packing"
bakkuru	HHHH	bakkuru	LHHH	"buckle"
panorama	HHHH	panorama	LHHH	"panorama"
baransu	HHHH	baransu	LHHH	"balance"
bandana	HHHH	bandana	LHHH	"bandana"
hiaringu	HHHHH	hiaringu	LHHHH	"hearing"
fiiringu	HHHHH	fiiringu	LHHHH	"feeling"
fiirudo	HHHH	fiirudo	LHHH	"field"
firutaa	HHHH	firutaa	LHHH	"filter"
huraito	HHHH	huraito	LHHH	"flight"
puraido	HHHH	puraido	LHHH	"pride"
*purantaa	HHHHH	pura´ntaa	LHLLL	"planter"
burandee	HHHHH	burandee	LHHHH	"brandy"
burando	HHHH	burando	LHHH	"brand"
*purannaa	HHHHH	pura´nnaa	LHLLL	"planner"
*purintaa	HHHHH	puri´ntaa	LHLLL	"printer"
*hureezu	HHHH	hure´ezu	LHLL	"phrase"
hurorida	HHHH	hurorida	LHHH	"Florida"
pureeto	HHHH	pureeto	LHHH	"plate"
hureemu	HHHH	hureemu	LHHH	"frame"
purobaidaa	HHHHHH	purobaidaa	LHHHHH	"provider"
*puropera	HHHH	purope´ra	LHHL	"propeller"
buronzu	HHHH	buronzu	LHHH	"bronze"
burondo	HHHH	burondo	LHHH	"blond"
bearingu	HHHHH	bearingu	LHHHH	"bearing"
peepaa	HHHH	peepaa	LHHH	"paper"
perikan	HHHH	perikan	LHHH	"pelican"
beruto	HHH	beruto	LHH	"belt"

pengin	HHHH	pengin	LHHH	"penguin"	
pointo	HHHH	pointo	LHHH	"point"	
booringu	HHHHH	booringu	LHHHH	"bowling"	
botoru	HHH	botoru	LHH	"bottle"	
*maaketingu	HHHHHH	maake´tingu	LHHLLL	"marketing"	
manikyua	HHHH	manikyua	LHHH	"manicure"	
miitingu	HHHHH	miitingu	LHHHH	"meeting"	
*misshon	HHHH	mi´sshon	HLLL	"mission"	
minichua	HHHH	minichua	LHHH	"miniature"	
minesota	HHHH	minesota	LHHH	"Minnesota"	
*memorii	HHHH	me´morii	HLLL	"memory"	
*raunji	HHHH	ra´unji	HLLL	"lounge"	
*rankingu	HHHHH	ra´nkingu	HLLLL	"ranking"	
ruijiana	HHHHH	ruijiana	LHHHH	"Louisiana"	
retaringu	HHHHH	retaringu	LHHHH	"lettering"	
*waiomingu	HHHHHH	waiomi´ngu	LHHHLL	"Wyoming"	

Unaccented Type L (9 Words)

Kansai Japanese		Tokyo Japanese		Gloss
okura	LLH	okura	LHH	"okra"
karee	LLH	karee	LHH	"curry"
*sutookaa	LLLLH	suto´okaa	LHLLL	"stalker"
zeratin	LLLH	zeratin	LHHH	"gelatin"
dokkingu	LLLLH	dokkingu	LHHHH	"docking"
baipasu	LLLH	baipasu	LHHH	"bypass"
manekin	LLLH	manekin	LHHH	"mannequin"
marason	LLLH	marason	LHHH	"marathon"
*rekoodingu	LLLLLH	reko´odingu	LHLLLL	"recording"

Bibliography

Akahori, Kanji (ed.). 1999. *Hyoojyun Pasokon Yougo Jiten* [A Standard Dictionary of Computer-related Words]. Tokyo: Syuwa System.

Akinaga, Kazue. 1958. Tokyo Akusento no Hoosoku ni tsuite [On the Laws of Tokyo Accent]. In H. Kindaichi, ed., *Meikai Nihongo Akusento Jiten* [Japanese Accent Dictionary]. 1–68. Tokyo: Sanseido.

Asano, Makiko. 1999. Gairaigo ni okeru Akusento Kinshi Ryooiki to Akusento gata no Henka [A Constraint-based Analysis of Loanword Accentuation in Japanese]. In Y. A. Sasaki, ed., *Gengogaku to Nihongo Kyoiku* [Linguistics and Japanese Pedagogy]. 65–79. Tokyo: Kuroshio Publishers.

Beckman, Jill. 1998. Positional Faithfulness. Ph.D. dissertation, Amherst: University of Massachusetts. [ROA–234, http://roa.rutgers.edu].

Benua, Laura. 1995. Identity Effects in Morphological Truncation. In J. Beckman, W. Dickey, and S. Urbanczyk, eds., *University of Massachusetts Occasional Papers in Linguistics* 18. 77–136. Amherst, MA: GLSA. [ROA–74, http://roa.rutgers.edu/].

Bloch, Bernard. 1950. Studies in Colloquial Japanese IV: Phonemics. *Language* 26. 86–125.

Downes, William. 1998. Language and Society: Second Edition. Cambridge: Cambridge University Press.

Fukazawa, Haruka, and Mafuyu Kitahara. 2005. Ranking Paradox in Consonant Voicing in Japanese. *Voicing in Japanese*. Berlin: Mouton de Gruyter.

Fukazawa, Haruka, Mafuyu Kitahara, and Mitsuhiko Ota. 1998. Lexical Stratification and Ranking Invariance in Constraint-based Grammars. *Proceedings of the CLS* 34. [ROA–267, http://roa.rutgers.edu].

Fukazawa, Haruka, Mafuyu Kitahara, and Mitsuhiko Ota. 2002. Constraint-based Modeling of Split Phonological Systems. *On'in Kenkyuu* [Phonological Studies] 5. 115–120.

Hamans, Camiel. 1997. Clipping in Modern French, English, German and Dutch. In R. Hickey and S. Puppel, eds., *Language History and Linguistc*

Modeling: A Festschrift for Jacek Fisiak on his 60th Birthday. 1733–1741. Berlin: Mouton de Gruyter.

Hayashi, Ooki (ed.). 1982. *Zusetsu Nihongo* [Illustrated Japanese]. Tokyo: Kadokawa Shoten.

Hayes, Bruce. 1980. *A Metrical Theory of Stress Rules*. Ph.D. dissertation, MIT. Published by Garland Press, New York, 1985.

Horiuchi, Katsuaki (ed.). 1996. *Katakana Gairaigo Ryakugo Jiten* [Abbreviated Loanword Dictionary]. Tokyo: Jiyuu Kokuminsya.

Inaba, Seiichiro. 2001. Ninchiteki Hyoosoo 3renhaku Futto to Rizumu Shidoo [Cognitive Surface Ternary Feet and Rhythm Instruction]. In M. Minami and Y. A. Sasaki, eds., *Linguistics and Japanese Language Education* II. 293–295. Tokyo: Kuroshio Publisher.

Itô, Junko. 1986. *Syllable Theory in Prosodic Phonology*. Ph.D. dissertation, Amherst: University of Massachusetts. Published by Garland Press, New York, 1988.

Itô, Junko. 1989. A Prosodic Theory of Epenthesis. *Natural Language and Linguistic Theory* 7. 217–259.

Itô, Junko. 1990. Prosodic Minimality in Japanese. In K. Deaton et al., eds., *Chicago Linguistic Society* 26: *Parasession on the Syllable in Phonetics and Phonology*. 213–239. Chicago: Chicago Linguistic Society, University of Chicago.

Itô, Junko, and Armin Mester. 1992. Weak Layering and Word Binarity. *LRC-92-09*, Linguistics Research Center, UCSC, Santa Cruz, CA.

Itô, Junko, and Armin Mester. 1995. Japanese Phonology. In J. Goldsmith, ed., *The Handbook of Phonological Theory*. 817–838. Oxford: Blackwell Publisher.

Itô, Junko, and Armin Mester. 1997a. Correspondence and Compositionality: The Ga-gyo Variation in Japanese Phonology. In I. Roca, ed., *Derivations and Constraints in Phonology*. 419–462. Oxford: Clarendon Press.

Itô, Junko, and Armin Mester. 1997b. Sympathy Theory and German Truncations. University of California, Santa Cruz ms. [ROA-211, http://roa.rutgers.edu/].

Itô, Junko, and Armin Mester. 1997c. Featural Sympathy. *Phonology at Santa Cruz* 45. 29–36.

Itô, Junko, and Armin Mester. 1998. Markedness and Word Structure: OCP Effects in Japanese. Santa Cruz: UCSC ms. [ROA–255, http://roa.rutgers.edu/].

Itô, Junko, and Armin Mester. 1999. The Phonological Lexicon. In N. Tsujimura, ed., *The Handbook of Japanese Linguistics*. 62–100. Oxford: Blackwell Publisher.

Itô, Junko, and Armin Mester. 2001a. Covert Generalizations in Optimality Theory: the Role of Stratal Faithfulness Constraints. *Studies in Phonetics, Phonology and Morphology* 7.2. 273–299.

Itô, Junko, and Armin Mester. 2001b. Structure Preservation and Stratal Opacity in German. In L. Lombardi, ed., *Segmental Phonology in Optimality Theory*. 261–295. Cambridge: Cambridge University Press.

Itô, Junko, and Armin Mester. 2003a. Lexical and Postlexical Phonology in Optimality Theory: Evidence from Japanese. ms., University of California, Santa Cruz.

Itô, Junko, and Armin Mester. 2003b. *Japanese Morphophonemics: Markedness and Word Structure*. Cambridge: The MIT Press.

Jorden, Elenor H. and Hamako I. Chaplin. 1976. *Reading Japanese*. New Haven and London: Yale University Press.

Jun, Jongho. 1995. Perceptual and Articulatory Factors in Place Assimilation: An Optimality Theoretic Approach. Ph.D. dissertation, UCLA.

Kager, René. 1999. *Optimality Theory*. Cambridge: Cambridge University Press.

Kanno, Ken. 1971. Gairaigo Akusento (3) [Loanword Accentuation (3)]. *Bunkyu Geppou* [Literature Research Journal] 3. 47–55.

Katayama, Motoko. 1995. Loanword Accent and Minimal Reranking in Japanese. *Phonology at Santa Cruz* 4. 1–12.

Kay, Gillian S. 1995. English Loanwords in Japanese. *World Englishes*. 14 (1). 67–76.

Kenstowicz, Michael, and Atiwong Suchato. 2004. Issues in Loanword Adaptation: A Case Study from Thai. ms., MIT.

Kenyon, John Samuel, and Thomas Albert Knott. 1944. *A Pronouncing Dictionary of American English*. Springfield: G. & C. Merriam Company.

Kindaichi, Haruhiko, and Kazue Akinaga (ed.). 2001. *Shinmeikai Nihongo Akusento Jiten* [Japanese Accent Dictionary]. Tokyo: Sanseido.

Kobayashi, Mina, Hiroko Quackenbush, and Atsushi Fukuda. 1991. Gairaigo ni mirareru Nihongokakisoku no Shuutoku [The Acquisition of English Loanwords in Japanese]. *Nihongo Kyooiku* [Japanese-language Education] 74. 48–59.

Kubozono, Haruo. 1988. *The Organization of Japanese Prosody*. Ph.D. dissertation, Edinburgh University. Published by Kuroshio Publishers, Tokyo, 1993.

Kubozono, Haruo. 1994. Syllable and Accent in Japanese: Evidence from Loanword Phonology, ms., University of California, Santa Cruz.
Kubozono, Haruo. 1995a. Constraint Interaction in Japanese Phonology: Evidence from Compound Accent. *Phonology at Santa Cruz* 4. 21–38.
Kubozono, Haruo. 1995b. *Go Keisei to Onin Koozoo* [Word Formation and Phonological Structure]. Tokyo: Kuroshio Publishers.
Kubozono, Haruo. 1999. Mora and Syllable. In N. Tsujimura, ed., *The Handbook of Japanese Linguistics*. 31–61. Oxford: Blackwell Publisher.
Kubozono, Haruo. 2003. The Syllable as a Unit of Prosodic Organization in Japanese. In C. Féry and R. van de Vijver, eds., *The Syllable in Optimality Theory*. 271–303. Cambridge, UK: Cambridge University Press.
Kubozono, Haruo and Satoshi Ohta. 1998. *Onin Koozoo to Akusento* [Phonological Structure and Accent]. Tokyo: Kenkyusha.
Labrune, Laurence. 2002. The Prosodic Structure of Simple Abbreviated Loanwords in Japanese: a Constraint-based Account. *Journal of Phonetic Society of Japan* 6. 98–120. [ROA–532, http://roa.rutgers.edu].
LaCharité, Darlene, and Carole Paradis. 2005. Category Preservation and Proximity versus Phonetic Approximation in Loanword Adaptation. *Linguistic Inquiry* 36. 223–258.
Ledefoged, Peter. 1993. *A Course in Phonetics*. 3rd edition. Fort Worth: Harcourt Brace Jovanovich.
Lombardi, Linda. 1999. Positional Faithfulness and Voicing Assimilation in Optimality Theory. *Natural Language and Linguistic Theory* 17. 267–302.
McCarthy, John. 1986. OCP Effects: Gemination and Antigemination. *Linguistic Inquiry* 17. 207–263.
McCarthy, John. 1999. Sympathy and Phonological Opacity. *Phonology* 16. 331–399.
McCarthy, John, and Alan Prince. 1990. Foot and Word in Prosodic Morphology: The Arabic Broken Plurals. *Natural Language and Linguistic Theory* 8. 209–282.
McCarthy, John, and Alan Prince. 1993a. Generalized Alignment. In G. E. Booji and J. van Marle, ed., *Yearbook of Morphology 1993*. 79–153. Dordrecht: Kluwer.
McCarthy, John, and Alan Prince. 1993b. Prosodic Morphology I: Constraint Interaction and Satisfaction. *Technical Report No.3, Rutgers University Center for Cognitive Science*. Cambridge, Massachusetts: MIT Press.

McCarthy, John, and Alan Prince. 1995. Faithfulness and Reduplicative Identity. In J. Beckman, W. Dickey, and S. Urbanczyk, eds., *University of Massachusetts Occasional Papers in Linguistics* 18. 249–384. Amherst, MA: GLSA.

McCawley, James D. 1968. *The Phonological Component of a Grammar of Japanese*. The Hague: Mouton & Co.

Mutsukawa, Masahiko. 2004. The Nativization and the Realization of English Word-final [r] in Japanese. *University of Washington Working Papers in Linguistics* 23: *Proceedings of the 20th Northwest Linguistics Conference*. 161–174. Seattle: University of Washington.

Mutsukawa, Masahiko. 2005a. Loanword Accentuation in Japanese. *Penn Working Papers in Linguistics* 11.1: *Proceedings of the 28th Annual Penn Linguistics Colloquium*. 199–212. Pennsylvania: Penn Linguistics Club.

Mutsukawa, Masahiko. 2005b. The Realization of the English Plural Morpheme in Japanese. *Proceedings of the 3rd Seoul International Conference on Phonology*. 159–183. Seoul: The Phonology- Morphology Circle of Korea.

Mutsukawa, Masahiko. 2007. English Compound Abbreviation in Japanese: A Case of Opacity. *Proceedings of the 4th International Conference on Phonology and Morphology*. 181–184. Seoul: The Phonology-Morphology Circle of Korea.

Mutsukawa, Masahiko. 2008a. Loanword Accentuation in Tokyo Japanese. *CLS 40-I: The Main Session*. 221–234. Chicago: Chicago Linguistic Society.

Mutsukawa, Masahiko. 2008b. The Realization of the English Plural Morpheme in Japanese and the Accessibility to the Morphological Information. *KLS 28*: Proceedings of the 32nd Annual Meeting of the Kansai Linguistic Society. 66–76. Kansai Linguistic Society.

Nakai, Yukihiko. 1988. Kyoto Hoogen ni okeru Gairaigo no Akusento ni tsuite [On Loanword Accentuation in Kyoto Japanese]. *Linguistic Research* 7. 130–152. Kyoto: Kyoto University.

Nakajo, Osamu. 1989. *Nihongo no Onin to Akusento* [Phonology and Accent of Japanese]. Tokyo: Keiso Shoboo.

National Language Research Institute. 1990. *Gairaigo no Keisei to sono Kyooiku* [A Study of Loanword Formation]. Tokyo: Ministry of Finance Printing Bureau.

Nihon Hoso Kyokai (ed.). 1998. *Nihongo Hatsuon Akusento Jiten* [Japanese Accent Dictionary]. Tokyo: Nihon Hoso Syuppan Kyokai.

Niikura, Shunichi. 1996. *Furansugo Handobukku* [A Handbook of French]. Tokyo: Hakusuisha.

Nishihara, Tetsuo, Jeroen van de Weijer, and Kensuke Nanjo. 2001. Against Headedness in Compound Truncation: English Compounds in Japanese. In J. van de Weijer and T. Nishihara, eds., *Issues in Japanese Phonology and Morphology*. 299–324. New York: Mouton de Gruyter.

Nishimura, Kohei. 2001. Lyman's Law in Japanese Loanwords. *Handout to Talk Presented at the Meeting of the Phonological Association in Kansai (PAIK)*, Kobe University, October 2001.

Ohso, Mieko. 1991. Eitango no Nihongoka [Japanization of English Loanwords]. *Nihongo Kyooiku* [Japanese Language Education] 74. 34–47.

Ono, Koji. 1991. Accentuation of Loan Words in Japanese. *Gengo Kyoiku* [Language Inquiry] 100. 9–20.

Paradis, Carole, and Darlene LaCharité. 1997. Preservation and Minimality in Loanword Adaptation. *Journal of Linguistics* 33, 379–430.

Peperkamp, Sharon, and Emmanuel Dupoux. 2003. Reinterpreting Loanword Adaptations: The Role of Perception. *Proceedings of the 15th International Congress of Phonetic Sciences*, 367–370.

Pierrehumbert, Janet, and Mary Beckman. 1988. *Japanese Tone Structure*. Cambridge, Massachusetts: MIT Press.

Poser, William J. 1984. The Phonetics and Phonology of Tone and Intonation in Japanese. Ph.D. dissertation, MIT.

Poser, William J. 1990. Evidence for Foot Structure in Japanese. *Language* 66. 78–105.

Prince, Alan. 1980. A Metrical Theory for Estonian Quantity. *Linguistic Inquiry* 11. 511–562.

Prince, Alan, and Paul Smolensky. 1993/2004. Optimality Theory: Constraint Interaction in Generative Grammar. *Technical Report No.2, Rutgers University, Piscateway*, NJ: Rutgers University Center for Cognitive Science. Revised version published 2004 by Blackwell. Page references to the 1993 version.

Shibatani, Masayoshi. 1990. *The Languages of Japan*. Cambridge, England: Cambridge University Press.

Shimmura, Izuru (ed.). 1955. *Kojien*: dai 1 pan [Comprehensive Japanese Dictionary. 1st edition]. Tokyo: Iwamura Shoten.

Shimmura, Izuru (ed.). 1969. *Kojien*: dai 2 han [Comprehensive Japanese Dictionary. 2nd edition]. Tokyo: Iwamura Shoten.

Shimmura, Izuru (ed.). 1983. *Kojien*: dai 3 pan [Comprehensive Japanese Dictionary. 3rd edition]. Tokyo: Iwamura Shoten.

Shimmura, Izuru (ed.). 1991. *Kojien*: dai 4 han [Comprehensive Japanese Dictionary. 4th edition]. Tokyo: Iwamura Shoten.

Silverman, Daniel. 1992. Multiple Scansions in Loanword Phonology: Evidence from Cantonese. *Phonology* 9. 289–328.

Smith, Jennifer L. 1998. Noun Faithfulness: Evidence from Accent in Japanese Dialects. *Japanese Korean Linguistics* 7. 611–627.

Smolensky, Paul. 1993. Harmony, Markedness, and Phonological Activity. Handout to Talk Presented at Rutgers Optimality Workshop 1, New Brunswick, N. J.. October 23. [ROA–87, http://roa.rutgers.edu].

Smolensky, Paul. 1996. The Initial State and 'Richness of the Base' in Optimality Theory. *Technical Report JHU-CogSci-96–4*, Cognitive Science Department, Johns Hopkins University.

Steriade, Donca. 2000. Padadigm Uniformity and the Phonetics-phonology Boundary. In M. B. Broe and J. B. Pierrehumbert, eds., *Papers in Laboratory Phonology* V. 313–334. Cambridge: Cambridge University Press.

Sugito, Miyoko. 1982. *Nihongo Akusento no Kenkyu* [Study of Japanese Accentuation]. Tokyo: Sanseido.

Szymanek, Bogdan. 1989. *Introduction to Morphological Analysis*. Warszawa: Wydawnictwo Naukowe.

Tanaka, Shin-ichi. 1992. Accentuation and Prosodic Constituenthood in Japanese. *Tokyo Linguistic Forum* 5. 195–216.

Tashiro, Koji. 1953. *Hyoojungo no Akusento Kyoohon* [Accent Textbook for Standard Japanese]. Osaka: Sogensha.

Tateishi, Koichi. 1989. Theoretical Implications of the Japanese Musicians' Language. *WCCFL* 8. 384–398.

Tateishi, Koichi. 2001. Onin Jisho Kurasu Seeyaku no Bunpu ni tsuite [On the Distribution of Constraints for Phonological Sub-lexica]. Paper Presented at the 26th Meeting of the Kansai Linguistics Society, Ryukoku University, Kyoto.

Tateishi, Koichi. 2003. Are Borrowed Morphemes Always Foreign? In T. Honma, M. Okazaki, T. Tabata, and S. Tanaka, eds., *A New Century of Phonology and Phonological Theory: A Festschrift for Professor Shosuke Haraguchi on the Occasion of His Sixtieth Birthday*. 258–267. Tokyo: Kaitakusha.

Tsuchida, Ayako. 1995. English Loans in Japanese: Constraints in Loanword

Phonology. *Working papers of the Cornell Phonetics Laboratory* 10. 145–164.

Tsujimura, Natsuko. 1996. *An Introduction to Japanese Linguistics*. Oxford: Blackwell Publisher.

Tsujimura, Natsuko (ed.). 1999. *The Handbook of Japanese Linguistics*. Oxford: Blackwell Publisher.

Vance, Timothy J. 1987. *An Introduction to Japanese Phonology*. New York: SUNY Press.

Wiese, Richard. 1996. *The Phonology of German*. Oxford: Oxford University Press.

Yip, Moira. 1991. Coronals, Consonant Clusters and the Coda Condition. In C. Paradis and J. Prunet, eds., *The Special Status of Coronals*. 61–78. San Diego, CA: Academic Press.

Yip, Moira. 2002. *Tone*. Cambridge: Cambridge University Press.

Yoshida, Yuko Z., and Hideki Zamma. 2001. The Accent System of the Kyoto Dialect of Japanese: A Study of Phrasal Patterns and Paradigms. In J. van de Weijer and T. Nishihara, eds., *Issues in Japanese Phonology and Morphology*. 215–241. New York: Mouton de Gruyter.

Index

A
[a:]]_PW   3, 67, 68, 69, 70, 71, 72, 73, 74, 75, 108, 126, 127, 128, 129, 139, 140, 142, 143, 149, 150
Accent(prominent μ)   33, 34
accent shift   24, 32, 33, 34, 48, 54
accessibility   3, 78, 99, 104, 148
affix   3, 77, 78, 80, 86, 87, 89, 90, 94, 95, 100, 101, 103
Align-R(Penult F, Accent)   33, 34
All-Ft-Left   133
All-Ft-Right   32
All-σ-Left   133, 136, 143
American English   1, 65
Anchor-L-BT   125, 126, 128, 145
antepenultimate   21, 22, 23, 25, 26, 28, 31, 34, 35, 45, 47, 52, 62
antepenultimate accent   15, 22, 24, 34, 46
assimilated   2, 13, 37, 49, 57, 58, 70, 75, 143, 149, 150
assimilation   2, 37, 49, 57, 108, 145, 146, 149, 150

B
bilinguals   2, 4, 9, 148
bimoraic   24, 26, 32, 107, 116, 117, 118, 125, 128, 129, 131, 132, 133, 135, 139, 142
bound morpheme   108, 133, 143, 144, 149

C
Coda-Cond   67, 68, 69, 110, 119, 129, 131, 132, 133, 134, 136, 140, 143, 144, 149
Coda-CondBM   134, 136, 140, 143, 144, 145, 149
Coda-CondPW   134, 135, 136, 138, 140, 143, 144, 149
coda condition   4, 108
Complex-Onset   67, 68
constraint reranking   3, 5, 75
context-free   3
context-free phonological adjustments   5, 9
Contiguity   119, 125, 126, 128, 129, 131, 138

D
default accent   15
default loanword accent   22

degenerate feet   24, 146
deletion   3, 57, 60, 66, 68, 70, 75, 76, 77, 78, 90, 99, 100, 101, 103, 104, 105, 125
Dep   67, 68, 129
Dep-BT   129, 131, 133, 138
Dep-IO   100, 101
Dep-IO(Aff)   100, 105
Dep-IO(Ph)   100, 105
Dep-IO(Ph Aff)   78, 100, 101, 104
devoiced vowel   23, 25, 47, 48, 55
devoicing   3, 68, 77, 78, 79, 80, 81, 82, 83, 87, 90, 91, 94, 95, 96, 97, 103, 104, 105
diachronic change   3, 75, 77, 78, 90, 96, 99, 104, 147
Dutch   107

E
English accent   15, 28, 30, 31, 32, 34, 35, 36, 44, 45, 46, 47, 52, 53, 54, 149
English accented   42
etymological   77, 86, 89, 90, 95, 103
etymology   12
extrametrical   23

F
FaithLoc(Accent)   33, 34
falling pitch   16, 39, 49
feet   24, 32, 34, 35, 36, 46, 48, 53, 54, 122, 141

foot   24, 25, 32, 34, 47, 122, 125, 141, 142, 146
French   107
FT-BIN   32

G

German   68, 103, 107, 108, 121, 123, 124, 132, 145

H

HEAD=H   40, 41, 50
heavy syllable   18, 21, 23, 54, 141
HH   40, 41, 50, 53
HL   37, 49, 150
host language   7, 8, 9, 63, 64, 148

I

I-CONTIG   100, 101, 102, 105
Ident   68
IDENT(CONSONANTAL)   67, 68, 74
IDENT(VOICE)$_{LOANWORD}$ 91, 95
IDENT(VOICE)$_{LOANWORD\ STEM}$ 90, 91, 93, 95
IDENT(VOICE)$_{STEM}$ 91
independent place of articulation   68, 133, 134, 143

J

Japanese lexicon   1, 2, 3, 5, 9, 12, 13, 26, 37, 49, 57, 58, 61, 68, 69, 70, 75, 77, 78, 89, 97, 102, 103, 104

Japanese phonetic inventory   3, 5, 9

L

language-specific   5, 8
LEFTMOST   33, 34, 35, 118, 145
Lexicon Optimization   6
LH   40, 41, 50
LH´   41, 50, 53
LH2   40
Light-Heavy   141, 142
Light-Heavy structure   4, 140, 141, 144, 146, 149
LL   40, 41, 50, 53
loanword adaptation   1, 2, 5, 7, 8
long vowel   21, 23, 34, 57, 58, 59, 61, 68, 69, 70, 117, 119, 126, 128, 129, 131, 143
Lyman's Law   80, 82, 105

M

Macedonian   22
MAX   3, 67, 68, 69, 70, 71, 73, 74, 75, 125
MAX-IO   100, 101
MAX-μ-BT   125
Mimetic   12
Mimetic sub lexica   70
monomoraic   26, 32, 55, 117, 126, 129, 131, 134, 139, 142, 143, 145

N

nativization   23, 24
nature of inputs   1, 7, 57, 147
NC   80, 82, 84, 85, 87, 90, 91, 93, 94, 95, 96, 98, 104, 105
No-D^2$_{PW}$ 90, 91, 93, 94, 96, 97, 104, 105
NONFINALITY   33, 34
NONHD/H   40, 50

O

OBLIGATORY CONTOUR PRINCIPLE   40
opacity   2, 4, 108, 109, 110, 111, 114, 124, 132, 143, 144, 145, 147, 149
opaque   108, 114, 143, 145, 149
Operative Level   1, 8, 57, 93, 96, 97, 98, 99, 104

P

PARSE-SYL   32
penultimate   22, 23, 25, 34, 47
perception   8, 57, 64, 65, 66, 69, 73, 74, 75, 76, 98, 147
Perceptual Level   1, 8, 57, 64, 65, 69, 75, 147
Perceptual Uniformity Hypothesis   8
phonetic representation   1, 3, 4, 7, 12, 55, 57, 75, 147
phonological adjustments   3
phonological representation   2, 4, 7, 8, 64, 147, 148
pitch-accent language   16

Polish   22
preantepenultimate   22, 23, 26, 28, 34, 45

Q

quadrimoraic   37, 48, 107, 117, 118, 120, 124, 125, 126, 128, 129, 131, 132, 138, 139, 142

R

recent loanwords   57, 58, 61, 66, 69, 70, 71, 75, 76, 149
resyllabification   145
Richness of the Base   5, 88, 111, 112, 114, 124
Rightmost   33, 34
Russian   22, 68, 103

S

Sino-Japanese   12, 70, 94
sonority   68
source language   1, 2, 3, 4, 7, 8, 9, 21, 22, 23, 24, 53, 57, 63, 64, 75, 147, 148
stem   2, 78, 81, 85, 86, 90, 91, 95, 98, 99, 100, 103, 104, 105, 108, 117, 134, 142, 143, 146, 149
sub-lexica   12
sublexica   1, 2, 77, 94
suffix   80, 82, 83, 84, 90, 98, 99, 104, 121, 123
Sympathy Theory   108, 109, 111, 112, 121, 124

T

trimoraic   4, 107, 108, 116, 117, 119, 120, 124, 126, 128, 129, 131, 132, 138, 139, 140, 142, 143, 144

Trunc=F   125, 126, 128, 131, 136, 139, 145
Turkish   22

V

vowel epenthesis   10, 11, 68, 100, 129

W

Weakly Parallel Model   2, 4, 108, 109, 110, 114, 115, 124, 132, 143, 144, 146, 149

Y

Yamato   12, 70, 77, 80, 82, 83, 86, 89, 90, 94, 95, 96, 98, 103

【著者紹介】

六川 雅彦（むつかわ まさひこ）

和歌山市出身。神戸市外国語大学外国語学部ロシア学科卒業。ミシガン州立大学言語学科修士課程、博士課程終了。言語学博士。現在、南山大学人文学部日本文化学科講師。

〈主要論文〉
「日本人の名前に見られる音韻的性差 — 音と意味の有縁性」『言語学と日本語教育 4』、くろしお出版 (2005)。"How Can Japanese People Tell the Gender of their Given Names?". *Proceedings of the Sixth Annual High Desert Linguistics Society Conference*. High Desert Linguistics Society (2007). "Phonology, Semantics, and Kanji in Japanese Given Names (1912–2005)". *Nanzan Studies on Japanese Language and Culture* 8. Nanzan University (2008). "Slips of the Ear in Japanese: Universal and Language-Specific Features and /u/ as a Non-back Vowel". *Nanzan Studies on Japanese Language and Culture* 9. Nanzan University (2009).

Hituzi Linguistics in English No. 15

Japanese Loanword Phonology
The Nature of Inputs and the Loanword Sublexicon

Nanzan University Monograph Series

発行	2009 年 3 月 31 日　初版 1 刷
定価	12000 円＋税
著者	ⓒ 六川雅彦
発行者	松本　功
装丁	向井裕一（glyph）
印刷所	互恵印刷株式会社
製本所	田中製本印刷株式会社
発行所	株式会社 ひつじ書房

〒 112-0011 東京都文京区千石 2-1-2 大和ビル 2F
Tel.03-5319-4916　Fax.03-5319-4917
郵便振替 00120-8-142852
toiawase@hituzi.co.jp　http://www.hituzi.co.jp/

ISBN978-4-89476-442-2　　C3080

造本には充分注意しておりますが、落丁・乱丁などがございましたら、小社かお買上げ書店におとりかえいたします。ご意見、ご感想など、小社までお寄せ下されば幸いです。